DEALING WITH JOSEF STALIN

"Papers Regarding the Anglo-Soviet Negotiations 1939, Russia No…. (1939)" is a document prepared for publication by The British Government in 1940, but withdrawn on the instructions of the Prime Minister, Neville Chamberlain, for reasons that are explained in the introduction to this book.

The collection, known as a 'Blue Book', was intended to describe the progress of negotiations between the Governments of the Soviet Union, Great Britain and France from March to September 1939, following the German invasion of Czecho-Slovakia

Prior to this edition this selection of papers has not been previously published and only two copies of the original proof of the Blue Book are to be found. The Government proof edition is reproduced here in full, with an explanatory introduction by Professor Sidney Aster of The University of Toronto.

DEALING WITH JOSEF STALIN

The Moscow Blue Book, *1939*

"Papers Regarding the Anglo-Soviet Negotiations 1939, Russia No.... (1939)"

With an Introduction by Professor Sidney Aster

Argonaut Papers

All rights reserved. No part of this publication may be reproduced, loaned, stored in a retrieval system, or transmitted in any form or by any means, electronic, mechanical, photocopying, recording or otherwise, without the permission of the publisher.

Applications for reproduction should be made by email to Tim Coates: tim.coates@yahoo.com

ISBN 978-1-84381-050-6

© Introduction: Sidney Aster 2009
© Text and edition: Tim Coates 2009

This work is previously unpublished but was prepared for publication by HMSO in 1940 under the title

"Papers Regarding the Anglo-Soviet Negotiations 1939, Russia No.... (1939)"

Argonaut Papers

A CIP catalogue record for this book is available from the British Library.

Printed in the UK by Lightning Source
Series Design: David Carroll

'The repackaging of classics is a tried and trusted winner, but Tim Coates has come up with something entirely original: the repackaging of history. He has transformed papers [from archives] ... into verbatim narratives, so, for instance, in UFOs in the House of Lords we get a hilarious recreation, directly from Hansard, of a nutty debate that took place in 1979 ... This is inspired publishing, not only archivally valuable but capable of bringing the past back to life without the usual filter of academic or biographer.' Guardian

'It is difficult to praise the idea, the format, the selection and the quality of the series too highly.' Times Higher Education Supplement

'Who, outside a few historians, knows that the British invaded Tibet? We approach these stories with an immediacy it would be impossible to contrive ... from one of the richest unexplored attics in the country.' Robert Winder, The Independent

'This is raw history ... An excellent series. It's particularly satisfying to see Goering getting a dressing down from a British diplomat.' (on Dealing with Hitler) Military Illustrated

'Very good to read ... insight into important things ... inexorably moving ... If you want to read about the Titanic, you won't read a better thing ... a revelation.' (on The Loss of The Titanic) Open Book, BBC Radio 4

'The account is humane, moving and beautifully told. Each pocket size edition tells a good story. This excellent series makes enjoyable reading. More please.' (on Tragedy at Bethnal Green) Times Higher Education Supplement

'Congratulations ... for unearthing and reissuing such an enjoyable vignette.') on Wilfred Blunt's Egyptian Garden) The Spectator

Sidney Aster

After receiving his Ph.D from the London School of Economics, Sidney Aster became a lecturer in Modern History at the University of Glasgow. He then returned to London where he worked as a freelance historian and was, for a time, research assistant to Sir Martin Gilbert, the official biographer of Winston Churchill. In 1976 he took up his present position as Professor of British and International History at the University of Toronto.

He is the author of numerous works including *1939: The Making of the Second World War*; *The "X" Documents*; *Anthony Eden; British Foreign Policy: A Guide to Research and Research Materials 1918-1945;* and *Appeasement and All Souls*.

He has contributed book reviews to The Daily Telegraph and academic journals.

He is presently writing the official biography of Sir Arthur (later Lord) Salter.

Professor Aster is a Fellow of the Royal Historical Society.

About the series

These are historic official papers which have not previously been available in a popular form. They have been chosen for the quality of their storytelling. Some subjects are familiar, but others are less well known. Each is a moment in history. A complete list is to be found at the back of this book.

Tim Coates studied at University College, Oxford and at the University of Stirling. After working in the theatre for a number of years, he took up bookselling and became managing director, firstly of Sherratt and Hughes bookshops, and then of Waterstone's. He is known for his support for foreign literature, particularly from the Czech Republic and for his work to improve public libraries. He specialises in the republishing of interesting archives. The idea for uncovered editions, the first series of these works, came while searching through the bookshelves of his late father-in-law, Air Commodore Patrick Cave OBE. He is married to Bridget Cave, has two sons and lives in London. He is the author of *Patsy: The Story of Mary Cornwallis-West* (published by Bloomsbury in 2003), *Delane's War* (published by Biteback Press, in 2009) and *Aldeburgh, a Portrait*, (published by Antique Collectors' Club in 2009). Tim Coates welcomes views and ideas can be e-mailed at timcoatesbooks@yahoo.com.

Introduction

by Professor Sidney Aster, University of Toronto.

A Blue Book Recalled: "Papers Regarding the Anglo-Soviet Negotiations 1939, Russia No.... (1939)"

British Prime Minister Neville Chamberlain rose in the House of Commons on 6 March 1940 and stated that his government had decided not to publish a Blue Book on the failed attempt in 1939 to negotiate an Anglo-French-Soviet alliance to deter Nazi Germany. Thereafter, copies of the Blue Book were destroyed and they disappeared from public memory first and then from historians' interest.[1] Such a fate is a disservice both to all the principals involved as well as the historian investigating the origins of the Second World War. The Blue Book might have provided information during the post-war period to explain the pre-1939 performance of British diplomats and politicians. It might also have afforded

---

[1] Parliamentary Debates, House of Commons Official Report, 5th Series [HC Debs.], 6 Mar. 1940, vol. 358, cols. 356-357. Frederick L. Schuman, Night Over Europe: The Diplomacy of Nemesis, 1939-1940 (New York, 1941), pp. 230-231 briefly referred to the Blue Book and speculated about its delayed publication. Copies of the Blue Book can be found in National Archives [NA], PREM1/409, and CAB67/4 W.P.(G.)(40)7, 10 Jan. 1940.

journalists and historians, who almost uniformly criticized Britain's failure to secure a version of the grand alliance against Nazi Germany, evidence about the difficulties of negotiating with the USSR. The Blue Book and its recall, therefore, offer a new perspective from which to examine Britain's diplomacy on the eve of the Second World War and the subject of Anglo-Soviet relations during the critical period of the "phony war" from September 1939 to May 1940 and afterwards.

British governments had historically published White Papers, and the more extensive Blue Books, in order to provide information, initially, to members of parliament.[2] After the First World War, and the backlash against pre-1914 "secret treaties and diplomacy", there was a growing demand for "open diplomacy", whereby parliament and public opinion would play stronger roles in formulating foreign policy. In the early 1920s, therefore, public pressure led to the publication of numerous Blue Books, many dealing with the USSR, and others tabling the texts of treaties or conference proceedings. In the later 1920s, especially when Sir Austen Chamberlain served as Secretary of State for Foreign Affairs, "a good deal of information was made available". The subjects included China, German disarmament, the Locarno treaties of 1925, the 1928 Kellogg-Briand pact, League of Nations issues and Anglo-Soviet relations.[3] Despite the impact of the Depression and the preoccupation with economic matters of the early 1930s, some foreign policy issues, for example the London Naval Conference, continued to be the subject of Blue Books. When Sir John Simon served as foreign minister from 1931 to 1935, he was less generous with regard to

---

[2] The following is based on Robert Vogel, <u>A Breviate of British Diplomatic Blue Books, 1919-1939</u> (Montreal, 1963), pp. xi-xxxiv. See also Harold Temperley and Lillian M. Penson, <u>A Century of Diplomatic Blue Books, 1814-1914</u> (Cambridge, 1938), and Oz Frankel, "Blue Books and the Victorian Reader", <u>Victorian Studies</u>, 46(2004), pp. 308-318.
[3] Vogel, p. xix.

such publications. Indeed, he "does not seem to have believed in the efficacy of Blue Books." [4] In the second half of the 1930s, despite such problems as the reoccupation of the Rhineland, the Ethiopian crisis, the Spanish Civil War and the Czechoslovakian dispute, even less information was provided than in the earlier inter-war period. "This failure", according to Robert Vogel, "marks a definite decline in the importance of the Blue Books."[5]

This trend accelerated during the Neville Chamberlain administration of 1937-1940. The few Blue Books published at the time provided scant information, while the historic British guarantees in 1939 to Poland, Romania and Greece went undocumented. After the outbreak of war on 3 September 1939, a consequence of the guarantee to Poland, some steps were taken to justify the decision to go to war. Between 1 September and 17 October, the government presented to parliament a brief White Paper and two Blue Books on the subject of Anglo-German-Polish relations.[6] The initial decision not to document the Anglo-French-Soviet negotiations of 1939, however, was consistent with earlier trends. Press conferences, the radio and informed newspaper reports seemed adequate

---

[4] Vogel, pp. xxii-xxiii.

[5] Vogel, p. xxv.

[6] See <u>Miscellaneous No. 8, Correspondence Between H.M. Government in the United Kingdom and the German Government, August 1939</u>; <u>Miscellaneous No. 9 (1939), Documents Concerning German-Polish Relations and the Outbreak of Hostilities Between Great Britain and Germany on September 3, 1939</u>, and <u>Germany No. 1 (1939), Final Report by the Rt. Hon. Sir Nevile Henderson, G.C.M.G., on the Circumstances Leading to the Termination of His Mission to Berlin</u>. The latter two collections were republished by The Stationery Office as <u>War 1939: Dealing with Adolf Hitler</u> (London, 1999) and are available in this series.

outlets for British government's intent on managing rather than informing public opinion.[7]

The Anglo-French-Soviet negotiations of April to August 1939 seemed destined to remain secret. During question period in the House of Commons on 4 October 1939, R.A. Butler, parliamentary under-secretary of state for foreign affairs, stated that a Blue Book on the negotiations raised "several important considerations." Frank K. Roberts of the Foreign Office Central Department, who had briefed Butler, pointed out that a Blue Book might drive the USSR closer to Germany. Furthermore, it would be difficult to select documents "to illustrate these lengthy and protracted negotiations", and public interest would focus on the military conversations of August which had to remain secret. Roberts had concluded that the negotiations were "a very long and complicated story in which we either appear in a humiliated rôle, or alternatively, by defending ourselves effectively, show up the Soviet government in such a light that our relations must inevitably suffer still further." He also added that the positions of Holland, Switzerland, and of Poland had been discussed and publication would "seriously annoy" them. On 11 October, Butler informed the House that a Blue Book was not being planned "at the present time." He added a factor that eventually proved decisive when he pointed out that during the negotiations with the USSR "we took into consideration the position of several other Governments."[8] The matter, however,

---

[7] See Richard Cockett, Twilight of Truth: Chamberlain, Appeasement and the Manipulation of the Press (London, 1989).

[8] HC Debs., 4 Oct. 1939, vol. 351, col. 1924, 11 Oct. 1939, vol. 352, cols. 307-308, minutes by F.K. Roberts, 4, 6 Oct. 1939, NA, FO371/23074, C15861/3356/18, C16431/3356/18. In late September, the Foreign Office rejected a request from the American journalist Louis Fischer for information for an

refused to go away. Butler responded to further questions on 25 October from Clem Attlee, the leader of the Labour party and MPs Geoffrey Mander and William Gallacher. He stated that no other governments would be approached for permission to proceed with a Blue Book and the decision not to publish stood. Roberts had indicated that doing so would cause "an explosion on their part".[9] On 8 November, when Butler again had to deal with the question, he merely resorted to his previous responses and emphasized the "great difficulties" involved.[10] There the matter appeared to rest.

The Blue Book

The Soviet invasion of Finland on 30 November 1939, however, offered the British too good a propaganda exercise to ignore. The Ministry of Information first requested permission from the Foreign Office to leak some "inspired comment" that would show that the tripartite negotiations failed "primarily due to Russia's imperialistic aims in Poland and the Baltic" and its demand for naval bases in Latvia, Estonia and Finland. Sir Orme Sargent, assistant under-secretary of state for foreign affairs, agreed that "a few divulgations" would be helpful. Lord Halifax, the secretary of state for foreign affairs, approved, provided "that we must not allow such anti-Bolshevik propaganda to get out of control …. [and] that it should not develop or degenerate into a clamour for war against the Soviet Government." The Ministry of Information prepared a briefing note and on 4 December The Times printed it almost

---

article on the 1939 negotiations. Minutes in NA, FO371/23074, C16202/3356/18.

[9] HC Debs., 25 Oct.1939, vol. 352, cols. 1369-1370, minute by Roberts, 23 Oct. 1939, NA, FO371/23074, C17297/3356/18.

[10] HC Debs., 8 Nov. 1939, vol. 353, col. 188.

verbatim.[11] Speaking to the War Cabinet the same day, Halifax acknowledged that the government had until then been "somewhat secretive" regarding the Anglo-French-Soviet negotiations. However, in light of the attack against Finland, he now believed that press revelations "within moderate limits" might stand the government in good stead with the Scandinavian countries. He expressed himself as satisfied with the "attitude" of the morning's press.[12]

The press leak prompted notice of a question in the House of Commons as to whether the government now intended to issue a Blue Book. Roberts believed that it would be entirely innovative to publish documents "relating to negotiations with a foreign power with whom we are still on ostensibly friendly relations without the consent of that Government." He also advised against "taking too hostile an attitude towards the Soviet Government if we can avoid it." Nonetheless, the forthcoming meeting of the League of Nations to discuss an appeal from Finland, with the possibility of Soviet expulsion, suggested that "the susceptibilities" of the USSR might soon be irrelevant. Butler replied in the House on 7 December that Halifax was "reconsidering" the issue of a Blue Book.[13]

In the following days, officials in the Foreign Office actively pursued the project. By 10 December Roberts and Sir William Strang, head of the Central Department, prepared what

---

[11] Minutes by R.L. Speaight 1 Dec., and Sargent, 2 Dec. 1939, NA, FO371/23074, C19731/3356/16, The Times, 4 Dec. 1939.
[12] CAB65/2, W.M. 103(39)12, 4 Dec. 1939.
[13] Minutes by Roberts and Cadogan, 6 Dec. 1939, FO371/23074, C19993/3356/18, HC Debs., 7 Dec. 1939, vol. 355, col. 840.

they termed "the skeleton".[14] The next day, the permanent under-secretary of state for foreign affairs, Sir Alexander Cadogan, wrote to Halifax:

> I think there would be advantage in publication if, as seems probable, it would show that we honestly did our best to obtain an agreement and that the delays and evasions came from the other side. In light of what has happened since, I think it will be clear that the suspicions which we tried to dismiss from our minds were unfortunately well-founded.

He added that an explanatory preface would be helpful and would "discreetly point the moral."[15] During the course of that same day, Halifax and Chamberlain approved publication of a Blue Book.[16] Further questions in parliament on 12 and 13 December indicated the growing interest from members, with one pointing out that the House "has never been officially informed of the character and scope of the Moscow negotiations." Speaking to the issue for the first time on 12 December, Chamberlain stated that the matter was "still under consideration". However, on 13 December he announced in the Commons that a Blue Book was in fact being prepared "showing the course of the negotiations which took place with the Soviet Government earlier in the year." Halifax spoke similarly in the House of Lords and confirmed that "recent

---

[14] Minute by Roberts, 10 Dec. 1939, FO371/23074, C19993/3356/18.
[15] Minutes by Cadogan and Halifax, 11 Dec. 1939, FO371/23074, C20386/3356/18.
[16] Minute by Roberts, 11 Dec. 1939, NA, FO371/23074, C20252/3356/18, FO371/23074, C20341/3356/18, minute by Strang, 11 Dec. 1939, NA, FO371/23074C20386/3356/18.

developments" had altered the government's position on the subject.[17]

The Blue Book was compiled with the intent to vindicate the British role in the tripartite negotiations and to discredit the USSR. However, the project quickly became subject to difficulties and doubts. The assembled documents certainly confirmed the expansionist impulses of the USSR. However, they also opened to criticism the British approach to the negotiations. As well, when the draft was circulated outside the Foreign Office, more doubts emerged, including outright opposition to its publication. These were sufficient ultimately to warrant the withdrawal and suppression of the Blue Book. The exercise and its final termination, therefore, in themselves raise several further questions. If ulterior motives tended to inspire publication of Blue Books, what then was the overriding intent of British policy towards the USSR in late 1939 and early 1940? What did the selection of documents indicate about British post-negotiation assessments of the failed exercise? When documents were edited, as many were, what prompted such excisions? An analysis of these and other considerations shed significant light on several issues rooted in the negotiations themselves and the wartime evolution of Anglo-Soviet relations.

On 12 December, even as the printers were setting up a proof, the first of several problems emerged. One concerned the military conversations held in Moscow in August and the "general principle of not revealing" its details. The solution was to write a memorandum on the subject that, it was thought, "would give the public all they need to know." This was to include reference to Soviet demands for naval bases in the Baltic States and permission to send Soviet troops across Poland

---

[17] HC Debs., 12, 13 Dec. 1939, vol. 355, cols.1051-1052, 1174; House of Lords Debates, 5th Series [HL Debs.], 13 Dec. 1939, vol. 115, cols. 265-266.

and/or Romania.[18] Then Roberts and Strang pointed out that the positions of Sir William Seeds, British ambassador in Moscow, and the Soviet ambassador in London, Ivan Maisky would have to be monitored while the papers were edited. There still remained "the difficulty of making intelligible to the ordinary reader the rather complicated questions" raised during the negotiations. As well, references to Romania were "to be amended sufficiently to avoid any necessity for consulting them", while "various minor changes" were to be made to give the USSR no "legitimate cause for offence". Finally, because the negotiations were tripartite, the French government would have to be consulted.[19] On 15 December a first draft of the Blue Book, circulated to 10 Downing Street among others, cautioned that the extensive list of approvals would delay publication.[20]

These were forthcoming in the following days. Roberts undertook the task of vetting the first proof, paying special attention to the several problematic areas. He also drafted the summary of contents intended as an introduction. "From the propaganda point of view", he noted on 16 December, "it is

---

[18] Minutes by Roberts, 12 Dec. 1939, Strang, 13 Dec. 1939 and Cadogan, 14 Dec. 1939, NA, FO371/23074, C20386/3356/18. On 14 December the memorandum on the military conversations was circulated and several amendments were incorporated, including those by Admiral Drax who had led the British military delegation. See details in NA, FO371/23074, C20955/3356/18.

[19] Minutes by Roberts, 10 Dec.1939, and Strang, 11 Dec. 1939, and Foreign Office to Lieut.-Col. L.C. Hollis, 14 Dec. 1939 and to E.H. Carr, 15 Dec. 1939, NA, FO371/23074, C20386/3356/18. This file also contains a list of the preliminary selection of 83 documents.

[20] Roberts to Rucker, 15 Dec. 1939, minutes by Cecil G. Syers, 15, 17 Dec. 1939, Rucker to Roberts, 21 Dec. 1939, NA, PREM1/409.

important to get the Blue Book out as soon as possible." Strang submitted the revised proof to Halifax who approved it, but suggested that Butler should preside over the final stages.[21] A meeting on 19 December, chaired by Butler, focused on five key points. In order to avoid embarrassment, it was decided to retain a series of documents concerning the alleged German threat to Romania in March 1939 and the Soviet proposal for a conference of major powers. Some of Seeds' more frank descriptions of Molotov were retained, to show both Molotov's "tiresome attitude" and "that Sir W. Seeds kept his end up well." References to Holland and Switzerland were to be excised wherever possible. Mention of the "secret protocol" would have to be made. Finally, Maisky's comments were to be retained, partly because he "used his position quite shamelessly to intrigue against His Majesty's Government and we need not treat him too tenderly." Although Cadogan later noted his agreement with regard to these conclusions, Halifax did not think it right to include Maisky's "personal observations of [a] controversial kind' and the advice was taken. An order for a printing of 100,000 copies was planned.[22] By 29 December 105 advance proof copies were distributed to various government departments, with additional copies going to the French, Polish and Romanian representatives in London.[23] The military departments were assured that their amendments to the memorandum on the staff conversations (document 77) had been incorporated.[24]

---

[21] Minutes by Roberts, 16 Dec. 1939, Strang, 17 Dec 1939., and Halifax, 17 Dec, 1939, NA, FO371/23074, C20926/3356/18.
[22] Note by Roberts, 16 Dec. 1939, Roberts to Halifax, 19 Dec. 1939, minutes by Strang, 20 Dec. 1939, Cadogan and Halifax 29 Dec. 1939, NA, FO371/23074, C20926/3356/18.
[23] Minute by Roberts, 29 Dec. 1939, NA, FO371/23074, C20926/3356/18.
[24] Roberts to Kirkpatrick, Admiral J.H. Godfrey and others, 29 Dec. 1939, NA, FO371/24395, C23/23/18. For some few later

The particular situation of Seeds at this time was pressing and complex. The Foreign Office had been discussing his future ever since the outbreak of the war. It was pointed out that for months Seeds had "been unable to do any serious business with the Soviet Government" and that "the value of the Embassy as a listening post is very slight."[25] In the event, on 22 December Seeds noted in his diary: "Received this morning tel. from Sir A. Cadogan suggesting I shd. go home on leave as they intend to publish a White Book on Anglo-Franco-Soviet pact negotiations, which might make my position here difficult for a time at least!" Seeds agreed to go on leave in early January.[26] He added: "I earnestly beg no papers will be published without my having had an opportunity to express my views." Seeds preferred to delay publication until after his departure from Moscow, and on 26 December he asked for a list of his telegrams and dispatches reproduced in the Blue Book. He continued:

> I strongly urge that all remarks of a personal nature be eliminated. No useful purpose would be served, and only dangerous resentment would be aroused by reference to

---

amendments made by Admiral Drax and the Polish government, see NA, FO371/24395, C189/23/18.

[25] Seeds to Halifax, 6 Dec. 1939, minutes by Maclean, Lascelles and Sargent, 8 Dec. 1939 and by Halifax, 17 Dec. 1939, and Sargent to Halifax, 22 Dec. 1939, NA, FO371/23678, N7134/57/38, Seeds to Halifax, 17 Dec. 1939, NA, FO371/23678, N7540/57/38. See also Sidney Aster, "Sir William Seeds: The Diplomat as Scapegoat", in Brian Farrell, ed., Leadership and Responsibility in the Second World War: Essays in Honour of Robert Vogel (London, 2005), pp. 142-148.

[26] Entry of 22 Dec. 1939, The Papers and Diaries of Sir William Seeds (in the possession of Corinna Seeds, Hydra, Greece), Seeds to Halifax, 22 Dec. 1939, NA, FO371/23683, N7861/105/38.

> Monsieur Molotov's 'inarticulate obstinacy' ... or to his bureaucratic mentality... We must count on Monsieur Molotov retaining his position (as a staunch and subservient creature of Stalin) whatever may happen to others and we may yet want Anglo-Russian relations to improve in his time.

Seeds received the list of documents the following day, with the reassurance that publication would be delayed until his return to London and after his final perusal of the collection.[27] He replied on 29 December that he found "nothing objectionable" and asked for only two omissions.[28] On 2 January 1940 Seeds was to leave Moscow, never to return.

Roberts sent Chamberlain's principal private secretary, A.N. Rucker, a copy of the advance proof on 29 December. He pointed out that Halifax had approved the document, and continued:

> We have also undertaken not to publish until Seeds has returned from Moscow and had an opportunity of seeing the documents. He is expected in London about January 8th. In preparing the documents we have paid special attention to the importance of safeguarding the position of Seeds and also that of Maisky.[29]

Rucker forwarded the proof to Chamberlain on 1 January 1940, noting that the summary of the contents "seems to me to be very useful and to make the Paper intelligible."

---

[27] Seeds to Halifax, 22, 26 Dec. 1939, Halifax to Seeds, 27 Dec. 1939, NA, FO371/23074, C21002/3356/18.
[28] Seeds to Halifax, 29 Dec.1939, and minutes by Roberts and Kirkpatrick, 30 Dec. 1939, NA, FO371/23074, C21058/3356/18.
[29] Roberts to Rucker, 29 Dec. 1939, NA, FO371/24395, C522/23/18.

However, Rucker added that "the consistency" of British policy, could have been increased with "a further short introduction". Chamberlain agreed on the value of an introduction, but noted that it "would be a formidable task & I rather doubt if there is anyone (except perhaps Van[sittart, chief diplomatic advisor]) in the F.O. who could do it."[30]

The relevant consultations began early in the New Year. On 3 January Cadogan met with the French Ambassador André Corbin who expressed his "misgivings". He worried that the Blue Book created a picture of the French government urging Britain to make concessions early in the negotiations. Cadogan thought it impossible to cancel publication at this stage and suggested further discussion. On 5 January Strang met with Maisky, explaining that Halifax wanted the ambassador to peruse the proof as a matter of courtesy. Maisky refused the invitation, stating that he wished thereby to avoid any responsibility for the contents. He also complained that publication "would damage Anglo-Soviet relations" and referred to rumours that it would be a prelude to breaking off diplomatic relations. Strang responded that

> ... this was certainly not our intention. Our intention was to meet a public demand for information as to what had happened, and we had done our best, in an objective spirit, to give the public as clear a view as possible of a very complicated series of negotiations, and to see that the Soviet case was stated, as well as our own.

---

[30] Rucker to Chamberlain 1 Jan. 1940, Minute by Chamberlain 1 Jan. 1940, NA, PREM1/409.

For the rest, he tried to calm Maisky's fears that a breach of relations was imminent.[31] The ambassador was not mollified and on 6 January wrote to Halifax that, while grateful to be informed of the proposed publication, neither he nor his government would have anything to do with the process.[32] The Romanian minister, Viorel Virgil Tilea, was handed his proof of the Blue Book and was informed that this was merely "an act of courtesy" and not intended to invite further comments.[33] Finally, E.H. Carr of the Ministry of Information prepared a summary for the use of press attachés abroad.[34]

The War Cabinet heard from Halifax on 9 January 1940 that the preparation of the Blue Book had taken longer than anticipated, "owing partly to reluctance in the first instance on the part of the French Government and partly to a certain nervousness on the part of the Romanians and of the Turks. In its present form, the Blue Book contained the text (subject to a few minor excisions) of all the relevant documents ...." He added that a short, "non-controversial" preface had been chosen instead of one of a "spirited nature" because he did not want to inflame public opinion. Besides, after the attack against Finland, "there were few people left in this country willing to make excuses for the Soviet Union."[35] The next day Halifax circulated the proof of the Blue Book to War Cabinet members. He noted that "before a final decision is taken regarding the contents of the Book I shall wish to hear any comments that Sir

---

[31] Minute by Strang, 5 Jan. 1940, NA, FO371/24395, C338/23/18.
[32] Maisky to Halifax, 6 Jan. 1940, NA, FO371/24395, C577/23/18.
[33] Minute by Sargent, 6 Jan. 1940, NA, FO371/24395, C511/23/18.
[34] For details see NA, FO371/24395,C515/23/18, C521/23/18, and FO371/24395, C575/23/18.
[35] CAB65/6 W.M.7(40)9, 9 Jan. 1940.

William Seeds, who has now returned to this country on leave of absence, may have to make."[36]

It was the circulation of the Blue Book to the French government that led shortly to a decisive outcome. On 11 January Corbin met with Halifax and explained that his government "was very uneasy about the whole question of publication." He feared that the Blue Book might support those who argued that the USSR was eager for an agreement from the outset while Britain and France held back. Others would find proof that Britain and France were prepared to sacrifice the interests of the states on the Soviet borders. Finally, publication would force the French to produce their own documents and these would reveal differences between the two governments. Halifax confessed that he "had never been much in favour of publication." However, once committed, "it would be difficult to cancel it entirely." He continued: "In this country there would no doubt be some who would hold that the failure of the negotiations was due to the stupidity of France and Great Britain, while others would say that it was due to the dishonesty of the Soviet Government."[37] Yet further observations came the next day in a detailed memorandum from Corbin. He expanded on "the possible inconveniences and disadvantages of publication", and he reiterated his "sérieuses réserves."[38] Halifax's minute already hinted at an impending change of mind: "We must talk about this. I don't much like going against the strong feeling of the French Gov't & there is something in their argument, tho' I think they exaggerate it." This led to a meeting in Halifax's room on 15 January where the

---

[36] CAB67/4 W.P.(G.)(40)7, 10 Jan. 1940.
[37] Halifax to Campbell, 11 Jan. 1940, NA, FO371/24395, C632/23/18.
[38] Memorandum by Corbin, 12 Jan. 1940, minute by Cadogan, 12 Jan. 1940, NA, FO371/24395, C671/23/18. Further French objections are detailed in Campbell to Strang, 11 Jan. 1940, NA, FO371/24395, C699/23/18.

suggestion was made to forego publication and produce instead "a narrative, incorporating or annexing such documents or extracts from documents as might be desirable to fill out the picture." At the same time, however, Chamberlain himself wrote that if the French government confirmed Corbin's objections, then "I think we ought to reconsider the question of publication. I don't think the Labour Party are anxious for publication."[39] On the latter account, he was soon to be proven very wrong.

Work on a narrative of the 1939 negotiations, presumably started at some earlier point, proceeded very quickly. On 16 January Roberts wrote that he had completed "a paper recapitulating in one connected story the course of the Anglo-Soviet negotiations." He pointed out that it was "not intended to be a tendentious document"; rather contained was "almost verbatim extracts", without "the telling propaganda remarks made by Sir W. Seeds, M. Molotov & M. Maisky". He admitted that it was "less effective propaganda" than the Blue Book. After examining the Roberts' paper, Strang wrote on 17 January: "I am very doubtful whether a narrative of this kind is suitable for publication." He continued:

> In the first place, it is from the French point of view as much open to objection as our Blue Book. In the second place, it is not nearly such good propaganda as the Blue Book, and being an ex parte statement much more open to criticism. The alternative seems to me to be a) to publish the Blue Book as it stands, or b) to publish nothing.

---

[39] Minute by Halifax, 13 Jan. 1940, minute by Strang, 15 Jan. 1940, NA, FO371/24395, C671/23/18, Syers to W.I. Mallet, 15 Jan. 1940, PREM1/409, also in NA, FO371/24395, C2855/23/18.

Strang noted that the Ministry of Information advocated publication because of its propaganda value in neutral countries. However, "I do not really see how we can go against the French in this matter." Assuming non-publication, Strang noted that he had, on Halifax's instructions, prepared a parliamentary statement, as well as some comments "explaining what we were seeking during the negotiations and why it was they broke down." Cadogan reminded Strang that Chamberlain was inclined, "one way or another, to defer publication". He personally believed that the draft statement "wd. have elicited such a storm of questions as to render publication almost inevitable. If we can simply delay publication, that wd. appear to be the best course .... I shd like to try, and to maintain, sheer dilatoriness for as long as possible."[40]

The subject of the Blue Book returned to the War Cabinet for discussion on 18 January. Halifax related what the French Ambassador regarded as likely "opportunities for attack":

> First, that the Blue Book showed that at the beginning of the negotiations the Soviet Government were willing to go further in the way of agreement than France or Great Britain. Secondly, that while the British and French Governments had begun by setting their face against sacrificing the interests of the small States bordering on Russia, they had finally given way to the Soviet Government on almost all points.
>
> The French Government also thought that publication of our Blue Book would oblige them to publish

---

[40] Minutes by Roberts, 16 Jan., Strang, 17 Jan., and Cadogan, 17 Jan. 1940, NA, FO371/24395, C2883/23/18. This file contains the 97 page typescript.

something themselves. This would give rise to acute domestic controversy in France.

Unable to change the ambassador's views, he had instructed the Foreign Office to prepare "a short historical narrative", likely however to be as contentious as a documentary collection. Halifax admitted that he was inclined "to pay regard to French susceptibilities in this matter." In addition, he was disposed to have the prime minister make a statement in parliament that publication "had better be deferred to a more appropriate time." The Cabinet conclusions noted, "publication at this juncture ... was inopportune." Although Halifax believed that Attlee "was not keen on publication", it was also decided that Chamberlain would consult further both with him and Archibald Sinclair, leader of the Liberal party.[41] On his return to the Foreign Office, Halifax minuted that the Cabinet had decided "to withhold publication"; Vansittart noted, "I am very glad to hear of this decision."[42] The Polish Ambassador Count Edward Raczynski wanted publication to "be put off altogether for the time being."[43]

After another conversation with Attlee, Chamberlain reported to the War Cabinet on 19 January that, "contrary to expectations", the Labour leader indeed wished to proceed with publication but promised to meet again with the prime minister.[44] At the War Cabinet meeting on 23 January Attlee's position created what Chamberlain described as "a somewhat difficult problem". A meeting between the two later in the day proved fruitless. This forced the government to provide "a

---

[41] CAB65/6, W.M.17(40)13, 18 Jan. 1940.
[42] Minutes by Halifax, 18 Jan. 1940, and Vansittart, 19 Jan. 1940, NA, FO371/24395, C2883/23/18.
[43] Raczynski to Strang, 19 Jan. 1940, NA, FO371/24395, C1702/23/18. See also minute by Strang, 19 Jan. 1940, NA, FO371/24395, C1074/23/18.
[44] CAB65/6, W.M.18(40)13, 19 Jan. 1940.

temporizing reply" to a parliamentary question the following day. Chamberlain told the Commons that he "was not able to fix a definite date." Asked further for confirmation that the delay was not being caused by any editing of the documents, he replied, "That is so." Although Attlee maintained his objection to withdrawing the Blue Book, Halifax later had the impression that he was not opposed to "dawdling" on the question.[45]

Any government enthusiasm about the Blue Book project diminished in the following weeks, but did not quite disappear. Members of the Foreign Office News Department continued to be troubled by ongoing press enquiries about the non-appearance of the Blue Book.[46] On 16 February Halifax told Corbin that Attlee's position might yet force the British government to proceed. When asked whether the French would publish their own collection, Corbin emphasized that such a move "would reveal some discordance at particular moments between British and French policy."[47] Several members of the Commons, however, continued to table questions on the reasons for the delay. Butler believed that Halifax "wants to dawdle" and himself concluded on 20 February that "the arguments for publication tend to dwindle as time passes." The following day, he informed the House that a date was not yet set and that consultations with Paris accounted for the delay. Undeterred, Mander tabled yet another question on the subject for 6 March.[48]

---

[45] CAB65/6, 21(40)13, 23 Jan 1940, HC Debs., 24 Jan. 1940, vol. 356, col. 550, minutes by Roberts, 23, 25 Jan. 1940, NA, FO371/24395, C1274,1339/23/18; minute by Halifax, 30 Jan. 1940, FO371/24395, C1108/23/18.
[46] Minute by Roberts, 8 Feb. 1940, NA, FO371/24395, C2799/23/18.
[47] Halifax to Campbell, 16 Feb. 1940, NA, FO371/24395, C2545/23/18.
[48] Minutes by Butler, 15, 20 Feb. 1940, NA, FO371/24395, C2799/23/18, HC Debs. 21 Feb. 1940, vol. 357, col. 1316.

With this in mind, Strang met with Cambon on 26 February to enquire whether the French government was still opposed to publication or would perhaps contribute their own documentary collection. The next day the British ambassador in Paris, Sir Ronald Campbell, was instructed to take the matter up with the Quai D'Orsay.[49] The response came on 5 March from Édouard Daladier, the French prime minister. He confirmed the French reservations and added that he too had resisted requests from the French Chamber for a parallel publication.[50] Thus, in reply to the question from Mander on 6 March, Chamberlain stated that, after further consultation with the French government, "we have reached a decision not to publish these documents at present." When questioned further, he added, "we have changed our minds."[51] On 20 March Attlee reminded Butler that parliament was promised "the facts." Butler responded that, after consultations with the French government and a review of the circumstances, the government "had decided not to publish." The last time the subject was raised in the Commons, on 9 October, Butler simply repeated these last comments.[52] And that was all that was ever revealed about the *volte face*.

Roberts immediately arranged for one final proof, with all amendments, to be available "if and when the matter comes up again." He also took steps to destroy all proofs in circulation.

---

[49] Minutes by Cadogan, 24 Feb., and Strang, 26 Feb., Strang to Cambell, 27 Feb. 1940, NA, FO371/24395, C2999/23/18. Butler noted on 28 February, "I am not too keen on publication - be it remembered." Ibid.
[50] Minute by Roberts, 5 Mar. 1940, NA, FO371/24395, C3237/23/18. See also Mack to Kirkpatrick, 6 Mar. 1940, NA, FO371/24395, C3561/23/18.
[51] Minute by Roberts, 5 Mar. 1940, NA, FO371/24396, C3564/23/18, HC Debs., 6 Mar. 1940, vol. 358, cols. 356-357.
[52] HC Debs., 20 Mar. 1939, vol. 358, cols. 1956-1957, HC Debs., 9 Oct. 1940, vol. 365, cols. 353-354.

The service departments quickly returned their copies, as did other ministries, most individuals and the Poles and French. [53] One holdout was Tilea, who was asked to return his copy on 15 March. He eventually complied under embarrassing circumstances. The translator at the Rumanian legation, instructed to summarise telegrams in the Blue Book relating to Romania, had instead brought the entire book to a commercial photocopier who then alerted the Foreign Office. On 12 April Sargent met with Tilea and heard the complicated story the latter had to offer. After a good deal of verbal jousting, Sargent afterwards noted that Tilea's story should be accepted, but advised putting the translator under MI5 investigation.[54]

Nonetheless, a leak had occurred. On 9 April, Seeds wrote to Strang and enclosed an article from The Nation, of 16 March 1940, by a United Press correspondent, Frederick Kuh. In the article, "Göring's Prophecy", Kuh claimed that, based on "authentic information", he could reconstruct the events leading to the Nazi-Soviet pact of August 1939. He continued: "Hitherto undisclosed facts, coupled with those we know, and all obtained from responsible, official sources, supply missing pieces of the jigsaw puzzle." The article included two direct quotations from Foreign Office correspondence. The first was the report Seeds had sent to Halifax on his conversation with Litvinov on 1 April. The second, a more sensitive one, reported on Seeds' interview with Molotov on 22 August, during which the ambassador accused Molotov of "bad faith". Given that the article quoted directly from these telegrams, the Foreign Office believed that Kuh "has seen the Blue Book (otherwise he

---

[53] Minute by Roberts, 13 Mar. 1940, NA, FO371/24396, C3564/23/18.
[54] Sargent to Tilea, 15 Mar. 1940, NA, FO371/24396, C3564/23/18, minutes by Roberts and Strang, 10 April, and Sargent, 12 Apr. 1940, NA, FO371/24396, C5577/23/18, Tilea to Sargent, 11 Apr. 1940, NA, FO371/24396, C5578/23/18.

wouldn't be such a fool as to quote)." One view was that the Poles were responsible.[55]

Kuh's diaries reveal that among his numerous contacts in the London diplomatic corps were Maisky[56] and Tilea[57] with whom he often discussed foreign policy issues. On 5 January Kuh had tea with Maisky at the Soviet embassy and the two discussed the Soviet military campaign against Finland. However, the entry for 11 January, far more revealing, consisted of almost three pages of notes on the background to the Nazi-Soviet pact. The notes were remarkably well-informed and clearly were a first draft of The Nation article. They referred specifically to, and quoted from, what Kuh writes was "Document 61 [sic] in the British Blue Book."[58] On another visit to the Soviet embassy on 3 February, Kuh found Maisky resigned to his isolation from the diplomatic corps and engaged in reading War and Peace.[59] Whoever made Kuh privy to the Blue Book - whether Maisky who had never accepted a copy, Tilea, or the Poles as the Foreign Office suspected - the information finally found its way into The Nation.

---

[55] Seeds to Strang, 9 Apr. 1940, and minutes by Roberts and Jebb, 12 Apr. 1940, NA, FO371/24396, C5530/23/18.
[56] See for example, entries of 30 Mar., 3 Apr., 5 May, 3 June, 1 Sept., 7, 14 Oct. 1939, Frederick Kuh Diaries, The George Washington University, The Melvin Gelman Library, Special Collections, Box 1, Folder 2.
[57] See for example, entries of 13, 14, 26 Apr., 1 Aug., 4 Oct. 1939, Kuh Diaries, Box 1, Folder 2.
[58] Entry of 11 Jan. 1940, Kuh Diaries, Box 1, Folder 2. The reference to document 61 is in error. Russia No. (1939), Papers Regarding the Anglo-Soviet Negotiations 1939 [hereafter, Blue Book] no. 15 records that conversation.
[59] Entry of 3 Feb. 1940, Kuh Diaries, Box 1, Folder 2.

The type of the Blue Book was finally destroyed in October 1941.[60] One proof copy, however, did remain in private hands. Strang had given his personal, annotated version to Seeds. This copy remained in Seeds' possession and survives among his private papers.[61]

The Blue Book Proof

The Blue Book proof, titled <u>Russia No. ... (1939), Papers Regarding the Anglo-Soviet Negotiations1939</u>, opened with a ten page "Summary of Contents". This began with a reference to Joseph Stalin's speech of 10 March 1939, in which he affirmed that the USSR stood "for the support of nations which were the victims of aggression". There followed a chronological narrative of the negotiations, highlighting British efforts to satisfy what were regarded as ever increasing Soviet demands. Emphasis was placed on British reluctance to force cooperation by East European or Baltic states fearful of association with the USSR. As for the final stage, the military conversations in Moscow from 11-25 August, the analysis highlighted Soviet demands to impose conditions of military cooperation upon the Polish and Romanian governments. In a final rebuke to the Soviet Union, the summary pointed to the astonishment of His Majesty's Government that the Soviet government should have concluded such an agreement with the German government at a moment when the tripartite negotiations had gone far towards a successful conclusion, and that they should have carried on the negotiations with Germany without a single word to His Majesty's Government or to the French government, with whom the Soviet government were already in treaty relations.[62]

---

[60] See FO371/24396, C3564/23/18.
[61] The Papers and Diaries of Sir William Seeds, (in the possession of Corinna Seeds, Hydra, Greece).
[62] <u>Blue Book</u>, xv.

A carefully chosen selection of 95 documents then followed. These included extracts from the 10 March 1939 speech by Stalin, ten House of Commons speeches by Chamberlain, one by Sir John Simon, the Chancellor of the Exchequer, two by Halifax in the House of Lords, the texts of the German-Soviet non-aggression pact of 23 August 1939 and the Soviet-Estonian treaty of 28 September 1939. The final extract was the League of Nations resolution of 14 December 1939 expelling the USSR. The remaining 83 documents derived from Foreign Office telegrams exchanged largely between Halifax and Seeds from 17 March to 22 August 1939.[63]

The Blue Book was intended for information but even more as a moral tale. The initial documents portray the British government as making the first approaches to the USSR for co-operation. However, the context - the alleged Nazi threat to Romania publicized by Tilea on 17 March 1939[64] - has been excised. This avoided the impression that Britain had reacted hastily, but was rather taking the initiative to meet any future crisis. Thus on 20 March Britain invited the USSR to join in a multi-lateral declaration to consult for purposes of joint resistance.[65] Evident from the outset as well were the special efforts made to safeguard the position of Seeds. The earliest instance of this was the exclusion of the fact that Seeds had been unable to explain to Litvinov on 18 March why the Romanian government had not directly approached the Soviet Union.[66] Of further interest is that the Blue Book omitted a

---

[63] All the Foreign Office documents were later published in Documents on British Foreign Policy, Third Series [DBFP], edited by E.L. Woodward and Rohan Butler, vols. iv-vii (London, 1951-53).
[64] See Sidney Aster, "Viorel Virgil Tilea and the Origins of the Second World War: An Essay in Closure," Diplomacy and Statecraft, 13(2002), pp. 153-174.
[65] See Blue Book, nos. 2, 4, 5, 6.
[66] DBFP, vol. iv, no. 403.

survey of the European situation submitted by Seeds on 21 March. He argued that it would be unwise to assume the USSR would intervene in a conflict in which it would benefit from non-intervention.[67]

Thereafter, the Blue Book followed the negotiations during March and early April when events overtook these early contacts. This led initially to the guarantee of Polish independence announced in the House of Commons on 31 March. The extract from Chamberlain's speech included his assurance that there were no "ideological impediments" to cooperation with the USSR.[68] The Blue Book documented the fact that Maisky had been informed of the guarantee prior to its announcement but that the Soviet proposal for a four-power declaration was likely dead.[69] Soviet negativity, at this juncture, was further detailed in the record of a conversation on 1 April, when Maxim Litvinov, the Soviet commissar for foreign affairs, threatened that the USSR "would stand aside".[70] Nonetheless, in an extract from Chamberlain's speech in the House of Commons on 3 April, and in a review of events that Halifax sent to Seeds on 4 April, the Blue Book underscored that Soviet petulance about being sidestepped was totally unwarranted.[71]

Precisely the same dilemma returned in mid-April. The Blue Book reproduced an extract from Chamberlain's speech to the Commons on 13 April, announcing the extension of the British guarantee system to Romania and Greece.[72] The following document, from British Ambassador in Paris, Sir Eric Phipps, simply reproduced the announcement from the French government on the same subject. The text also referred to

---

[67] Seeds to Halifax, 21 Mar. 1939, DBFP, vol. iv, no. 476.
[68] Blue Book, no. 13.
[69] Blue Book, no. 14.
[70] Blue Book, no. 15.
[71] Blue Book, nos. 16, 17.
[72] Blue Book, no. 19.

ongoing "contact" with other countries, including the USSR.[73] A House of Commons exchange on 13 April led to another review of Anglo-Soviet contacts and emphasized "the closest touch" being kept with the USSR and that there was "no objection in principle" to a military alliance with the Soviets.[74]

When the British returned to the charge, however, it was more of a step backwards than a headlong rush into a military alliance. On 14 April Halifax suggested to Maisky that the Soviet Union make a unilateral declaration of support for Romania and, possibly, Poland. Maisky replied that he had been told to concentrate solely on Romania.[75] Halifax then instructed Seeds to request that the Soviet government make such a declaration, with its assistance available, "if desired."[76] Seeds met with Litvinov the next day. However, the Blue Book pointedly omitted Litvinov's comment that the French government had already broached the subject of "mutual military assistance" between France and the USSR.[77] In another meeting on 16 April, Litvinov advised Seeds that the USSR wished to know, in advance of any declaration, both how far the United Kingdom was prepared to go and what was expected from the USSR.[78]

---

[73] Blue Book, no. 20.
[74] Blue Book, no. 21.
[75] Blue Book, no. 23.
[76] Blue Book, no. 22. The reversal of order might have suggested that it was Britain that initiated this latest proposal.
[77] Compare Blue Book, no. 24 and DBFP, vol. v, no. 182. Nonetheless, reference to this French proposal, which the Soviets later described as a "proposal for a Franco-Soviet pact of mutual assistance", was contained in a later submission from the USSR. See Blue Book, no. 26 and DBFP, vol. v, no. 201.
[78] Blue Book, no. 25. This document omitted a reference to the fact that Romania and Poland were not pressed on the

Without awaiting a response, Litvinov summoned both Seeds and the French ambassador, Paul-Émile Naggiar on 18 April. He unexpectedly announced that the Soviet Union was prepared to negotiate a comprehensive agreement for a diplomatic and military alliance. During that period, not documented by the Blue Book, Seeds advised Halifax that the Soviet proposals were serious and he urged Halifax not to merely reiterate that the British "would lend all support 'in their power'."[79] On his return to London from Moscow, Maisky was told by Halifax on 29 April that a reply would be forthcoming.[80]

On 4 May Seeds signaled that Vyacheslav Molotov had replaced Litvinov as foreign commissar.[81] His view, not reproduced in the Blue Book, was that the change possibly signaled the abandonment of collective security and a turn towards isolation.[82] Maisky reassured Halifax on 6 May that the appointment of Molotov signified no change in policy. Halifax then explained why Britain was reluctant to embrace a triple alliance, including the fact that automatic Soviet support would cause difficulties to Romania and Poland. Maisky replied that the Soviet approach was "the more logical, the more complete and the more effective."[83] Acting then on instructions that the Soviet proposal for a triple alliance was premature, Seeds met Molotov on 8 May. In what Seeds afterwards described as a "most unpleasant ten minutes", Molotov probed him about the different British and French responses to the Soviet triple

---

nature of any assistance from the USSR. Cf., DBFP, vol. v, no. 193.
[79] Seeds to Halifax, 25 April 1939, DBFP, vol. v, no. 282.
[80] Blue Book, no. 27. For a complete record of this discussion, see DBFP, vol. v, no. 316. For Seeds' second intervention, see Seeds to Halifax, 3 May 1939, DBFP, vol. v, no. 344.
[81] Blue Book, no. 29.
[82] DBFP, vol. v, nos. 359, 509.
[83] Blue Book, no. 30.

alliance proposal.[84] The Blue Book omitted this paragraph in order to suppress instances of Anglo-French divergences. The following day, Halifax spoke with Maisky and tried to assuage Soviet fears that the British proposal might find the USSR at war in advance of Britain and France.[85] The record of this conversation in the Blue Book was followed by an extract from the House of Commons question time on 10 May. Chamberlain reassured the House that the negotiations were proceeding amicably and he even ventured that an Anglo-Soviet alliance was "not excluded."[86]

The Soviet response, when it came on 14 May, proposed "three indispensable conditions": an Anglo-French-Soviet treaty of mutual assistance; a guarantee of the states of central and eastern Europe, including, Latvia, Estonia and Finland; and a military agreement.[87] The British government, up to the eve of the signature of the Nazi-Soviet pact on 23 August, was to spend all its time, first resisting and then conceding on all three issues. Although Seeds provided his own reflections on these proposals, and Halifax responded to the ambassador,[88] the Blue Book omitted these and fell back on a parliamentary statement. Speaking in the Commons on 19 May, Chamberlain stressed that Britain was after "a peace front" and "not an alliance" and acknowledged that "a sort of veil, a sort of wall" existed between London and Moscow.[89] Halifax covered much the same ground when he next met on 21 May with Maisky. However, Halifax's grim conclusion - "I think the

---

[84] Blue Book, nos. 31, 32. The adjective "relentless" was omitted. See DBFP, vol. v, nos. 421, 436.
[85] Blue Book, no. 33. A similar and equally fruitless conversation took place on 11 May between the two. See Blue Book, no. 35 and DBFP, vol. v, no. 494.
[86] Blue Book, no. 34.
[87] Blue Book, no. 36.
[88] See e.g., DBFP, vol. v, nos. 530, 533, 546, 554.
[89] Blue Book, no. 37.

choice before us is disagreeably plain", either a collapse of the negotiations or agreeing to the Soviet proposals - was omitted from the Blue Book.[90]

The British government conceded but not entirely. The Blue Book then guided the reader with an extract from Chamberlain's comments in the Commons on 24 May, indicating that he anticipated "full agreement at an early date". On 25 May Seeds received the detailed draft agreement, intended as a joint Anglo-French approach. While agreeing to a mutual assistance pact and military conversations, the draft was linked surprisingly to the covenant of the League of Nations, and carefully protected the preferences of specific countries with regard to cooperation with the USSR.[91] After presenting the draft to Molotov two days later, Seeds wrote that he was "astounded" at Molotov's negative reaction to the linkage to the League and his conclusion that this would result in the "the maximum of talk and the minimum of results." The Blue Book omitted Seeds' further observation that Molotov "seemed to be either blindly acting on instructions or else incapable of understanding."[92] Halifax shared Seeds' views and instructed the ambassador on 29 May to return to the charge with further reassurances regarding the references to the League and the timing of military conversations.[93] Seeds did this the same day, only to be further grilled by Molotov. Seeds' frustrated observations were not included in the Blue Book. He wrote: "…it is my fate to deal with a man who is totally ignorant of

---

[90] Blue Book, no. 38. The text of this document, in paragraph 4, was altered when it was reprinted in DBFP, vol. v, no. 581 to eliminate a reference to the differences between British and French proposals. In addition, paragraph 20 in DBFP, vol. v, no. 582, a continuation of the conversation, was also omitted from the Blue Book.
[91] Blue Book, nos 39-43.
[92] Blue Book, no. 44, DBFP, vol. v, no. 648.
[93] Blue Book, no. 45.

foreign affairs and to whom the idea of negotiation – as distinct from imposing the will of his party leader – is utterly alien. He has also a rather foolish cunning of the type of the peasant."[94]

At this seeming impasse, the Blue Book then produced its longest document: an eight-page record of Molotov's speech at the 31 May session of the Supreme Council of the USSR. Molotov acknowledged that the democracies were finally searching "to create a united front of peace-loving States against aggression." He then revealed that Soviet-German commercial negotiations were proceeding. All of this, in Molotov's words, proved that Soviet foreign policy was "peaceful and directed against aggression."[95] It was these concluding words that the Blue Book presumably hoped would stick in Molotov's throat after the Nazi-Soviet pact and the attack against Finland.

At their next meeting on 2 June, Molotov gave Seeds and Naggiar the Soviet response to the 29 May Anglo-French draft. Seeds pointed out that the Soviets had added yet another demand, namely that the political and military agreements would enter into effect simultaneously [article six].[96] On 6 June Halifax asked Seeds to return for intensive briefings. Seeds declined because of ill health, and was informed the next day that the Foreign Office would be sending someone "to assist" him.[97] The Blue Book documented none of this, but substituted a speech by Chamberlain to the Commons on 7 June in which he revealed that a member of the Foreign Office was going to

---

[94] Blue Book, no. 46; DBFP, vol. v, no. 665.
[95] Blue Book, no. 47. Further extracts in DBFP, vol. v, no. 687.
[96] Blue Book, no. 48. The Blue Book omitted a suggestion by Naggiar to add a secret protocol covering Soviet border states.
[97] DBFP, vol. v, nos. 720, 722, 724, 729, 734.

Moscow "to accelerate the negotiations".[98] The following day Halifax briefed Maisky on British reaction to the Soviet draft treaty of 2 June. Halifax enumerated three problem areas: naming states who did not want to be guaranteed; making the alliance dependent on the conclusion of military talks; and the inclusion of a no separate peace provision. He also informed Seeds that William Strang of the Foreign Office Central Department would travel to Moscow to assist in the negotiations.[99] The Blue Book then reprinted a long memorandum of instructions carried by Strang to Moscow. This indicated areas of agreement and disagreement and included a draft Anglo-French-Russian agreement.[100]

The Blue Book reported nothing of a conversation Halifax had with Maisky on 12 June where ongoing problems, such as guarantees to the Baltic states, were discussed.[101] Nor did it record that Seeds had finally ensured that both he and Naggiar were to act "jointly and simultaneously" when meeting with Molotov.[102] However, on 20 June Seeds provided a review of the complex, sometimes acrimonious, discussions on 15 and 16 June in the Kremlin. He also confessed that he found it "somewhat irritating to be interrogated" by Molotov. This telegram was followed by no less than six enclosures which detailed British reservations regarding Soviet proposals.[103]

---

[98] Blue Book, no. 49. The text of Chamberlain's speech was sent to Seeds. DBFP, vol. v, no. 735.
[99] Blue Book, no. 50. Halifax's conclusion that Maisky's "general attitude was friendly and not at all unhelpful" was excised. See DBFP, vol. vi, no 5.
[100] Blue Book, nos 51-52. Cf. DBFP, vol. vi, annex 1 to no. 35.
[101] DBFP, vol. vi, no. 38.
[102] DBFP, vol. vi, no. 49.
[103] Blue Book, no. 53. Enclosure 1-5 reprinted material from Blue Book no. 51, the "Memorandum of Instructions". Enclosure six was a translation of the Soviet reply of 16 June

As the Blue Book attested, progress was slow in June, consisting of ongoing British concessions to the Soviets. On 19 June Halifax agreed to drop any reference to the League of Nations in the interests of "early and rapid progress."[104] Seeds and Naggiar met with Molotov on 21 June, with most of the discussion centred on article one and the question of naming, or not, the eight eastern European countries bordering on the Soviet Union.[105] Molotov's reply, a day later, declared that the Soviet version of article one, as offered on 2 June, stood as "*ne veriateur*". This left Halifax writing to Seeds on 22 June that he was "bewildered" by Molotov's attitude and "stubborn pertinacity" and confessing, "I realise the difficulty of dealing with a man of such inarticulate obstinacy."[106]

An exception to the Blue Book practice of omitting Seeds' personal observations was made for a 23 June telegram. In this, Seeds tried to explain Molotov's suspicious mind and then hinted at acceding to Soviet preferences regarding a list of states to be guaranteed. He also commented on what the Soviets regarded as "loopholes" in the British approach.[107] Seeds' input possibly reinforced Halifax comment to Maisky

---

1939, as in <u>DBFP</u>, vol. vi, no. 69. <u>Blue Book</u> no. 54 was a record of the meeting on 16 June. The <u>Blue Book</u> omitted Seeds' comments (<u>DBFP</u>, vol. vi, no 73) that Molotov had a "suspicious mind" and "I fear we shall have trouble over this point later [regarding Poland's position]." The <u>Blue Book</u> also did not reproduce the record of the first meeting on 15 June. See <u>DBFP</u>, vol. vi, no. 60.

[104] <u>Blue Book</u>, no 55.

[105] <u>Blue Book</u>, nos. 56-57. Paragraph10 in <u>DBFP</u>, vol. vi, no. 123 was omitted.

[106] <u>Blue Book</u>, no. 60. The <u>Blue Book</u> omitted four paragraphs dealing with British objections and possible alternatives to the Soviet version of article one. Cf. <u>DBFP</u>, vol. vi, no 127.

[107] <u>Blue Book</u>, no. 61. Cf. <u>DBFP</u>, vol. vi, no. 139.

that same day, "that saying 'No' to everything was not my idea of negotiation."[108]

On 27 June Halifax attempted to meet the Soviet position with a renewed formulation of article one. Although avoiding naming specific eastern European states, it did give the Soviets freedom of action in the case of aggression against a border state. The Blue Book, however, omitted the telling paragraph in which Halifax noted his reluctant agreement, in the last resort, to listing the eastern border states if the Netherlands and Switzerland were included, and if this list was to remain secret.[109] The Blue Book followed this with another lengthy Soviet extract, this time from a 29 June article in Pravda. It was likely included because of its conclusion, ironic in retrospect, that Britain and France were preparing "their own public opinion for an eventual deal with the aggressors."[110]

When Seeds and Naggiar met with Molotov on 1 July, they agreed that the list of guaranteed states would be left to a secret protocol. Molotov then raised a new question. He insisted that the phrase "indirect aggression" against the border states be added to article one, with its definition relegated to an unpublished annex to the treaty.[111] Although considerable discussion of this issue passed between Seeds and Halifax, the Blue Book instead jumped to a further meeting in Moscow on 3 July and the Soviet refusal to include Holland and Switzerland in the secret protocol.[112] On 6 July Halifax informed Seeds that, while he was prepared to concede this point, he found the Soviet definition of indirect aggression "completely

---

[108] Blue Book, no. 62. There were two minor omissions. Cf. DBFP, vol. vi, no. 135.
[109] Blue Book, no. 63. Cf. DBFP, vol. vi, no. 151.
[110] Blue Book, no. 64.
[111] Blue Book, nos. 65-68.
[112] Blue Book, no. 69.

unacceptable."[113] Instead, Halifax proposed speaking only of aggression "to be understood as covering action accepted by the State in question under the threat of force by another Power and involving the abandonment by it of its independence or neutrality."[114] The Blue Book omitted Halifax's suggestion that if difficulties were prolonged, he was prepared to fall back to a simple tripartite agreement on mutual assistance.[115] On the same day, as well, Halifax met with Maisky who was non-committal about the idea of reverting to a simple tripartite pact of mutual assistance.[116]

After another fruitless meeting in Moscow on 9 July, Seeds observed, "we can carry negotiations no further without further instructions." With so much of the discussion centred on minute points of phrasing, the Blue Book then reproduced a very edited version of the emerging document. Seeds' observation that reverting to a tripartite agreement would be fraught with difficulties was omitted.[117] When Halifax next communicated with Seeds on 12 July, he affirmed that Molotov's 9 July definition of "indirect aggression" was unacceptable, not least because it would "undermine [Britain's] ... moral position in Europe". He concluded that the government "might have to reconsider their whole position."[118]

---

[113] As in Blue Book, no. 68: "an internal coup d'etat or a reversal of policy in the interest of the aggressor."

[114] Blue Book, no. 70. A telegram from Halifax to Seeds stating that he was not prepared to make entry into force of any agreement dependent on the conclusion of a military agreement, which is in fact what transpired, was not included in the Blue Book. See DBFP, vol. vi, no. 252.

[115] See DBFP, vol. vi, no. 253.

[116] Blue Book, no. 71. Maisky's response that the Baltic states, according to his information, would not really object to being guaranteed, was omitted. See DBFP, vol. vi, no. 255.

[117] Blue Book, nos. 72-73. Cf. DBFP, vol. vi, no. 281-282.

[118] Blue Book, no. 74.

With the pace of the negotiations in mid-July slowed and the issues complex, the Blue Book became selective in an attempt to unfold a coherent narrative.[119]

When the negotiations resumed on 18 July, no progress was made on the question of defining "direct and indirect" aggression. As well, Molotov stood firm on the argument that the political and military agreements "formed one organic and inseparable whole." Seeds urged a trade-off between Soviet flexibility on defining aggression in return for British flexibility regarding article six.[120] In the following five days, although considerable discussion took place on the British side, no records found a place in the Blue Book. In a letter to Halifax, Strang described the negotiations as "a humiliating experience" and observed that Britain would have to pay the Soviet price.[121] On 21 July Halifax telegraphed Seeds that the government would meet Soviet demands on article six.[122]

When the talks resumed in Moscow on 23 July, Seeds informed Molotov that the British government had conceded on article six. Molotov then stated that article one and the protocol did not raise any "insuperable difficulties" and that the military talks should begin at once and in Moscow. In a document not included in the Blue Book, Seeds afterwards

---

[119] Thus the Blue Book omitted such documents as DBFP, vol. vi, nos. 300, 301, 305, 312, 324, and most significantly, no. 329 in which Halifax indicated to Seeds that the British were prepared to begin military discussions conditional on the Soviets abandoning their insistence on simultaneous signature with the political accord.

[120] Blue Book, no. 75. Some convoluted details of the conversation were left out of the Blue Book. See DBFP, vol. vi, no. 338. DBFP, vol. vi, nos. 339, 342, 349 have further details.

[121] Strang to Halifax, 20 July 1939, DBFP, vol. vi, no. 376.

[122] DBFP, vol. vi, no. 378, 381.

observed that he was "not optimistic" about the success of military talks, although he considered that the initiative would have positive results elsewhere.[123] Halifax also emphasized the "deterrent value of Staff conversations" when he met with Maisky on 25 July.[124] That same day, Halifax informed Seeds that the British were prepared to begin the military talks immediately.[125] Molotov received this information on 27 July when the talks resumed. The Blue Book, however, omitted the subsequent acrimonious exchange about what publicity was to be given to the opening of the military talks. Molotov demanded that no statement was required.[126]

Halifax and Seeds continued to exchange telegrams, omitted from the Blue Book, on the vexed question of "indirect aggression", Halifax taking a much firmer line.[127] Instead, the Blue Book highlighted government statements in parliament between 31 July and 3 August, underscoring the complexities of trying to define "indirect aggression", and trumpeting the dispatch of a military mission before the conclusion of a political agreement as evidence of *bona fides*.[128] The Blue Book followed this with a Tass communiqué in which Butler was taken to task for not differentiating the question of infringing the independence of the Baltic states, the British position, with a firm definition of "indirect aggression", the Soviet position.[129]

On 2 August Seeds informed Molotov of the composition of the British military delegation. Molotov again

---

[123] Blue Book, no. 76; DBFP, vol. vi, no. 416. Seeds expressed the same reserve again on 26 July. See DBFP, vol. vi, no 456.
[124] Blue Book, no. 78.
[125] Blue Book, no. 77.
[126] Blue Book, no. 79; DBFP, vol. vi, no. 473.
[127] See e.g., DBFP, vol. vi, nos. 474, 483, 493, 497.
[128] Blue Book, nos 80-82.
[129] Blue Book, no. 83.

complained about Butler's comments, while Seeds did his best to defend the British position. The Blue Book contained an extensively edited record of this acrimonious and ultimately futile exchange. A most telling omission was Seeds' conclusion: "I feel our negotiations have received severe set-back."[130] Nor did the Blue Book publish Seeds' follow up telegram on 3 August, in which he suggested that if the government intended to take a firm line on the question of "indirect aggression", then "a pause in the conversations ... would do no harm." Finally, Seeds observed that the French were inclined to accept the Soviet formulation.[131] However, the Blue Book continued with one last telegram from Halifax to Seeds recounting a meeting between Butler and Maisky in a further attempt to calm the waters. The Blue Book, however, deleted Maisky's admission that the Tass version of Butler's speech was "not correct."[132]

The Blue Book narrative continued with the text of the proposed agreement as of 2 August, indicating the substantial measure of agreement reached since April.[133] Then an "Explanatory Memorandum" summarized the military conversations held in Moscow from 11-25 August, and emphasized that it was the Nazi-Soviet pact of 23 August that had destroyed any prospects of a grand alliance against Hitler.[134] There followed <u>Tass</u> communiqués announcing, first, the conclusion of a German-Soviet commercial agreement and then

---

[130] <u>Blue Book</u>, no. 84. The annex to no. 84 contained the British draft definition of "indirect aggression" handed to Molotov on 2 August. Cf. <u>DBFP</u>, vol. vi, no. 525. On 4 August Halifax instructed Strang to return to London. See <u>DBFP</u>, vol. vi, no. 540.

[131] <u>DBFP</u>, vol. vi, no. 527.

[132] <u>Blue Book</u>, no. 85. Cf. <u>DBFP</u>, vol. vi, no. 544.

[133] <u>Blue Book</u>, no. 86. See <u>DBFP</u>, vol. vi, no. 493 for a similar summary as of 29 July.

[134] <u>Blue Book</u>, no. 87. This was actually prepared on 12 December 1939.

the impending visit to Moscow of Joachim von Ribbentrop, the German Foreign Minister.[135] Halifax then instructed Seeds to see Molotov and he also accused the Soviets of acting in "bad faith."[136] This was precisely what Seeds stated when he met with Molotov on 22 August. The ensuing conversation consisted mainly of recriminations in which Molotov countered accusations of "bad faith" with "a lack of sincerity" on Britain's part.[137]

Among the closing documents in the Blue Book was an extract from a speech given by Halifax on 24 August in the House of Lords. He expressed his dismay at the secret German-Soviet negotiations leading to the signature of a non-aggression treaty and reiterated that Britain stood by its obligations to Poland.[138] The intent of the Nazi-Soviet agreement was underlined with a reprinting of the German-Soviet agreement of 28 September dividing Poland and the Estonian-Soviet mutual assistance pact of the same day.[139] The Blue Book concluded with resolutions by the League of Nations Assembly and Council on 14 December expelling the USSR.[140]

---

[135] Blue Book, nos. 88-89.
[136] Blue Book, no. 90.
[137] Blue Book, no. 91. An attempt by Molotov to show a divergence between the British and French governments on the issue of the passage of troops through third party states was omitted from the Blue Book. See DBFP, vol. vi, no. 165.
[138] Blue Book, no. 92.
[139] Blue Book, nos 93-94.
[140] Blue Book, no. 95.

Conclusion

A Blue Book on the Anglo-Soviet-French negotiations of 1939 had initially been resisted on several grounds. Arguments that the Soviets should not be pushed further into the German camp; that to select documents of a sensitive nature would be difficult; that publication would require the agreement of other countries; and that Britain's negotiating tactics themselves might be open to criticism initially overshadowed the project. However, the Soviet attack against Finland completely altered the climate and publication was approved. A Blue Book was suddenly regarded as a useful propaganda effort. Although the exercise ended with a reversion to total silence, it was revealing at several levels. In terms of intent, the Blue Book proceeded along a strictly defined path. The position of Seeds was carefully safeguarded. He was recalled from Moscow on 22 December to spare him any difficulties that publication might produce. He also reviewed the selection of documents both before and soon after his return to London on 8 January 1940. As well, the Blue Book only reproduced his telegrams detailing conversations with Litvinov and afterwards with Molotov. Telegrams of a personal, reflective or advisory nature were omitted. So too were others which revealed the occasional difficulties he initially had with the French ambassador on questions of coordination and several more where Seeds' thinking appeared to be ahead of the Foreign Office. The intention to safeguard Maisky is marginally problematic. The Blue Book included records of his conversations with Halifax, but these were rarely revealing. It is likely that the purpose was to avoid any worsening of Anglo-Soviet relations in early 1940.

Given these strictures, it is easy to agree with Strang who, on 5 January 1940, stated that the objective of publication was "to see that the Soviet case was stated, as well as our own."[141] Yet this was a double-edged sword. No doubt, a reader of the Blue Book could follow the unfolding of the Soviet end of the negotiations, although without any insight into such questions as motive. On the other hand, what was clearly revealed, and the sticking point of the negotiations, was Soviet thinking on the definition of "indirect aggression" and cross border transit rights. Such issues threatened the sovereignty of both large and small nations. And it is the rectitude of such issues, resisted earlier by the British, that the Foreign Office wished the Blue Book to unequivocally convey. However, publication finally was stalled because of both direct and indirect influences. As the weeks of 1940 passed, the urgency behind the exercise abated. This was partly due to the ongoing and ultimately unfinished negotiations with Labour leaders who wanted the Blue Book to appear. Countering this was the adamant and finally decisive opposition of both the French and to a lesser extent the Polish governments. The war effort needed Anglo-French co-operation. The war effort, as 1940 unfolded, also required improving relations with the USSR. A combination of all of these factors, therefore, allowed the Blue Book to wither on the vine. Writing in 1941, a Foreign Office official noted that the type for the Blue Book at last could be destroyed with Britain and the Soviet Union finally in alliance against Nazi Germany.

The failure to publish the Blue Book in 1940 was remedied with the publication of <u>Documents on British Foreign Policy, 1919-1939, Third Series</u>, Volumes IV-VII (1951-1954). These volumes revealed the tripartite negotiations as preserved in the Foreign Office archives. Other internal documentation, including officials' minutes and related files, were opened in 1969 when the 50-year rule of secrecy was reduced to 30 years. Orthodoxy, revisionism and neo-revisionism have subsequently

---

[141] Minute by Strang, 5 Jan. 1940, NA, FO371/24395, C188/23/18.

produced very different interpretations of the negotiations. These have ranged through criticism of the Chamberlain government's handling of the negotiations, to a defense based on expediency, to a more recent reversion towards criticism of the British approach and greater sympathy towards the Soviet position. The fact of the matter is that, despite a voluminous quantity of materials, consensus still eludes the historians of the 1939 negotiations, much as it did the original compilers of the Blue Book.

PAPERS REGARDING THE ANGLO-SOVIET NEGOTIATIONS, 1939.

SUMMARY OF CONTENTS.

M. STALIN'S speech of the 10th March, 1939, in which he stated that the Soviet Union stood "for the support of nations which were the victims of aggression and were fighting for the independence of their country" (document 1), encouraged His Majesty's Government to hope that the Soviet were prepared to co-operate in an effort to restrain farther aggression in Europe.

On the 17th March, two days after the German occupation of Prague, His Majesty's Government consulted the Soviet Government about current reports that German aggression against Roumania was imminent. His Majesty's Government enquired whether the Soviet Government would actively assist the Roumanian Government if requested by the latter to do so (document 2). In reply, the Soviet Government proposed an immediate six-Power conference at Bucharest, to be attended by representatives of the British, Soviet, French, Polish, Turkish and Roumanian Governments. M. Litvinov informed Sir W. Seeds that the Soviet Government had refused "to recognise the seizure of Czecho-Slovakia on the ground that no Head of State had a legal or constitutional right to sign away his country's independence" (documents 3 and 4).

In an interview with the Soviet Ambassador on the 19th March Lord Halifax explained the practical difficulties in the way of a conference at Bucharest, and suggested that more effective and rapid results might be obtained by a four-Power declaration associating Great Britain, France, Poland and the Soviet Union (document 5). On the 21st March Sir W. Seeds put forward to the Soviet Government a proposal for a four-Power declaration between the British, French, Polish and Soviet Governments for mutual consultation in the event of a threat to the independence of any European State (documents 6 and 7). Although the Soviet Government were disappointed that their proposal for a conference in Bucharest had not been accepted (documents 7 and 8), they agreed on the 22nd March to associate themselves with a four-Power declaration (documents 9 and 10).

During the visit of the Secretary of the Department of Overseas Trade to Moscow towards the end of March, Mr. Hudson had two conversations with M. Litvinov in which the latter enlarged upon the theme of the failure of the democracies to withstand German aggression and the probability that "a Europe entirely German would shortly be bounded simply by Great Britain and the Soviet Union" (document 16). M. Litvinov had also complained of the "cold-shouldering of the Soviet Union," but the Prime Minister gave an assurance in the House of Commons on the 31st March that there were no ideological impediments between the United Kingdom and the U.S.S.R. (document 13), and on the 3rd April he informed the House of Commons that ideological differences would not be allowed to prevent Anglo-Soviet collaboration in resistance to aggression (document 17).

On the 28th March the Prime Minister informed the House of Commons that His Majesty's Government were "actively continuing their consultations with other Governments," and that what they had in mind went "a great deal further than consultation". He added that "His Majesty's Government had made perfectly clear to the other Governments with whom they were in consultation what His Majesty's Government were prepared to do in certain circumstances" (document 11).

On the 29th March M. Maisky asked Sir A. Cadogan to explain the exact meaning of the Prime Minister's statement. Sir A. Cadogan explained that the Polish Government were reluctant to associate themselves with action clearly directed to meet possible German aggression and therefore likely, in their view, to precipitate it. It was therefore useless to pursue the idea of a four-Power declaration, and His Majesty's Government were contemplating instead the possibility of giving assurances to the Polish and Roumanian Governments involving direct military assistance.

M. Maisky remarked that such a course "would be a revolutionary change in British policy. It would increase enormously the confidence of other countries and might have a very great effect" (documents 10 and 12). His Majesty's Government, with the object of steadying the European situation, gave a unilateral pledge to Poland on the 31st March. The French Government authorised the Prime Minister" to make it plain that they stood in the same position in this matter as His Majesty's Government" (document 13).

This was afterwards converted, on the 6th April, into a reciprocal Anglo-Polish declaration. The Soviet Government were kept fully informed, and the Prime Minister's statement of the 31st March (document 13) was communicated to M. Maisky earlier in the day. Although he was unable to express his Government's views at short notice, he informed Lord Halifax that the Soviet position "had been defined by M. Stalin a short time ago as assistance against aggression for those who fought for their independence, and therefore they were certainly prepared to help Poland or any other country that was attacked and resisted, but the Soviet Government had no desire to force themselves on anybody. Although they thought it groundless, they understood the fear of the Poles, which was that, if Soviet troops came into Poland, Polish conditions were such that the contacts that would be made would probably produce disturbing effects on Polish society."

In view of this the Prime Minister had stated in the House of Commons on the 31st March that "he had no doubt that the principles on which we are acting are fully understood and appreciated by the Soviet Government" (documents 13 and 14).

On the 1st April, however, M. Litvinov contested the latter statement and attempted to maintain that His Majesty's Government had neither consulted nor informed the Soviet Government of their action. He even expressed "doubts whether we would regard an attack on Danzig or the Corridor as threatening Poland's independence" (document 15).

On the 4th April a telegram was sent to Sir W. Seeds recapitulating the close consultation which had in fact, taken place between His Majesty's Government and the Soviet Government during the last half of March and the encouragement which the latter had given to His Majesty's Government to expect that their declaration of assistance to Poland was in accordance with the Soviet Government's policy (document 18).

On the 13th April His Majesty's Government also gave a unilateral undertaking to assist Roumania and Greece (document 19). The French Government gave a similar undertaking and confirmed the Franco-Polish alliance in a declaration published on the 13th April (document 20). On the 13th April Sir John Simon referred in a statement in the House of Commons to the exchanges which had taken place with the Soviet Government (document 21). The Soviet Government were informed of the British undertakings to Poland and Roumania and invited on the 15th April, in view of M. Stalin's statement of the 10th March, to support them by a declaration that the assistance of the Soviet Union would be available, if desired, for any European neighbour of the Soviet Union which found itself the victim of aggression and resisted it (documents 22 and 24). On the 14th April M. Maisky informed Lord Halifax that, in view of the action taken by His Majesty's Government, the Soviet Government were prepared to take part in giving assistance to Roumania and enquired as to the best methods by which assistance could be given. M. Maisky felt that the guarantee of His Majesty's Government to Roumania was right and that the British pledge given to the Roumanian Government would steady the situation (document 23). On the 16th April M. Litvinov said that, before replying to the British proposal for a Soviet unilateral declaration, he wished to know how far Great Britain and other countries were prepared to go when it came to the point, and what was expected of the Soviet Union (document 25).

On the 18th April M. Litvinov communicated to the British and French Governments a proposal in writing for an Anglo-Franco-Soviet agreement for mutual assistance, implying military assistance against aggression. The three parties were also to assist all the Eastern European States bordering on the U.S.S.R. against aggression and to conclude a military pact as soon as possible (document 26). On the 29th April Lord Halifax explained to M. Maisky that we were in consultation with the French Government about the Soviet proposal, and asked him to make clear to his Government that we had not asked the Soviet Government to take action except in circumstances in which the British and French Governments would already be automatically involved. On the 29th April Sir W. Seeds was instructed to remove any misunderstanding regarding the attitude of His Majesty's Government (document 28).

Whilst the final reply of His Majesty's Government to the Soviet proposals was still under consideration, M. Litvinov was on the 4th May relieved of his post as Commissar for Foreign Affairs (document 29). On the 6th May the Soviet Ambassador assured Lord Halifax that M. Litvinov's departure would not imply any change of policy, and that the Russian proposals (document 26) still held the field (document 30). A similar statement was made to Sir W. Seeds by M. Molotov on the 8th May (document 32).

On the 8th May the British and French Ambassadors communicated the reply of their Governments to M. Molotov, who had succeeded M. Litvinov as Commissar for Foreign Affairs. They pointed out the difficulties of guaranteeing Soviet assistance to States such as Poland and Roumania, which were chary of invoking Soviet support, and reverted to the original British proposal for a unilateral Soviet declaration consonant with the position of the Soviet Union as a Great Power, which would only commit the Soviet Government to action after Great Britain and France had already been involved in virtue of their existing obligations (document 31). M. Molotov suggested that the Polish Government might no longer be reluctant to accept Soviet assistance. He cross-examined Sir W. Seeds regarding the British attitude towards Holland, Belgium and Switzerland and expressed himself in favour of early military conversations. Although repeating that Soviet policy had not changed, he said that it was liable to be altered if other States changed theirs (document 32). Further enquiries regarding the British proposal were made by M. Maisky on the 9th May (document 33).

On the 10th May the Prime Minister made a statement in the House of Commons regarding the progress of the Anglo-Soviet negotiations (document 34).

On the 11th May M. Maisky expressed to Lord Halifax some doubts regarding the position of the Baltic States under the British proposals, and suggested that His Majesty's Government were not prepared for complete reciprocity in this respect. Lord Halifax expressed the hope that it might be possible to clear up any difficulties personally with the Soviet representative at the forthcoming Council meeting at Geneva (document 35).

On the 14th May M. Molotov rejected the British proposal on the grounds (1) that it did not involve true reciprocity; (2) that it left the north-west frontier of the Soviet Union uncovered: and (3) that it did not provide the Soviet Government with any guarantee against direct aggression. He insisted upon a concrete tripartite pact and military conversations (document 36).

On the 19th May the Prime Minister made a statement in the House of Commons in which he pointed out that the British Government had "never desired to ask the Soviet Government to do anything which they were not prepared to do themselves." Since His Majesty's Government had already undertaken commitments to certain States, any inequality was in favour of the Soviet Union and not of the United Kingdom. The Prime Minister regretted the decision of the Soviet Government not to be represented by M. Molotov or M. Potemkin at Geneva, although the Council meeting had been postponed for a week to permit this (document 37).

On the 21st May Lord Halifax discussed the position with M. Maisky, who was representing the Soviet Government at the Council meeting at Geneva. The latter insisted on the necessity of a triple reciprocal mutual guarantee against direct aggression, but "he agreed that assistance could not be forced on those who did not desire it." He said that "the essential thing was to prevent war,' and that "the Soviet Government were anxious that there should be no outbreak of war anywhere." Lord Halifax expressed his disappointment that whereas "we had made very great efforts to meet their (the Soviet Government's) point of view, they had not changed their position at all and had made little or no advance to meet us"(document 38).

On the 24th May the Prime Minister made a further statement in the House of Commons to the effect that Lord Halifax had had satisfactory conversations with the French Government in Paris and with M Maisky at Geneva, and that he hoped that "as a result of proposals which His Majesty's Government were now in a position to make on the main questions arising it would be found possible to reach full agreement at an early date." (Document 39).

On the 27th May the British and French Ambassadors in Moscow saw M. Molotov, and put forward a revised text for a tripartite agreement for mutual assistance in certain eventualities. This text differentiated between States such as Poland, Roumania and Belgium which had accepted guarantees and others such as Finland and the Baltic States, which were known to be unwilling to accept them. It also provided for action in conformity with the principles of the Covenant.

M. Molotov appeared entirely to misunderstand the purport of these revised proposals and even suggested that "Great Britain and France were apparently satisfied with a state of affairs where Russia would be bombed by the aggressor while Bolivia blocked all action at Geneva." His attitude was such that Sir William Seeds could not omit mention of the fact that M. Molotov might "merely be manoeuvering to close the negotiations," although he assumed that this was not the case (documents 40-44).

On the 29th May Sir W. Seeds attempted to remove M. Molotov's misapprehensions particularly as regards action in accordance with League principles and the need for meeting the susceptibilities of other Powers. M. Molotov was insistent on the necessity for military conversations, and discussed the precedent of the German entry into Prague in March. Sir W. Seeds explained that His Majesty's Government could not impose guarantees of protection on independent nations against their will (documents 45 and 46).

On the 31st May M. Molotov made a. speech to the Supreme Council of the U.S.S.R., in which he stated the Soviet objections to the latest British proposals. He referred to what he termed the absence of reciprocity and of a guarantee in the case of aggression against the States to the north-west of the U.S.S.R. He also objected to the dependence of the proposed negotiations on the Covenant of the League. He required as a minimum (1) an effective tripartite pact of mutual assistance against aggression of a purely defensive nature; (2) a tripartite guarantee against aggression to the states of Central and Eastern Europe including all European States bordering on the U.S.S.R.; and (3) a concrete tripartite agreement as to the forms and extent of immediate and effective assistance to be rendered. M. Molotov repeated M. Stalin's statement of the 10th March that the Soviet Union "stood for the cause of peace and for the prevention of any sort of development of aggression... The Soviet Union could not fail to take its place in the foremost ranks of the united front of peaceful States who were really resisting aggression" (document 47).

On the 2nd June M. Molotov communicated to the British and French Ambassadors a revised text of the proposed agreement in which he insisted upon (1) the naming of eight States, including Finland, Estonia and Latvia, as those which the contracting parties agreed to defend against aggression; and (2) the simultaneous entry into force of military and political arrangements (document 48).

On the 7th June the Prime Minister made a statement in the House of Commons referring to the points upon which agreement had been reached with the Soviet Government. He said that in order to remove the remaining difficulties and accelerate the negotiations a representative of the Foreign Office would be sent to Moscow to assist His Majesty's Ambassador. The Prime Minister also stated that the Finnish, Estonian and Latvian Governments had made it clear that in view of their intention to maintain strict neutrality they did not wish to receive a guarantee as a result of the present negotiations between Great Britain, France and Russia (document 49).

On the 8th June Lord Halifax had a further talk with M. Maisky who "seemed to think this (i.e. the decision to send a Foreign Office representative to Moscow) a very reasonable proposal and spoke in terms of warm appreciation of Mr. Strang's ability, if he was the representative of the Foreign Office to he selected" (document 50).

Mr. Strang left for Moscow on the 12th June with a memorandum and instructions for Sir W. Seeds (document 51). Although far-reaching concessions were made to meet the Soviet point of view His Majesty's Government maintained their opposition to naming the Baltic States in the treaty, in view of the reluctance of these States to be associated with it and suggested an alternative method of covering their case. In that event, however, His Majesty's Government would have to insist upon also dealing with the case of the Netherlands and Switzerland, which occupied a similar position in relation to their own security to that of the Baltic States in relation to the U.S.S.R. His Majesty's Government also explained their opposition to the simultaneous entry into force of the military and political agreements.

M. Molotov received the two ambassadors and Mr Strang on the 15th and 16th June, but little progress was made, particular difficulty being caused by the Soviet Government's insistence upon naming the various States concerned (documents 53 and 54). The difficulties of His Majesty's Government in regard to the Baltic States and the reluctance of the Polish and Roumanian Governments to receive guarantees from the Soviet Union were again explained to M. Molotov on the 21st June, and, in an effort to secure early progress, His Majesty's Government agreed (1) to start Staff conversations immediately on the signature of the agreement, and (2) to omit the reference to the Covenant of the League in paragraph 1 (document 55 and documents 57 and 58). M. Molotov nevertheless expressed his personal view that the proposals made to him "did not represent any progress" (document 56). On the 22nd June M. Molotov informed the two ambassadors that the Soviet Government had rejected their proposals as unacceptable (document 59).

On the 22nd June Lord Halifax, in a telegram to Sir W. Seeds, expressed his bewilderment at the attitude of M. Molotov since we had made so many concessions to his point of view (document 60). On the 23rd June Sir W. Seeds telegraphed his estimate of Soviet policy, in the course of which he suggested that they "had it in mind to secure our assistance or at the least our apparent connivance, should they ever find it expedient to intervene in the Baltic States" (document 61). Lord Halifax attempted on the 23rd June, without success, to obtain some explanation of the Soviet attitude from M. Maisky. In reply to a point-blank question by Lord Halifax. M. Maisky said that the Soviet Government certainly wanted a treaty. Lord Halifax pointed out that they had not "budged a single inch and that we had made all the advances and concessions... Saying 'No' to everything was not his idea of negotiation and it had a striking resemblance to Nazi methods" (document 62).

On the 27th June Lord Halifax put forward a further proposal for dealing with the difficulty of the Baltic States and of other Eastern European Powers without arousing their opposition (document 63).

On the 29th June an article appeared in *Pravda* signed by a prominent member of the Politburo, M. Zhdanov, suggesting that the British and French Governments did not want a real agreement or one acceptable to the U.S.S.R. He concluded by suggesting that "the only thing they really wanted was to talk about an agreement and, by making play with the obstinacy of the Soviet Union, to prepare their own public opinion for an eventual deal with the aggressors" (document 64).

On the 1st July the two ambassadors submitted to M. Molotov the new Franco-British proposals (document 63). These included the suggestion that the Baltic States might be dealt with in an unpublished annex in this case, however, provision would have to be made for the ease of the Netherlands and Switzerland. M. Molotov agreed to the principle of the unpublished protocol, but refused to include the Netherlands and Switzerland, on the grounds (1) that this was an afterthought, and (2) that the Soviet Union had no diplomatic relations with either of them. He also raised the question of "indirect aggression," and demanded a very liberal interpretation of this phrase. He continued to insist upon the simultaneous entry into force of the military and political agreements (documents 65-69).

On the 6th July the two ambassadors were authorised to agree to the omission of the Netherlands and Switzerland but to refuse to agree to the simultaneous entry into force of the military and political agreements or to the very wide definition of "indirect aggression" suggested by M. Molotov, which would appear to justify the worst suspicious of Finland and the Baltic States regarding Soviet interference in their internal affairs (documents 70 and 71).

On the 9th July some progress was achieved with M. Molotov. He remained, however, adamant as regards his definition of "indirect aggression" and the question of military conversations. He suggested that the treaty should, for example, cover the case of "the employment of German officers or instructors by the Estonian or Latvian army, and the consequent transformation of those armies into instruments of aggression against the Soviet Union" (documents 72 and 73).

On the 12th July the ambassadors were authorised to agree to the inclusion of a formula regarding "indirect aggression" in the actual text of the treaty instead of in an unpublished protocol. M. Molotov was to be reminded that he had made no attempt to meet them in return for the concessions made by His Majesty's Government regarding (1) the demand that the treaty should cover the case of the Baltic States; (2) the abandonment of the demand that the Netherlands and Switzerland should be covered by the agreement; (3) the agreement to provide for the case of "indirect aggression"; (4) the reluctant agreement to define "indirect aggression"; (5) the readiness to insert this definition in the agreement itself : and (6) the agreement to include a clause prohibiting the signature of a separate peace. It was pointed out that the Soviet insistence that the political agreement should be dependent on the military agreement suggested that the Soviet Government hoped to force the acceptance of military conditions which would be against our better judgment (document 74).

On the 17th July the ambassadors saw M. Molotov, put the above points and assured him that their two Governments were willing to open military conversations (document 75).

On the 23rd July the ambassadors saw M. Molotov again and informed him that their governments were prepared to meet him regarding the simultaneous entry into force of the military and political agreements. M. Molotov expressed satisfaction, but insisted that, to save time and to deter the aggressors, military conversations should start at once without waiting for full agreement on the two outstanding points of the political agreement (document 76). His Majesty's Government agreed to this suggestion on the 25th July, although they pointed out that they continued to attach capital importance to finding a satisfactory formula for article 1, i.e., one which would not give the Baltic States cause for alarm (documents 77-79).

On the 31st July the Prime Minister stated in the House of Commons that British and French military representatives would be sent to Moscow as soon as possible for military conversations, and that the political discussions should continue concurrently with these conversations (document 80). In the course of a debate later in the day the Prime Minister disposed of the accusation that there had been excessive delay in the course of the negotiations with the Soviet Government and, when summing up the debate, the Parliamentary Under-Secretary of State for Foreign Affairs referred to the difficulty which had been caused by the position of the Baltic States (document 81).

On the 3rd August the Secretary of State referred to the Anglo-Soviet negotiations in a speech in the House of Lords (document 82).

Mr. Butler's reference in the House of Commons on the 31st July (document 80) to the position of the Baltic States was misinterpreted in a Tass communiqué published in Moscow on the 2nd August (document 83). M. Maisky agreed with Mr. Butler on the 4th August that his remarks had been misinterpreted, and that the Tass communiqué (document 83) had been the result of a misunderstanding (document 85). M. Molotov was informed on the 2nd August of the composition of the British and French military missions to Moscow. The remaining difficulties in the political agreement were also discussed, but M. Molotov used Mr. Butler's remarks as a pretext to adopt an unhelpful and critical attitude (document 84). The substantial measure of agreement which had been reached by the three Governments almost entirely as a result of British and French concessions to the Soviet point of view is, however, shown in document 86, containing the English text of the agreement as it stood after the last meeting with M. Molotov on the 2nd August, before the opening of the military conversations.

The course of the military conversations from the 11th-25th August is described in document 87. The main difficulties arose out of (1) the Soviet intimation that they desired His Majesty's Government and the French Government to make arrangements whereby Finnish, Latvian and Estonian bases would be at the disposal of British, French and Soviet naval forces, and (2) the Soviet demand that the Polish and Roumanian Governments should agree in advance to allow Soviet troops to operate in their territory in the event of German aggression, and to draw up, at an early date, the plans necessary to provide for this eventuality. It had been impossible to reach agreement on these points when an announcement appeared in the Soviet press on the 21st August regarding the conclusion of a Soviet-German economic agreement (document 88). This was followed on the 22nd August by a Tass communiqué, announcing the decision to conclude a Soviet-German non-aggression pact and Herr von Ribbentrop's impending visit to Moscow (document 89).

On the 22nd August Sir W. Seeds, on instructions, expressed to M. Molotov the astonishment of His Majesty's Government that the Soviet Government should have concluded such an agreement with the German Government at a moment when the tripartite negotiations had gone far towards a successful conclusion, and that they should have carried on the negotiations with Germany without a single word to His Majesty's Government or to the French Government, with whom the Soviet Government were already in treaty relations. Sir W. Seeds referred to this as an act of bad faith. M. Molotov attempted to excuse himself on the plea that the military missions had arrived at Moscow without instructions enabling them to remove Polish or Roumanian objections to the use of their territory by Soviet troops. Even at this stage M. Molotov did not, however, exclude the continuation of the Anglo-Franco-Soviet negotiations. He said "that it all depended on the German negotiations and perhaps after a bit, say a week, we might see" (documents 90 and 91). In a speech in the House of Lords on the 24th August Lord Halifax publicly expressed the British Government's view of the conduct of the Soviet Government and announced that it did not affect British obligations towards Poland and other countries (document 92).

On the 28th September the Soviet Government reached an agreement with the German Government for the partition of Poland. The text of this agreement, together with a joint German-Soviet declaration and a letter from M. Molotov to Herr von Ribbentrop of the same date is published as document 93.

On the 28th September the Soviet Union signed a pact of mutual assistance with Estonia granting to the Soviet Union the right to station military forces in Estonia (document 94). Similar treaties were concluded by the Soviet Union with Latvia and Lithuania.

On the 30th November Finland was attacked by Soviet forces. On the 3rd December the Finnish Government appealed to the League and on the 14th December the Assembly and the Council of the League of Nations condemned Soviet aggression against Finland. The Soviet Union was declared to be no longer a member of the League (document 95).

List of Persons Mentioned in the Documents Showing their Official Positions

Moscow

Josef Stalin,   Leading Statesman, Secretary of the Communist Party

Maxim Litvinov,   Soviet People's Commissar for Foreign Affairs, relieved of this post on 4 May, 1939

M. Molotov,   Soviet President of the People's Commissars for Foreign Affairs, appointed on 4 May, 1939

M. Zhdanov,   Deputy of the Supreme Council of the Soviet Union

M. Potemkin,	Deputy Commissar for Foreign Affairs
Marshall Voroshilov,	Military Delegation for Anglo-French-Soviet Conversations in Moscow
Army Commander B Shaposhnikov,	the same
Flagman Flotta H Kuznetsov,	the same
Army Commander A Loktionov,	the same
Corps Commander I Smorodinov,	the same
Sir William Seeds,	British Ambassador in Moscow
Admiral Sir Reginald Plunkett-Ernle-Erle-Drax,	British Military Mission to the Soviet Union
Major General T Heywood,	the same
Air Marshall Sir Charles Burnett,	the same
M. Naggiar,	French Ambassador at Moscow
General Doumenc,	French Military Mission to the Soviet Union
General Valin,	the same

Count von der Schulenburg, German Ambassador at Moscow

London

M. Maisky, Soviet Ambassador at London

Neville Chamberlain, Prime Minister

Sir John Simon, Chancellor of the Exchequer

Viscount Halifax, Secretary of State for Foreign Affairs

Mr. R. S. Hudson, Parliamentary Under Secretary for Foreign Affairs and Secretary of the Department of Overseas Trade

Sir Alexander Cadogan, Permanent Under Secretary of State for Foreign Affairs

Mr W. Strang, Foreign Office official, sent to Moscow on 12 June 1939

Mr R. A. Butler, Parliamentary Under-Secretary of State for Foreign Affairs

Arthur Greenwood MP	Deputy Leader of the Labour Party
Hugh Dalton MP	Member of the Labour Party, Parliamentary Under-Secretary of State for Foreign Affairs

<u>Berlin</u>
Herr von Ribbentrop,	Minister for Foreign Affairs

<u>Warsaw</u>
Colonel Beck,	Minister for Foreign Affairs

<u>Paris</u>
M. Daladier,	President of the Council and Minister of War

PAPERS REGARDING THE ANGLO-SOVIET NEGOTIATIONS, 1939.

No. 1.

Extract from the Speech by M. Stalin on March 10, 1939, at the 18th Congress of the All-Union Communist Party.

THE foreign policy of the Soviet Union is clear and explicit:-

1. We stand for peace and the strengthening of business relations with all countries. That is our position and we shall adhere to this position as long as these countries maintain like relations with the Soviet Union, and as

long as they make no attempt to trespass on the interests of our country.

2. We stand for peaceful, close and friendly relations with all the neighbouring countries which have common frontiers with the U.S.S.R. That is our position: and we shall adhere to this position as long as these countries maintain like relations with the Soviet Union, and as long as they make no attempt to trespass, directly or indirectly, on the integrity and inviolability of the frontiers of the Soviet State.

3. We stand for the support of nations which are the victims of aggression and are fighting for the independence of their country.

4. We are not afraid of the threats of aggressors and are ready to deal a double blow for every blow delivered by instigators of war who attempt to violate the Soviet borders.

Such is the foreign policy of the Soviet Union.

No. 2.

Viscount Halifax to Sir W. Seeds (Moscow).

(Telegraphic.) *Foreign Office, March 17, 1939.*

HIS Majesty's Government are considering their position in the event of Roumania becoming victim of German aggression, but an essential element in their judgment would be the knowledge of what would he the attitude of other Governments.

2. Please enquire immediately of Soviet Government whether they can give any indication that they would, if requested by Roumanian Government, actively help the latter to resist German aggression.

No. 3.

Sir W.Seeds to Viscount Halifax.

(Telegraphic.) *Moscow, March 18, 1939.*

YOUR telegram of 17th March. (No. 2)

I have just seen M. Litvinov, who promised to give a reply later.

Meanwhile, he put to me questions which he said his colleagues would certainly ask. Had I any indication of the line which His Majesty's Government were proposing to take themselves? Did we wish the Soviet Union to take engagement while leaving our own hands free? I said in a problem affecting this part of Europe His Majesty's Government quite properly wanted to know the attitude of countries principally concerned: that would he the obvious basis of our decision later.

He said at least I could tell him what was official reaction of His Majesty's Government to seizure of Czecho-Slovakia. What reply were we making to notes which we, like the Soviet Government, had doubtless received from the German Government announcing the *fait accompli*? I said I could for the moment only point to the Prime Minister's speech as showing our attitude. But this did not seem to satisfy him possibly on the same grounds that the local press pretend that the changed attitude to Germany of *The Times* may be only for temporary and internal consumption.

No. 4.

Sir W. Seeds to Viscount Halifax.

(Telegraphic.) *Moscow, March 18, 1939.*

MY telegram of 18th March. (No. 3)

M. Litvinov has informed me that he immediately laid my earlier request before his Government. Latter took the view that no good purpose would be served by various Governments enquiring of each other in turn what action others would take before making up their own minds. The Soviet Government therefore proposed that delegates appointed by British, Soviet, French, Polish, Turkish and Roumanian Governments should meet to discuss possibilities of common action. He himself thought that Bucharest would be most suitable venue. I promised to transmit suggestion to His Majesty's Government in case events should require further consultations.

He said that the Soviet Government had replied to the German Ambassador's notes with a refusal to recognise seizure of Czecho-Slovakia on the ground that no head of State had legal or constitutional right to sign away his country's independence.

No. 5.

Viscount Halifax to Sir W. Seeds (Moscow).

Foreign Office, March 19, 1939.

Sir,

THE Soviet Ambassador asked to see me this afternoon. M. Maisky said that he had no doubt I had received information from your Excellency as to the two conversations that you had had with M. Litvinov. M. Maisky said that he wished to develop somewhat the arguments that had been in M. Litvinov's mind in regard to the method of procedure that he had suggested by way of conference between Great Britain, France, Poland, Russia, Turkey and Roumania at Bucharest. In M. Litvinov's view this would be the quickest method of attaining results and, although he was open-minded about the venue of such a conference, he thought the psychological effect of holding it at Bucharest would be valuable both at Bucharest and at Berlin.

2. I told M. Maisky that we had had an opportunity of considering this proposition this morning and that we were wholly at one with M. Litvinov in feeling the desire for finding means to make speedy progress. We certainly had no wish to waste time in prolonged and argumentative diplomatic exchanges. At the same time, we were sensible of two difficulties in the proposal that M. Litvinov had made. First, we could hardly in present circumstances manage to send a responsible Minister to take part in the conference, and, if this were not possible, the desired advantage in the way of quick decision would not, in fact, be obtained. Secondly, and perhaps more important, we thought that to hold such a conference as M. Litvinov suggested without a certainty that it would he successful was dangerous.

3. We were at present employed upon the consideration of a proposal not altogether dissimilar, but one which we thought was perhaps better calculated to yield the results we all desired. I was not in a position at present to speak in detail of this, as we were having a further meeting this afternoon to consider it, but in essence our notion was that it might be possible quite quickly to find means by which Great Britain, France, Poland, Turkey

and Russia could publicly assert their solidarity of attitude in a form that would, I thought, achieve both the principal objects that M. Litvinov, not less than we ourselves, had in view. If some such public action could speedily be taken, it would at once constitute a plain signal of danger to the German Government and might be expected to afford a rallying point and vitalising force for the smaller States. Provided we could get so far, I thought that it would then become desirable that we should together consider what precise action it would be in the power of each of us to take in particular circumstances, and with that examination we should also hope to associate the giving of encouragement to the smaller States to act in concert both with one another and with ourselves. M. Maisky did not press me closely upon the details of what I had said to him and seemed prepared to give general agreement to the line that I had indicated. He did ask me whether we should rule out the idea of a conference to which I replied that we "should certainly not rule it out;" but that I thought it was desirable to make further progress, as I thought we might expect to do more rapidly by the method I had outlined, before attempting to decide whether or not the conference procedure would be appropriate at a later stage. I told him that I should hope to be in a position to telegraph further instructions to your Excellency this evening for communication to the Soviet Government.

No. 6.

Viscount Halifax to Sir W. Seeds (Moscow).

(Telegraphic.) *Foreign Office, March 20, 1939.*

MY telegram of 17th March. (No. 2)

Recent German absorption of Czecho-Slovakia shows clearly that German Government are resolved to go beyond their hitherto avowed aim of consolidation of German race They have now extended their conquest to another nation, and if this should prove to be part of a definite police of domination there is no State in Europe which is not directly or ultimately threatened.

2. In the circumstances thus created it seems to His Majesty's Government in the United Kingdom to be desirable to proceed without delay to the organisation of mutual support on the part of all those who realise the necessity of protecting international society from further violation of the fundamental laws one which it rests.

3. As a first step they propose that the French, Soviet and Polish Governments should join with His Majesty's Government in signing and publishing a formal declaration, the terms of which they suggest should be on the lines of the following: -

> 'We the undersigned, duly authorised to that effect, hereby declare that, inasmuch as peace and security in Europe are matters of common interest and concern, and since European peace and security may be affected by any action which constitutes a threat to the political independence of any European State, our respective Governments hereby undertake immediately to consult together as to what steps should be taken to offer joint resistance to any such action.'

4. It appears to us that the publication of such a declaration would in itself be a valuable contribution to the stability of Europe, and we should propose that publication should be followed by an examination by the signatories of any specific situation which requires it, with a view to determining the nature of any action which might be taken.

5. Please endeavour immediately to obtain the views of Governments to which you are accredited. His Majesty's

Government would be prepared to sign declaration immediately the three other Governments indicate their readiness to do so.

6. We should propose to say nothing of this to the other Governments concerned before the four Powers are agreed on the declaration.

N.B.- A similar telegram was addressed to Paris and Warsaw.

No. 7.

Sir W. Seeds to Viscount Halifax

(Telegraphic.) *Moscow, March 21, 1939.*

YOUR telegram of 20 March. (No. 6)

I saw M. Litvinov this afternoon and gave him substance of paragraphs 1 and 2 of your telegram as well as text of proposed declaration.

2. He said that in view of misleading reports published in the press of all countries (except in Soviet Union) he had been compelled to issue to-day an official communiqué stating that in reply to our enquiries about his Government's attitude he had suggested a six Power conference. He understood from the Soviet Ambassador in London that you considered his suggestion premature.

3. I pointed out that the present proposal of His Majesty's Government in no way rendered his suggestion premature: it only proposed earlier step, which would be clearer warning to potential aggressors and was easier to decide on owing to the smaller number of Powers concerned at the outset.

4. He answered that agreement on your present proposal

would be more easily attained by a conference, otherwise each Government concerned would suggest amendments of text and endless telegraphing would ensue. I argued that the substance of the declaration was such that truly peace-loving Governments could not fail to subscribe to it, and that any amendments would therefore be only slight and speedily settled.

5. M. Livitnov expressed the belief that the Polish Government would not commit themselves to a declaration of the nature proposed.

6. He reverted several times to the fact that his suggestion was regarded as "premature," and I observe that that word concludes the communiqué to which I alluded and which I have only this moment received.

7. Text of communiqué follows in my immediately succeeding telegram.

No. 8.

Sir W. Seeds to Viscount Halifax.

(Telegraphic.) *Moscow, March 21, 1939.*

FOLLOWING is text of Tass communiqué referred to in my immediately preceding telegram (No. 7):-

"Foreign press have been spreading rumours to effect that Soviet Government recently proposed to Poland and Roumania its aid in case they became victims of aggression. Tass is authorised to declare that this does not correspond to reality. Neither Poland nor Roumania appealed to Soviet Government for aid or informed Soviet Government of any danger threatening them. It is true that on 18th March British Government, having informed Soviet Government that there were serious reasons for fearing an act of violence against Roumania, enquired as to possible position of Soviet Government in such an eventuality. Soviet Government in reply to this enquiry made proposal of calling Conference of representatives of most interested States, namely, Great Britain, France, Poland, Roumania, Turkey and U.S.S.R. Such a Conference in opinion of Soviet Government would give best possibility for clarifying real situation and ascertaining position of each of participants. British Government, however, believed that this proposal was premature."

No. 9.

Sir W. Seeds to Viscount Halifax.

(Telegraphic.) *Moscow, March 22, 1939.*

MY telegram of 21st March. (No. 7)

M. Litvinov sent for me this evening and informed me as follows: -

"We are in agreement with the British proposal and accept text of declaration. The Soviet Government will give its signatures as soon as both France and Poland have accepted the British proposal and promised their signatures."

2. The Soviet Government suggest that the declaration should be signed by the Prime Minister as well as by the Minister for Foreign Affairs of each country. They are also anxious that not only the Balkan but also Baltic and Scandinavian countries should be invited to adhere after publication.

No. 10.

Viscount Halifax to Sir W. Seeds (Moscow).

Foreign Office, March 28, 1939.

Sir,

The Soviet Ambassador called on the 23rd March on Sir A. Cadogan and told him, although he understood we had already received news to that effect through your Excellency, that the reply of his Government to our enquiry about the four-Power declaration was in the affirmative.

2. Sir A. Cadogan said that we had already received this information from you and that we appreciated the prompt affirmative reply given by the Soviet Government. At the same time we had been somewhat disconcerted at the proposal of the Soviet Government to make a public announcement on the subject today. M. Maisky at once said that he understood that his Government had now revised their decision on this point and would not be publishing.

3. He then went on to question Sir A. Cadogan as to the general progress of our negotiation. Sir A. Cadogan told him that so far we were without a final answer from the Polish Government. He enquired whether the Polish Government appeared to be making any serous difficulty. Sir A. Cadogan said that it was easy to understand that the Polish Government at this juncture

should feel themselves to be in a difficult position: they had told us, in fact, that the matter would require very careful consideration. It was not unnatural that they might hesitate before committing themselves in peace time to joining openly a *bloc* which was obviously designed for resistance to German expansion. Sir A. Cadogan was bound to say in all frankness that their hesitation on this point seemed to be increased by the reflection that, if they joined a bloc which included the Soviet Government, that in itself would expose them all the more to German indignation. However, Sir A. Cadogan repeated that they appeared to be still considering the matter and we would of course keep closely in touch with M. Maisky.

4. He then enquired whether, if we secured the declaration, we should then proceed to get in touch with other Powers. In his view it would be advisable to secure the co-operation of as many countries as possible. Sir A. Cadogan said that that would no doubt come up for consideration in the course of the exchanges of views which would follow on the declaration, but, as a personal observation, he suggested that it might perhaps be as well to start with certain countries who appeared to be more directly in the road of German advance and who were already organised in some treaty arrangements.

No. 11.

Statement by the Prime Minister in the House of Commons on March 28, 1939.

Mr. Arthur Greenwood asked the Prime Minister whether he has any statement to make with regard to the European situation.

The Prime Minister: I need not repeat the statement which I made last Thursday on behalf of His Majesty's Government, but I can inform the House that His Majesty's Government are actively continuing their consultations with other Governments upon the issues arising from recent events. During the progress of these consultations, the House will appreciate that it is essential that their confidential character should be respected, and hon. members will not, I trust, press me to make statements which could not in any case be complete, until we are in possession of the final views of the other Governments concerned.

Mr. Greenwood: While one realises the difficulties of complete disclosure at this stage, in view of the general uneasiness which I think there is in this country and in the House, would it be possible, for the enlightenment of the public here and the public abroad and of certain other Powers for the right hon. gentleman to go just a little bit further to remove the apprehensions that there are in the minds of members in all parts of the House, as to whether the declaration which has been submitted to certain Powers is one merely for consultation, or whether it is one which is a policy of mutual aid which might involve military commitments? If the House could have some guidance on that matter it might feel more at rest than it is at this time.

The Prime Minister: I quite appreciate the right hon. gentleman's desire to have as much information as possible, and particularly to remove what he, I think rightly describes as misapprehensions. He will appreciate, on the other hand, that it is extremely difficult and delicate to throw all the cards on the table while the game is not yet complete. It will, at any rate, be readily understood, from what I have said previously, that what the Government have in mind goes a great deal further than consultation. I do not think I should like to go any further into details at this moment.

Mr. Dalton: May I take note of what the right hon. gentleman has said, that what the Government have in mind goes further than consultation? Have the Government made clear the contents of their minds to those foreign Powers with whom they have communicated, and particularly has it been made clear to Poland that His Majesty's Government would be willing, in conjunction with other great Powers, to come to Poland's assistance if she is to be the next victim of German aggression?

The Prime Minister: I think I must still maintain a certain reserve on this matter. I will say this, that the Government have made perfectly clear to the other Governments with whom they are in consultation what His Majesty's Government are prepared to do in certain circumstances.

Mr. Greenwood: May I assume that the right hon. gentleman will take every possible step to speed up the negotiations that are taking place, and may I assume quite definitely that perhaps at a very early date the House will want a discussion of the position?

The Prime Minister: I appreciate that, but I would like to assure the right hon. gentleman and the House generally that the Government fully realise the urgency of this matter and the desirability of coming to a conclusion at the earliest possible moment. At the same time it will be realised that there is more than one Government involved, and that the issue is not solely in the hands of His Majesty's Government.

No. 12.

Viscount Halifax to Sir W. Seeds (Moscow).

Foreign Office, April 4, 1939.

Sir,

AT the end of a conversation with Sir A. Cadogan on the 29th March, the Soviet Ambassador referred to the Prime

Minister's statement in the House of Commons on the 28th March (No. 11) and in particular to his replies to supplementary questions by Mr. Greenwood, M.P. and Mr. Dalton, M.P. As regards the former, M. Maisky drew attention to the Prime Minister's words: "It will, at any rate, be readily understood from what I have said previously that what the Government have in mind goes a great deal further than consultation." As regards the latter, he drew attention to the words: "I will say this, that the Government have made perfectly clear to the other Governments with whom they are in consultation what His Majesty's Government were proposing to do in certain circumstances." M. Maisky said he was rather puzzled by these replies. In the first place, he was not aware that His Majesty's Government were proposing to go further than consultation and, in the second place, his Government had not, so far as he was aware, been kept informed as to what action His Majesty's Government was prepared to take beyond consultation.

2. In regard to the first point, Sir A. Cadogan reminded M. Maisky that the proposal for consultation contemplated consultation with a view to concerting measures, and therefore went a little bit further than pure consultation, and M. Maisky accepted this. In regard to the second point, he was reminded of a conversation that Sir A. Cadogan had a short while ago with him when he asked whether he could be told anything in regard to the result of our soundings of other Governments on the proposed four Power declaration. As Sir A. Cadogan had then hinted to his Excellency, it appeared that the Polish Government at least would be unwilling to be associated openly with the Soviet Government in any such declaration. Their attitude on this point was, as we understood it, due not to any feeling of hostility towards the Soviet Government, but to the reflection that such open association with them would, in the circumstances, merely increase the fury and indignation of the German Government. Sir A. Cadogan said that we had had to recognise that it was useless to pursue the idea of the four-Power declaration, and His Majesty's Government had therefore

been considering what other line they could usefully take. It seemed that in present circumstances the countries nearest to the German menace and most exposed to attack were Poland and Roumania, and His Majesty's Government had come to the conclusion that it was essential to ascertain what the spirit of resistance of those two countries would be and in what way it could best be fortified. They were therefore contemplating the possibility of giving assurances, together with the French Government, to the Polish and Roumanian Governments in the hope that that would encourage them successfully to resist further German expansion. If those countries were determined to resist and were ultimately engaged in a conflict with Germany, they would no doubt be glad of the sympathy and, indeed, of the active assistance of the Soviet Government, if the latter were disposed to accord it, in whatever way might seem most suitable and effective.

3. M. Maisky asked whether what we were contemplating involved direct military assistance to Poland and Roumania, to which Sir A. Cadogan replied that that was what those countries would require, and that we were indeed contemplating the possibility of giving assurances to that effect. Sir A. Cadogan said that the matter was at the moment still under consideration, and his Excellency must not take it from him that a firm decision had been taken, though he personally thought that it was likely that His Majesty's Government would be ready to give such assurances.

4. M. Maisky asked whether the French Government agreed to this course, to which Sir A. Cadogan replied that we had been discussing it with them and they appeared to be sympathetic to it. M. Maisky remarked that, if we adopted this course, that would be a revolutionary change in British policy and might have most far-reaching results. It would increase enormously the confidence of other countries and might have a very great effect.

5. Sir A. Cadogan said that he knew I would wish to keep in touch with his Excellency and keep him informed of developments, and that when the final decision had been taken I would doubtless inform him of it.

No. 13.

Statement by the Prime Minister in the House of Commons on March 31, 1939.

The Prime Minister: As the House is aware, certain consultations are now proceeding with other Governments. In order to make perfectly clear the position of His Majesty's Government in the meantime before those consultations are concluded, I now have to inform the House that during that period, in the event of any action which clearly threatened Polish independence; and which the Polish Government accordingly considered it vital to resist with their national forces, His Majesty's Government would feel themselves bound at once to lend the Polish Government all support in their power. They have given the Polish Government an assurance to this effect.

I may add that the French Government have authorised me to make it plain that they stand in the same position in this matter as do His Majesty's Government.

Mr. Arthur Greenwood: May I, in one sentence, transgress in order to say that I am quite sure that this House realises the potentialities that might arise from the statement which the right hon. gentleman has made. It may prove to be in its consequences as momentous a statement as has been made in this House for a quarter of a century. It is very difficult with such recent statements before us to say very much, but may I ask the right hon. gentleman one or two questions which I do not think he has made quite clear in his statement. I would like to ask him whether the statement which he has now read is to be regarded as the first step in a developing policy to deter or restrain aggression, and, if so, will the Government take immediate, active and energetic steps to bring into this arrangement other Powers? Will he especially think of the value of the Union of Soviet Socialist Republics together with other Powers, large and small? Will he do so with the wider object of obtaining the maximum amount of co-operation in the defence of peace? Will he consider now the advisability of an immediate conference of those Powers who might be prepared to range themselves on the side of peace as against aggression?

The Prime Minister: I will try to answer the questions which the right hon. gentleman has put to me. I think the statement makes it clear that what I have said is intended to cover what I may call an interim period. The Government, as has already been announced, are in consultation with various other Powers, including, of course, the Soviet Government. My noble friend the Foreign Secretary saw the Soviet Ambassador this morning, and had very full discussions with him on the subject. I have no doubt that the principles upon which we are acting are fully understood and appreciated by that Government. The House is aware that we are expecting a visit next week from Colonel Beck, the Foreign Secretary of Poland. There will then be an opportunity of discussing with him the various further measures that may be taken in order, as the right hon. gentleman has put it, to accumulate the maximum amount of co-operation in any efforts that may be made to put an end to aggression, and to substitute for it the more reasonable and orderly method of discussion.

Mr. Greenwood: There is a point to which the right hon. gentleman did not refer: the possibilities of a conference. May I put this point, and I want to put it quite frankly, as I think the House will not be without a feeling of responsibility at this moment. Can the right hon. gentleman say whether in his view he would welcome that maximum cooperation from all powers, including the U.S.S.R.?

The Prime Minister: Yes, we should welcome the maximum amount of cooperation. On the question of a conference, in our view it is a matter of practical expediency. We have no theoretical views about a conference. If it proved to be the best way we should not hesitate to use it. If we find there is a more effective way of achieving our object, we might dispense with a conference.

Mr John Morgan: Can the right hon. gentleman give us an assurance that there are no ideological impediments between us and the U.S.S.R.?

The Prime Minister: Yes, I have no hesitation in giving that assurance.

No. 14.

Viscount Halifax to Sir W. Seeds (Moscow).

Foreign Office, March 31, 1939.

Sir,

I ASKED the Soviet Ambassador to come and see me this morning and began by apologising for having been obliged, through no fault of my own, to postpone the appointment I had made with him yesterday.

2. I knew, however, that he had seen Sir Alexander Cadogan two days ago, who had kept him informed of the lines on which we were proceeding and which had been rendered necessary by the particular position of the Polish Government, of which he was, of course, very well aware. I then told the Ambassador that it had appeared to us of considerable importance to secure the

position, pending the conclusion of the consultations in which we were engaged. There had been many rumours in circulation about Germany's intentions against Poland, of which, as the Prime Minister had already stated in the House of Commons, we had no official confirmation. None the less, we thought that it would be valuable at the present juncture that there should be no doubt as to the position of this country. Accordingly, I told him that the Prime Minister was making a statement in the House of Commons this afternoon promising support to the Polish Government in certain circumstances should the need for this arise. I then read M. Maisky the statement that the Prime Minister proposed to make.

3. His first comment was that the phrase "lend the Polish Government all support in their power" might be argued to be a phrase capable of being greatly minimized by those who, whether honestly or from a desire to make mischief, would profess doubts as to the genuine character of British intentions.

4. I said that, of course, nothing could prevent people who wished to make mischief from making it, but that the Polish Government had appeared to welcome our suggestion, and that the decision on behalf of His Majesty's Government was, from the point of view of British policy, a grave and momentous decision. M. Maisky agreed and I pointed out to him that this was only an interim arrangement pending the conclusion of the wider discussion.

5. Having regard to the importance of avoiding any unnecessary appearance of divisions between the Governments concerned, I asked the Ambassador whether there was anything that the Prime Minister could say on the lines of assuming that the Soviet Government would not disapprove or even would approve the general line we were taking. I was not surprised that M Maisky took the opportunity of saying that, as he had not been consulted yesterday, it was obviously impossible for him to

say at a moment's notice what the position of his Government would be. It had been defined by M. Stalin a short time ago as assistance against aggression for those who fought for their independence, and therefore they were certainly prepared to help Poland or any other country that was attacked and resisted, but the Soviet Government had no desire to force themselves on anybody. Although they thought it groundless, they understood the fear of the Poles, which was that, if Russian troops came into Poland, Polish conditions were such that the contacts that would be made would probably produce disturbing effects on Polish society.

6. I suggested to M. Maisky that the Prime Minister might say we had every reason to suppose, from the declaration of the principles on which Russian foreign policy rested, that they would not find themselves other than in agreement with our declaration, or something to that effect. The Ambassador did not feel any great difficulty with this being said, for what it was worth, on the Prime Minister's own authority, and agreed with me when I said there were plenty of people trying to make mischief between his Government and our Government, and possibly between his Government, His Majesty's Government and the Polish Government. The purpose of all who wished to stand together, being essentially agreed, must be to avoid giving mischief-makers any encouragement. To this virtuous sentiment M. Maisky readily assented, and I said I looked forward to the opportunity next week of discussing these difficult matters with Colonel Beck and, so far as I could, without breach of Colonel Beck's confidence, I looked forward to a further opportunity of discussing them with M. Maisky. The Ambassador thanked me for what I had said, and repeated that his Government had no wish to force themselves on anybody, and would therefore take no initiative.

7. In reply to an enquiry by the Ambassador as to what was the present position as to the suggested Four-Power

declaration, I said that in that form the project was evidently bound to encounter difficulty, but that we were hopeful of being able to achieve substantially the ends we had in view by the rather different approach we were now making.

8. As he was leaving, the Ambassador asked me whether Colonel Beck was proposing to visit France on his return from this country, but I told him that I had no further information on this matter than had appeared in the press.

No.15.

Sir W. Seeds to Viscount Halifax.

(Telegraphic.) *Moscow, April 1, 1939.*

MOSCOW press published full reports yesterday of proceedings in the House of Commons, but omitted any mention of Prime Minister's expressed belief that Soviet Government understood and appreciated principles on which His Majesty's Government were acting.

2. I have just seen M. Litvinov, who made it quite clear that His Majesty's Government's action is misunderstood and not at all appreciated. He claimed at first that we had never informed the Soviet Government that proposed four-Power declaration had been dropped. I contested this and an examination of Soviet Ambassador's telegrams from London eventually absolved us of that charge. Nevertheless, he said fact remained that in response to our approach Soviet Government had first suggested six-Power conference, and, secondly, agreed to sign a four-Power declaration; each proposal had been summarily dropped. Now His Majesty's Government, of their own initiative, were engaged on a new plan of which he knew little. Soviet Government had had enough and would henceforward stand apart free of any commitments.

3. I denied that His Majesty's Government were in any way responsible for failure of the two proposals in question, which, as he well knew, failed only because of certain international suspicions which seemed to clog every means of approach. Surely in Soviet Union, where we were always attacked for alleged capitulations, a welcome should be accorded to a momentous change of front. Soviet Ambassador had been, and would be, kept informed - in accordance with our desire to maintain close touch with Soviet Government.

4. But he was not to be moved, and in spite of my argument that Prime Minister's statement covered only an interim arrangement and must not therefore be picked to pieces, he expressed doubts whether we would regard attack on Danzig or Corridor as threatening Poland's independence. In any ease we could pursue our own policy; the Soviet Government would stand aside - a course which might possibly be in their best interests.

No. 16.

Sir W. Seeds to Viscount Halifax.

Moscow, April 3, 1939.

My Lord,

I HAVE the honour to report that the visit to Moscow of Mr. Hudson and his mission gave frequent occasion for an informal interchange of views on the general international situation. More normal conversations were limited to two in number.

2. The first, on the 23rd March, was in fact on M. Litvinov's initiative, as he took opportunity of Mr. Hudson's first courtesy call in my company to express his views at considerable length. These were on the lines used by him in previous conversations with myself, and could be divided into (1) a recital of the past

errors of the "capitulating" Western democracies, and of the efforts of the Soviet Government to guide Europe in the right path, and (2) a recommendation of a conference of Powers, great and small, to remedy the vile and dangers of the present situation.

3. M. Litvinov's historical review was most comprehensive, and began as far back as the adhesion of the Soviet Union to the League of Nations. Developed with his usual mastery of the subject, it exhibited the constant retreat of the Western democracies from one position after another, culminating in the Munich capitulation and the cold-shouldering of the Soviet Union.

4. M. Litvinov was quite clear on those points. Touching but lightly, as he generally does in conversation with me, on British weakness (in contradistinction to his habit when conversing with a French representative), he said that France was practically done for; she was, as he put it, full of German agents, disaffected and disunited, at the mercy of certain leading politicians whom he profoundly distrusted. He foresaw, in the not far-distant future, a Europe entirely German from the Bay of Biscay to the Soviet frontier, and bounded, as it were, simply by Great Britain and the Soviet Union, Even that would not satisfy German ambitions, but the attack, he said smiling happily, would not be directed to the East.

5. Mr. Hudson countered with a description, most valuable, as coming from one in the know, of the change of heart which had occurred both in the Government and people of Great Britain, and so of the remarkable progress of our rearmament which had completely reversed the previous situation. Having, as I think, considerably impressed his hearer, he mentioned your Lordship's anxiety that Powers interested in the preservation of peace should maintain close contact and should act in concert so far as possible.

6. This led to a discussion as to which particular Powers should be included in any such concert or contact, M. Litvinov maintaining the necessity of including the largest possible number, both small and great, while Mr. Hudson argued that it was for the big Powers, especially Great Britain and the Soviet Union, to give a lead which the others would probably follow. Both agreed that in any case the fullest measure of resistance, whether diplomatic or military or economic, should come into review at any such conference.

7. A further conversation between M Litvinov, Mr. Hudson and myself was arranged, at which I asked his Excellency to define more particularly what he had in mind. It then became clear that M. Litvinov had only been envisaging a conference with the South Eastern and Baltic and Scandinavian countries to follow the Four-Power declaration, which was then the subject of negotiation, as a later development of his suggestion which I had forwarded to your Lordship by my telegram of the 22nd March. (No. 9)

No. 17.

Extract from the Prime Minister's Speech in the House of Commons on April 3, 1939.

I DO not wish, today, to attempt to specify what Governments we may now, or in the near future, find it desirable to consult with on the situation, but I would make the one allusion to the Soviet Union, because I quite appreciate that the Soviet Union is always in the thoughts of hon. members opposite, and they are still a little suspicious as to whether ideological differences may not be dividing us upon what otherwise would obviously be in the interests of both to do. I do not pretend for one moment that the ideological differences do not exist; they remain unchanged. But, as I said on Friday in answer to a question, our point is that whatever may be those ideological differences they do not really count in a question of this kind. What we are concerned with is to preserve our independence and when I say 'our independence' I do not mean only this country's. I mean the independence of all States which may be threatened by aggression in pursuit of such a policy as I have described.

Therefore, we welcome the co-operation of any country, whatever may be its internal system of government, not in aggression, but in resistance to aggression.

No. 18.

Viscount Halifax to Sir W. Seeds (Moscow).

(Telegraphic.) *Foreign Office, April 4, 1939.*

YOUR telegram of 1st April. (No. 14)

I approve your language. I cannot find any justification for M. Livitnov's attitude. Soviet Ambassador here has been kept informed at every stage.

2. On 19th March (No. 5), I explained to him the difficulties we saw in M. Livitnov's proposal for a conference at Bucharest and said that, while we did not rule it out, we had a proposal of our own, not altogether dissimilar, which we thought was better calculated to achieve the results we wanted.

3. That proposal (the four – Power declaration) was put to the Soviet Government by your Excellency on 21st March (No. 7). On the following day Soviet Government informed you that they accepted text of declaration, and would sign "as soon as both France *and Poland* have accepted and promised their signatures."

4. On 23rd March (No. 10) we expressed to the Soviet Ambassador our appreciation of this reply, but intimated that while, while we had as yet no final answer from the Polish Government, we understood that latter would hesitate before committing themselves.

5. On 29th March (No. 12) Soviet Ambassador was told that, in view of the Polish attitude, we had to recognise that it was useless to pursue the idea of a four – Power declaration, and that we had therefore been considering what other line we could usefully take. He was told that the reason for this change of plan was that it now appeared that the Polish Government would be unwilling to be associated openly with the Soviet Government in any such declaration. Their attitude on this point, as understood here, was due not to any feeling of hostility to the Soviet Government, but to reflection that such open association with them would merely increase indignation of the German Government. When I spoke to the Soviet Ambassador on 31st March (No. 14) he said that the Soviet Government, although they thought it groundless, understood the fear of the Poles, which was that, if Soviet troops came into Poland, Polish conditions were such that the contacts that would be made would probably produce disturbing effects on Polish society.

6. The Soviet Ambassador was on 29th March (No. 12) given a provisional outline of the new course we were contemplating, which would involve our giving assurances, together with France, to Poland and Roumania. Soviet Ambassador recognised that this would be revolutionary change in British policy, and that it would increase enormously the confidence of other countries. It was made clear in the conversation that we had no intention of excluding the Soviet Government, since the Soviet Ambassador was told that Poland and Roumania were engaged in conflict with Germany they would no doubt be glad of the active assistance of the Soviet

Government, if the latter were disposed to accord it, in whatever way was most suitable and effective.

7. Before any further statement on this new proposal could be made to the Soviet Ambassador circumstances arose which made it necessary for the Prime Minister to make a declaration in the House of Commons on afternoon of 31st March. Soviet Ambassador was informed of purport of that statement on the morning of 31st March before it was made. (No. 14)

8. If M. Litvinov complains that it is not true to say, as the Prime Minister did, that he had "no doubt that the principles on which we are acting are fully understood and appreciated by the Soviet Government," the answer is that the Soviet Ambassador told me on 31st March that Soviet policy had recently been defined by Stalin as assistance against aggression for those who fought for their independence, and therefore they were certainly prepared to help Poland and any other country that was attacked and resisted. The principles by which His Majesty's Government were moved to make their Polish declaration were precisely the same; and it seemed therefore self-evident that these principles would he both understood and appreciated by Soviet Government.

No. 19.

Extract from Statement of the Prime Minister in the House of Commons on April 13, 1939.

I TAKE this opportunity of saying, on behalf of His Majesty's Government, that they attach the greatest importance to the avoidance of disturbance by force or threats of force of the *status quo* in the Mediterranean and the Balkan Peninsula. Consequently, they have come to the conclusion that, in the event of any action being taken which clearly threatened the independence of Greece or Roumania, and which the Greek or Roumanian Governments respectively considered it vital to resist with their national forces, His Majesty's Government would feel themselves bound at once to lend the Greek or Roumanian Government, as the case might be, all the support in their power. We are communicating this declaration to the Governments directly concerned, and to others, especially Turkey, whose close relations with the Greek Government are known. I understand that the French Government are making a similar declaration this afternoon. I need not add that the Dominion Government, as always, are being continuously informed of all developments.

No. 20.

Sir E. Phipps to Viscount Halifax.

(Telegraphic.) *Paris, April 13, 1939.*

FOLLOWING is translation of French Government's declaration issued this afternoon:-

"The French Government has to-day published the decisions taken yesterday by the Council of Ministers.

In communicating them to the press M. Daladier, President of the Council, Minister for National Defence and War accompanied them by the following declaration:-

"I defined the policy of France in the speech which I delivered by radio on the 29th March. I then said that Europe was in a state of watchfulness and that France, decided to maintain peace in freedom and honour should first strengthen her own defences and increase her bonds of solidarity with all peoples who were resolved to stand up to aggression. Since then it is in this sense that we have acted. We did so without verbal manifestations and without vain provocations. Action in order to be effective, has no need to be accompanied either by speeches or by threats.

"That is why we have taken military measures which guarantee the frontiers of France and her Empire against any surprise. The Government thanks, in the name of France, all those men who have rejoined their posts in their regiments, in their squadrons and in their ships, all those who contribute to assure the security of their country. It wishes to thank all those who in our national defence factories, in whatever capacity, are making a vigorous effort of which I register the happy results every day. It renders homage to the entire people who, in France and in her overseas territories, give admirable example of calm and resolution.

"At the same time following the same methods, we have pursued the diplomatic action necessary for the maintenance of peace by strengthening the common bonds (*"solidarities"*) which must unite before the common peril all the countries which are resolved to preserve their liberty. We remain in permanent contact with the Governments of Great Britain, the United States, Russia, Poland and the Balkan *Entente*. Our aim, which I am convinced we shall attain, is to organise this necessary collaboration between all the nations who do not think of threatening the vital interests of any people whatever, who do not refuse to undertake in good faith any examination of present problems, and who are determined to oppose any attempt at domination. Need I add that our close and deep entente with Great Britain has never been stronger than today.

"I therefore address to the French nation the following declaration which has been drafted in agreement by the Government of the Republic and the Government of Great Britain:-

"The French Government attaches the greatest

importance to preventing any modification of the *status quo* in the Mediterranean and in the Balkan Peninsula imposed by force or threat of force.

"Taking into consideration the special anxieties to which the events of recent weeks have given rise, the French Government has consequently given to Roumania and Greece the particular assurance that, in the event of an action being undertaken which should clearly threaten the independence of Roumania or Greece, and which the Roumanian Government or the Greek Government should consider it in its vital interest to resist with its national forces, the French Government will consider itself bound immediately to lend that Government all assistance in its power.

"The English Government has adopted the same attitude.

"Moreover, the French Government has been pleased, by the conclusion of the reciprocal engagements of Great Britain and Poland, who have decided to grant each other Mutual support in order to defend their independence if it were threatened directly or indirectly. The Franco-Polish Alliance is, moreover, confirmed by the French Government and the Polish Government in the same spirit. France and Poland guarantee each other immediately and directly against any direct or indirect threat against their vital interests.

"We are communicating this declaration to all the interested Governments, and in particular to Turkey.

"The protection of the territory of France and her Empire against any direct or indirect attack on her integrity and her rights, the search, with the sole desire for peace, for all the *ententes* appropriate for ensuring the joint protection of peoples against any enterprise threatening their independence - such is the policy which the French Government has followed, in full consciousness of its responsibilities and with the inflexible determination not to recoil before any of the duties imposed on it by the protection of the destinies of France."

No. 21.

Extract from Speech by Sir J. Simon in the House of Commons on April 13, 1939.

AT the very outset of this new policy we did as I think the House knows, earnestly invite the speedy co-operation of Russia. Very shortly after the German occupation of Czecho-Slovakia, we invited the Soviet Government to join in a four-Power declaration. The Soviet Government responded quite promptly, and said that they would agree to join in a four-Power declaration as soon as France and Poland had adopted and had promised their signatures. As the hon. gentleman said, we got to rather a delicate point, and I think the House knows that it, unfortunately, proved impossible to realise that precise project, and we were obliged to adopt a different course, not with a different object but a different method. Then a suggestion was made by Russia. They suggested a conference of Powers.

Mr. Dalton: The right hon. gentleman is giving it in the wrong order. The conference came first.

Sir J. Simon: I am obliged to the hon. gentleman. They were both quite early, and in neither case was our action in any sort of way disparaging or discouraging. With regard to Russia's proposal for a conference - I think it was to be a conference at Bucharest - I wish to say, as has been said before, that His Majesty's Government had no sort of objection to that proposal because it came from Soviet Russia. The proposal had to be examined, judged and pronounced upon purely as a practical issue. Everybody who has attended a conference knows that the most important thing to secure is that one does not start the conference until one has some solid reason for thinking it will be successful. A conference that breaks down in confusion does far more harm than discussions through other channels. The difficulty we felt had nothing to do with the fact that the proposal was made by Soviet Russia. It was purely a question of what was the most effective and prompt machinery for getting agreement between the Powers concerned. There would have been great difficulties in having conference but we should have tried to get over them if we had been able to persuade ourselves that that method was the best method. We never resisted the proposal because it came from Soviet Russia. We were never less inclined to approve of it on that account. We regarded it and I am sure Soviet Russia understands this - simply as a question of procedure and method, our object being to get as quickly as possible the greatest amount of agreement we could.

Recent events in Europe, both in March and in April, gave rise inevitably to anxiety in certain countries that their independence was in jeopardy, and that the matter was as urgent as a matter could be. It might have been a matter of days or hours. To meet that danger - not behind the back of Soviet Russia, not with any disinclination to make use of her help, but because we were faced with this immediate and urgent business, and in full accord with the French Government - we felt impelled to make what contribution we could to the restoration of confidence by giving the assurances of which the House knows. Therefore, we took on special commitments to those countries whose independence was exposed, or might be exposed, to an immediate menace. Throughout those negotiations we have kept Soviet. Russia in the closest touch with ourselves, and I will give the House a short account of some of the actual steps that were taken.

On the 29th March the Soviet Ambassador was told that we had to recognise that it was useless to pursue the idea of a four-Power declaration, and that we, therefore, had been considering what other line we could usefully take. The Soviet Ambassador was given a provisional outline of the new course we were contemplating, which would involve us giving assurances, together with France, to Poland and Romania. The Soviet Ambassador recognised that this would be a revolutionary change in British policy and that it would increase enormously the confidence of other countries. It was made clear in the conversations that we had no intention at all of excluding help from the Soviet Government, if the latter were disposed to afford it, in whatever way was most suitable and effective.

Circumstances then arose, however, which made it necessary for the Prime Minister to make the declaration regarding Poland on that Friday; but before it was made the Soviet Ambassador was informed of the purport of the statement. As soon as ever it was arranged, it was communicated to him. The Soviet Ambassador told the Foreign Secretary, on the 31st March, that Soviet policy had recently been defined by M. Stalin as assistance against aggression for those who fought for their independence, and the Foreign Secretary received that definition as one would expect it to be received by all of us who wish to get the maximum help from all possible quarters. I think the House will see that the principles by which His Majesty's Government were moved to make their Polish declaration were precisely the same as M. Stalin's own declaration.

It seemed to us, and it seems to us now, self-evident that these principles were not misunderstood by the Soviet Government, and I wish the House plainly to understand that while these things are more difficult to negotiate with a very large number of Powers than might appear, there is no truth in the suggestion that we have been seeking to find means of avoiding taking Soviet Russia into that system which it is our object to build up as a system of peace against aggression. Since then my Noble Friend has seen the Soviet Ambassador on more than one occasion and has kept him fully informed of the progress of events. I have endeavoured to state what has happened checking it by the documents which I have before me, and I say that it shows that there is no justification for the suggestions which have been made, and indeed, considering the peril in which the free countries of the world now stand, we should be fools if we did not recognise where assistance might be drawn and gladly received.

Mr. Dalton: May I just remind the right hon. gentleman of a question I put? Have the Government at any time proposed to the Russians a definite military alliance between this country, France and the Soviet Union ? Have they proposed it and, if so has it been rejected?

Sir J. Simon: I beg the right hon. gentleman's pardon. I had intended as a matter of fact to say a word about that. I will meet the point and deal with it in another way. There is no objection on our part in principle to such a proposition at all. These things are not always as simple as they may appear, but whatever is the most effective way of organising the forces of peace is the way that His Majesty's Government will wish to choose. I do not think, powerful as Russia is, that we ought to concentrate the whole of our gaze simply upon that Great Power we have to remember that there are others even nearer to danger than Russia is. But, though I cannot say that that particular proposition has been made the hon. gentleman and the House may take it that the Government is raising no objection in principle to any such proposition.

No. 22.

Viscount Halifax to Sir W. Seeds (Moscow).

(Telegraphic.) *Foreign Office, April 14, 1939.*

IN spite of difficulties which stand in the way of any close association of the Soviet Government in the system of international collaboration which His Majesty's Government and the French Government are engaged in organising, I am reluctant to abandon my efforts to secure some measure of co-operation from the Soviet Government.

2. These difficulties arise not merely from the reluctance of certain Governments to be openly associated in any way with the Soviet Union and from any suspicion, real or assumed, that the Soviet Government may have of the intentions of His Majesty's Government and the French Government, but also from a natural tendency of the Soviet Government to stand aloof, a tendency which may be enhanced by the very success of our efforts to secure the collaboration of other Governments.

3. We gave full weight to the Soviet proposal for a conference and we only abandoned our own suggestion for a four-Power declaration when it was clear that the attitude of the Polish Government made its conclusion impossible. We have explained our difficulties to the Soviet Government at every stage and made clear to them the reasons why we have found it necessary to embark on the course we are now pursuing. That course has already been attended by a great measure of success, and we consider it vital to press on with it in order to secure the adherence of as many Powers as possible.

4. The Soviet Government have criticised our action on what seems to me the rather academic ground that any attempt

to make a stand at one point merely diverts the probability of an attack to another. But this criticism whether well founded or not, seems to me to have lost a good deal of its force now that His Majesty's Government and France have supplemented the arrangement they reached with Poland by an undertaking to go to the help of Roumania in the event of a threat to the independence of Roumania which the latter considered it vital to resist. The Soviet Union are also aware that His Majesty's Government are in consultation with the Turkish Government; and it is their intention, in concert with the French Government, to reach, if possible, with Turkey an agreement on the same principle as the recent agreement with Poland.

5. The situation which His Majesty's Government and the French Government contemplate, therefore, is one in which they will have given guarantees to the two countries, Poland and Roumania which cover the greater part of the western frontier of the Soviet Union and to a country Turkey, which is a friendly neighbour of the Soviet Union in the Black Sea. In making these arrangements, His Majesty's Government and the French Government have not regarded the principle of reciprocity as being in all cases indispensable.

6. His Majesty's Government have noted M. Stalin's recent statement that the Soviet Union stands for the rendering of support to nations which are victims of aggression and which fight for their independence. It would therefore seem to be in complete accord with this policy were the Soviet Government now to make a public declaration on their own initiative in which, after referring to the general statement of policy alluded to above find to statements recently made by His Majesty's Government and the French Government they would repeat that in the event of any act of aggression against any European neighbours of the Soviet Union which was resisted by the country concerned, the assistance of the Soviet Government would be available, if desired, and would be afforded in such

manner as would be found most convenient. A positive declaration by the Soviet Government at the present moment would, I believe, have a steadying effect upon the international situation and would be a concrete application of the general policy of the Soviet Government as stated above.

7. I shall he glad if you will speak to M. Litvinov on the lines of the present telegram and enquire whether it would be possible for the Soviet Government to act in the sense suggested.

No. 23.

Viscount Halifax to Sir W. Seeds (Moscow).

Foreign Office, April 14, 1939.

Sir,

THE Soviet Ambassador called on me this afternoon to inform me, on instructions from his Government, that, in view of the interest shown by His Majesty's Government in the fate of Greece and Roumania, the Soviet Government were prepared to take part in giving assistance to Roumania. The Soviet Government wished to learn the views of His Majesty's Government as to the best methods in which such assistance could given and as to the part the various Powers concerned could play in helping Roumania.

2. I thanked M. Maisky for his communication and told him that I had had it in my mind to ask him to come and see me in order to tell him that I was proposing to inform the Soviet Government that I had been thinking over my last conversation with the Ambassador and had been trying to find a way of bridging the differences between our points of view

of which we both were aware. I had had it in mind that the Soviet Government might perhaps feel that the position had been modified by the guarantee which we had given to Roumania. I had been looking again at the speech of M. Stalin, to which the Ambassador had drawn my attention and had been wondering whether, in view of what we had already done for Poland and Roumania and hoped to do for Turkey, and in view of the fact that in these cases we were not insisting on strict reciprocity, the Soviet Government would consider making a similar unilateral declaration in respect of Roumania and perhaps of Poland, such as would put our two countries on a similar footing and thereby contribute towards meeting the differences in our points of view. This, I added, seemed to be in harmony with the communication which the Ambassador had just made to me, and I accordingly proposed to instruct you to speak to M. Litvinov on the above lines. I suggested that it might be helpful if I were also to send instructions to Warsaw and Bucharest urging that, if the Soviet Government were to make the Unilateral declarations which I had proposed, these would be unlikely to cause the Polish and Roumanian Governments any embarrassment and should be given favourable consideration.

3. M. Maisky said that he did not know what his Government's reaction would be to the proposal for unilateral declarations which I had made. I pointed out that my proposal only gave precision to what I understood that M. Stalin had said, but Maisky repeated that he was unable to say whether his Government would think such a step necessary. His instructions referred solely to Roumania.

4. I told Maisky that I had always taken the view that wherever the attack might come the problem which would arise would always be essentially the same. This, M. Maisky said, brought one back to the idea of collective security. To this I replied that there was, however, a difference, in that under the

old idea of collective security we sometimes deluded ourselves into thinking that words were the same as action. I added that I was most grateful to the Ambassador for his communication, which I would convey immediately to the Prime Minister.

5. Before leaving. M. Maisky said that at his last interview he had formed the impression that the guarantee from this country to Roumania was not imminent, and that he had, therefore, been completely surprised to learn yesterday of the pledge which we had given, and he asked why we had changed our minds. I replied that I would tell him frankly that, although we had thought it desirable to clarify the attitude of Poland and Turkey before giving a guarantee, the French Government had felt that the danger to Roumania was pressing and that it would therefore be unwise to delay, and that we had accordingly agreed to give our guarantee forthwith. M. Maisky told me that he felt sure that we had done right. Roumania was, in his view, in much greater danger than Poland, and the pledge we had given to the Roumanian Government would steady the situation.

No. 24.

Sir W. Seeds to Viscount Halifax.

(Telegraphic.) *Moscow, April 15, 1939.*

YOUR telegram of 14th April. (No. 22)

I spoke to M. Litvinov as instructed. He gave proposal a friendly hearing and promised to consult his Government. He was inclined to think that a unilateral declaration bound the Soviet Government without committing anyone else and without knowing nature or method of assistance which might be required from this country. I pointed out that His Majesty's

Government; were committed up to the hilt, that question of actual assistance was too complicated and too dependent on the course of events to allow of settlement at present, and that a unilateral declaration was most consonant with the position of Soviet Union as a Great Power.

2. He told me he had just instructed Soviet Ambassador in London to come to Moscow for consultation.

No. 25.

Sir W. Seeds to Viscount Halifax.

(Telegraphic.) *Moscow, April 16, 1939.*

MY immediately preceding telegram. (No. 24)

I saw M. Litvinov again this afternoon. He said that the Soviet Government wished first of all to have reply to enquiry made by their Ambassador (No. 24) as to nature of assistance which would be required from the various Powers concerned for protection of Roumania.

2. I reminded him of what you had said to the Ambassador at the time and of appreciation which I had conveyed to M. Litvinov personally yesterday in accordance with your instructions (No. 23) when I had pointed out that your proposal for a declaration was not only in harmony with the Ambassador's communication but also extended it in accordance with the Soviet Government's own idea that it was advisable to cover as many points as possible instead of only one.

3. He said that the Ambassador had been, on his Government's instructions, answering a specific question you

had addressed to him: Soviet Government had, through the Ambassador, replied to His Majesty's Government that they were ready in principle to come to Roumania's assistance, but that they wanted to know how far Great Britain and other countries were prepared to go when it came to the point and what was expected from the Soviet Union. They wanted an answer to that before considering a declaration which, if made at present, would commit them blindly. To my argument that examination of the means of assistance would take time, M. Litvinov asked why there was any need for urgency. Did we really think an attack was imminent? What were Poland and Roumania doing? Negotiating perhaps with Germany? Roumanian Minister for Foreign Affairs was going to Berlin and it would be foolish to make a declaration at a time when Roumania might be willingly signing away something at Germany's command.

4. I pointed out that engagements which His Majesty's Government had taken were an answer to those questions: we had made our position clear to the world and hoped that Soviet Union would similarly announce publicly the determination to help the victims of aggression; we knew and welcomed Soviet Government's readiness to assist Roumania but Europe was still in the dark. He said, when pressed, it might come to a public declaration but repeated that at present they must have the facts to go on.

5. On terminating a friendly interview, I said while disappointed I was glad that the Soviet Government's attitude in regard to assistance to Roumania marked at any rate a step in advance.

No. 26.

Sir W. Seeds to Viscount Halifax.

(Telegraphic.) *Moscow, April 18, 1939.*

M. LITVINOV has now handed me in writing following proposal which is also being communicated to Soviet Ambassador in Paris:-

"Subsequent to English enquiry regarding consent of Soviet Union to render assistance to States lying on its borders against aggressors, Soviet Government also received a French proposal on lines of bilateral obligations regarding mutual military assistance against aggressors. As we regard this proposal as an acceptable one in principle and wish to extend M. Bonnet's idea, and as we are also desirous of placing relations between the three States on a solid foundation, we are endeavouring to combine English and French proposals in the form of following propositions which we submit for consideration of British Government:

1. "England, France and Soviet Union to conclude with one another an agreement for a period of five to ten years, by which they would oblige themselves to render mutually forthwith all manner of assistance, including that of a military nature, in case of aggression in Europe against any one of the contracting Powers.

2. England, France and Soviet Union to undertake to render all manner of assistance, including that of a military nature, to Eastern European States situated between Baltic and Black Seas and bordering on Soviet Union, in case of aggression against these States.

3. England, France and Soviet Union to undertake to discuss and to settle within shortest period of time extent and forms of military assistance to be rendered by each of these States in fulfilment of paragraphs 1 and 2.

4. English Government to explain that assistance promised to Poland concerns exclusively aggression on the part of Germany.

5. The treaty of alliance, which exists between Poland and Roumania, is to be declared operative in case of aggression of any nature against Poland and Roumania, or else to be revoked altogether as one directed against Soviet Union.

6. England, France and Soviet Union to undertake, following outbreak of hostilities, not to enter into negotiations of any kind whatsoever, and not to conclude peace with aggressors separately from one another and without common consent of the three Powers.

7. An agreement on above lines to be signed simultaneously with terms of convention, which has been described above under paragraph 3.

8. The necessity recognised for England, France and Soviet Union to enter into joint negotiations with Turkey, having in view conclusion of a special agreement on mutual assistance."

M. Litvinov explained that French Chargé d'Affaires, when supporting yesterday His Majesty's Government's proposal for a unilateral declaration by Soviet Government, had stated French Government were not thereby withdrawing their own proposal for a Franco-Soviet pact of mutual assistance. Present Soviet proposal was as stated above a combination of both, clause 2 being specially designed to meet His Majesty's Government's suggestion.

Clause 4 was, he said, inserted because recent British declaration of assistance to Poland might be read as implying the possibility of aggression by Soviet Union.

Clause 5 was required in view of the fact that existing Polish-Roumanian Treaty had been originally aimed at the Soviet Union only.

Clause 7 was necessary as previous experience had shown that difficulties arose where military agreements were only negotiated subsequently to political conventions.

Clause 8 was designed to cover possibility that. Turkish Government might wish to confine its liabilities to Balkan or Mediterranean areas.

No. 27.

Viscount Halifax to Sir W. Seeds (Moscow).

Foreign Office, April 29, 1939.

Sir,

I ASKED the Soviet Ambassador to call on me today on his return from Moscow. I told his Excellency that we had hoped to be in a position before now to send a reply to the carefully considered and very valuable proposals that we had recently received from the Soviet Government. The nature of the Soviet proposals had been such that we had felt it necessary to consult the French Government before ourselves sending a reply.

2. Meanwhile there was one matter in regard to which I

could not but think that the Soviet Government were under some misapprehension as to the attitude of His Majesty's Government. It seemed to me, reading the Soviet Government's proposals, that they feared lest under our suggestions it might so turn out that the Soviet Government would be committed in certain circumstances to help Poland and Roumania, without Great Britain and France themselves being involved. If this was, in fact, in the mind of the Soviet Government, it was a mistaken conclusion, inasmuch as the whole essence of our suggestion had been that, owing to the particular political difficulties of which we were all aware, the Soviet Government might offer their assistance in whatever form might seem appropriate, if, and when desired, but only in the circumstances in which our own guarantees would be *ex hypothesi* having been called into operation. The Ambassador said that this was an important point and that he would have made it plain to M. Litvinov.

3. From this we turned to a short discussion on Herr Hitler's speech. The Ambassador's judgment of this was what I naturally anticipated. He said it was remarkable for Herr Hitler to suggest that it was profitable for anybody to enter into discussions with the German Government with the object of making new treaty arrangements at a moment he was unilaterally terminating two of the engagements to which he was hitherto bound. The Polish Treaty had five more years to run and its value had been solemnly reasserted only three months ago when Herr von Ribbentrop visited Warsaw, and the Anglo German Naval Agreement also contained no provision for unilateral denunciation. The moral was sufficiently plain. Whether Herr Hitler believed his own case or not, it was clear that no certainty or assurance could attach to any treaty or arrangement made with him. In these circumstances the Ambassador was concerned to stress the unfortunate impression that would be created if His Majesty's Government were to make any response to Herr Hitler's invitation to discuss matters arising out of the denunciation of the Anglo-German Naval Agreement. Any such

action on our part would emphasise the doubts that had been aroused b y the return of Sir Nevile Henderson to Berlin. There was only one policy to pursue and that was to strengthen the anti-aggression front and make it as wide as possible.

4. I told the Ambassador that that we should certainly take no decision on the matters he had raised without very careful consideration, and that, for the present, we were contenting ourselves with acknowledging the note about the Naval Agreement, and should make any further observations after due time for reflection.

5. M. Maisky asked whether we expected to be able to send our reply to the Soviet Government in the course of next week, and I told him that, while it was impossible for me to be sure about any precise date, I should certainly wish to do so at the earliest possible moment. The Ambassador said that he was at my disposal if there were any points arising out of the Soviet Government telegram about which we felt further elucidation to be necessary, and I assured him that I, on my side, also held myself available for consultation at any time that he might desire.

No. 28.

Viscount Halifax to Sir W. Seeds (Moscow).

(Telegraphic.) *Foreign Office, April 29, 1939.*

YOUR telegram of 18th April. (No. 26)

1. His Majesty's Government have considered the latest Soviet proposal and are in consultation with the French Government as to the reply to be returned to it. They are also in communication with the Polish and Roumanian Governments. I

hope to be able to send you instructions before very long. Meanwhile, I would ask you to clear up with M. Litvinov the misunderstanding referred to in your telegram of 16th April. (No. 25)

2. I do not recall having put to the Soviet Ambassador a direct question as to what form of assistance the Soviet Government could give to Roumania. Nor was I conscious that the Soviet Ambassador regarded himself as giving a reply to a specific question of mine when, on 14th April, he informed me that the Soviet Government were prepared to take part in giving assistance to Roumania, and asked our views as to the best methods by which such assistance could be given and as to the part the various Powers concerned could play in helping Roumania.

3. I did not think it necessary to discuss with him in detail at that stage the answer to these enquiries of his, since his communication to me had synchronised with a new suggestion of my own (communicated to you in my telegram of 14th April (No. 21) and summarised by me to the ambassador) which it seemed to me might bridge the differences between the points of view of the two Governments.

4. I do not understand why Soviet Government should affect to believe that His Majesty's Government are not committed by the declarations they have made to Poland and Roumania. The language of those declarations (as also of the declaration to Greece) make it clear that, in the event of any action being taken which clearly threatened the independence of these countries and which the latter considered it vital to resist, His Majesty's Government would feel themselves bound at once to lend them all the support in their power. The first condition is that there should be resistance to a clear threat to national independence. If such resistance were offered, His Majesty's Government would intervene.

5. It was on the strength of that definite commitment on our part that I suggested that the Soviet Government should for their part make the declaration which I have proposed to them.

No. 29.

Sir W. Seeds to Viscount Halifax.

(Telegraphic.) *Moscow, May 4, 1939.*

ACCORDING to decree published in front page in this morning's press, M. Molotov, President of Council of People's Commissars, has been appointed Commissar for Foreign Affairs in addition to his other duties.

2. Inconspicuous four-line notice on back page of newspapers states that Presidium of Supreme Council of Union of Soviet Socialist Republics has released M. Litvinov at his own request from his duties as Commissar for Foreign Affairs.

3. M. Litvinov gave me no inkling of this when I saw him yesterday.

No. 30.

Viscount Halifax to Sir W. Seeds (Moscow).

Foreign Office, *May 6, 1939.*

Sir,

I ASKED the Soviet Ambassador to call on me this morning. I told his Excellency, as I had informed him last week, that we had been in consultation with other Governments concerned as to the proposals received from the Soviet Government, and that we were now, so far as these consultations were concerned almost ready to submit our reply to the Soviet Government. We had, in deference to the views expressed by the Soviet Government, somewhat modified our own suggestions and the formula that we had put forward though I must tell him that on the main line we were still disposed to feel that our method of procedure seemed to us the best.

2. Before communicating, however, with his Government, I should like to ask him if he felt able to tell me whether the recent changes in personnel in Moscow should be held to signify any change in policy. Should we assume that the Russian proposals still held the field?

3. M. Maisky at once replied that no change of policy was to be assumed from the recent departure of M. Litvinov and that accordingly the Russian proposals did still hold the field. I said that I was glad to hear this, and that, in the light of this knowledge, I hoped we should be able to make our communication to Moscow in the course of the next day or two. The Ambassador asked me whether I could give him any indication of what were the modifications that we had introduced. I said that I thought our reply would take the form of a somewhat detailed examination of the proposals actually made by the Soviet Government, and that, in particular, it would

make plain what had not been plain in the earlier suggestion, i.e., that we were not inviting the Soviet Government to accept any commitment except in conditions under which this country and France would themselves be actively engaged in hostilities. In the course of discussion, in which the Ambassador developed familiar arguments in support of the Russian plan, I told his Excellency that what I conceived to be the real difference between us was that the Russian plan, in fact, amounted to a triple alliance between Great Britain, France and Russia. For that from our point of view there was no doubt a great deal to be said, but it did seem to us very clearly to involve this consequence. Inasmuch as in the circumstances which we had in contemplation we should be involved in hostilities on behalf of Poland or Roumania, the Russian plan did automatically involve, through the terms of the hypothetical alliance, Soviet support for Poland and Roumania, and this was exactly what all our information led us to believe would cause great embarrassment to those countries, and in their view might very well provoke the very thing we all wished to avert. The difference between us was really one of form, though admittedly the difference of form was of great importance, and the practical result of the plan we suggested would, in fact, be the same as that desired by the Soviet Government, with only this difference that our plan did not carry the great disadvantages of causing immediate difficulties to those whom we both desired to help. I begged the Ambassador, even if he could not bring himself to think that we were right in preference for our own proposals, to assure his Government that they were put forward in all good faith and sincerely designed to effect the purpose of providing deterrents to aggression which we, not less than the Soviet Government, desired to do. With this the Ambassador readily concurred while still expressing regret that we felt difficulty about accepting what seemed to him the more logical, the more complete and the more effective Russian plan.

No. 31.

Viscount Halifax to Sir W. Seeds (Moscow).

(Telegraphic.) *Foreign Office, May 6, 1939.*

YOUR telegram of 18th April. (No. 26)

1. His Majesty's Government have given careful and sympathetic consideration to the counter-proposal of the Soviet Government communicated in your telegram under reference. They much appreciate the readiness which the Soviet Government have shown in making their contribution towards the object which both Governments have in view. His Majesty's Government regret that they have not been able to return their comments on the Soviet plan at an earlier date. But such delay as has occurred has been unavoidable not only because they have felt it right themselves to examine the Soviet plan with all the care that so important a proposal deserves, but also because they have been in duty bound to communicate with other interested Governments before reaching their own conclusions.

2. I have already instructed you in my telegram of 29th April (No. 28) to clear up a misunderstanding which had apparently arisen as to the intention underlying the proposal made by His Majesty's Government to the Soviet Government on 14th April. I would take this opportunity of repeating that when His Majesty's Government made their proposal to the Soviet Government it was no part of their intention that the Soviet Government should commit themselves to intervene on behalf of Poland and Roumania irrespective of whether Great Britain and France had already intervened. If the Soviet Government wished to make their own intervention contingent on that of Great Britain and France, His Majesty's Government for their part would have no objection.

3. Furthermore His Majesty's Government would point out that in the formula suggested by them to the Soviet Government on 14th April the reason for confining Soviet assistance to cases in which assistance was desired and to forms which would be acceptable to the Governments concerned, is to he found in the attitude of the Governments to which assistance would be rendered rather than that of His Majesty's Government themselves. Our object is to arrange early help and protection for Poland and Roumania as the countries most immediately threatened, in the form best calculated to act as an effective deterrent to all aggression upon them. It seemed to His Majesty's Government that the formula which we suggested to the Soviet Government taken together with the assurances already given to Poland and Roumania by Great Britain and France would be the best way of securing this, though in effect we were asking the Soviet Government to commit themselves less completely than we were committed ourselves, in that they were only invited to pledge themselves to give assistance if desired, and *ex hypothesi* only to intervene when France and Great Britain do so.

4. Our main criticism of the new proposal now made by the Soviet Government is that, though logically complete, it takes too little account of practical difficulties and would require too long a time for its negotiation. Under point 2 of the Soviet proposals the Soviet Union would be bound automatically to render military assistance to Poland and Roumania in case of aggression against those States. We know the difficulties that this presents to the Polish and Roumanian Governments. The same difficulty exists indirectly in connection with point 1. A promise by the Soviet Government of automatic assistance to His Majesty's Government in cases where the latter are involved in war in discharge of commitments in favour of Poland and Roumania would seem inevitably to involve Polish and Roumanian Governments in the same position as that which they find so embarrassing in the case of direct assistance.

5. In the arrangements which we have in mind the key positions are occupied by Poland and Turkey. In the case of Turkey no difficulty arises so far as the Soviet Union is concerned. With Poland however, as has already been pointed out, the case is different. The hesitation of the Polish Government to be too closely associated with the Soviet Union in political arrangements is well known to the Soviet Government. The Polish Government are convinced that if they were to enter into any public association with the Soviet Union, this would be regarded by the German Government as an unnecessary provocation and would involve grave risk of war which ought to be avoided. The same considerations apply in the case of the Roumanian Government.

6. For these reasons we believe the time is not yet ripe for the comprehensive counter-proposal which the Soviet Government have made to us. His Majesty's Government are still disposed to feel that the better plan is to start from what is immediately practical and to build upon that basis. The primary task must be to erect the first essential barrier against aggression in Eastern Europe by making arrangements for the safety of those States most directly menaced. In this task His Majesty's Government would always attach great importance to the association with their efforts of the Soviet Government. They are in fact fully conscious that the support that might be afforded by the Soviet Government to Eastern European countries would be of the utmost value in case of war, and that the prospect of such support would act as at powerful deterrent against aggression. Their whole effort has accordingly been directed to finding means by which the difficulties alluded to above may be avoided or overcome. It was with this purpose that His Majesty's Government proposed that the Soviet Government should of their own volition make a declaration which they are convinced would steady the situation by showing the willingness of the Soviet Government to collaborate and which at the same time would not disturb the possible

beneficiaries of Soviet assistance. By this proposal the Soviet Government would lend their assistance, in whatever form seemed most desirable, to States victims of aggression and themselves determined to resist, who wished to take advantage of it. The original proposal made to the Soviet Government was designed for the purpose of giving effect to this idea.

7. His Majesty's Government have, however, in the light of the Soviet counter-proposal and of their consultations with other Governments, revised the proposal which they originally made to the Soviet Government, and they would now submit it in the following form:-

> "It is suggested that the Soviet Government should make a public declaration on their own initiative in which after referring to the general statement of policy recently made by M. Stalin, and having regard to statements recently made by His Majesty's Government and the French Government accepting new obligations on behalf of certain Eastern European countries the Soviet Government would undertake that in the event of Great Britain and France being involved in hostilities in fulfilment of these obligations; the assistance of the Soviet Government would be immediately available if desired, and would be afforded in such manner and on such terms as might be agreed."

8. You will observe that this formula does, in fact, give the Soviet Government a reciprocal assurance of common action, since the declaration which we would suggest to be made by them only places them under a conditional obligation, in a case where *ex hypothesi* Great Britain and France are already engaged.

9. You should speak to Commissar for Foreign Affairs on the foregoing lines.

No. 32.

Sir W. Seeds to Viscount Halifax.

(Telegraphic.) *Moscow, May 8, 1939.*

YOUR telegram of 6th May. (No. 31)

I called on M. Molotov this afternoon.

2. On my mentioning M. Litvinov's departure, he at once said that Soviet policy had not changed, that their proposals still held good, and that they were awaiting an answer.

3. I then spoke as instructed, and finally gave him, with some alterations, paragraphs 6 (from words "In this task" onwards) and 7 of your telegram.

4. He listened attentively and proceeded to subject me to cross-examination on following points:-

> (a) Did we mean to start military conversations at once? I said military questions would doubtless be discussed later on if necessity arose under last line of suggested declaration. He said that, if that were so, His Majesty's Government had changed their minds, as Sir J. Simon's statement in House of Commons (on 13th April (No. 21) was in favour of far-reaching military agreement. I answered that I did not remember statement in question. I eventually said that His Majesty's Government considered issue of suggested declaration by Soviet Government without starting military talks was all that was required at the moment, but I was sure that, if friendly consideration were given to our suggestion, His Majesty's

Government would be glad to discuss such points as might arise therefrom.

(b) M. Molotov said that I had laid stress on Poland's reluctance to be associated publicly with Soviet Union in the matter of possible assistance, but his own information was that Polish Government had now changed their attitude in this respect. I answered that such was not the impression so far as I knew, either of His Majesty's Government or of French Government. He said Poland was only directly mentioned in point 2 of Soviet Proposals, but what about point 1? Did Polish Government's objection hold good as to that point? I refused to be drawn, and insisted that Soviet proposals had been considered as a whole. I gave similar reply to question why His Majesty's Government had not given considered answer to each point of Soviet proposals.

5. Asked whether His Majesty's Government had given guarantees to Holland, Belgium and Switzerland, I pointed out that the Low Countries had always been considered a vital point in Great Britain's defences.

6. M. Molotov said the Soviet Government would give careful consideration to our views. He repeated that Soviet policy had not changed, but added cryptic remark that it was liable to be altered if the other States changed theirs.

7. I should add that he commented unfavourably on our delay in answering. I repeated what I had previously said as to necessity for consulting other Governments. When he finally pointed out that Soviet Government had always replied to us within three days instead of three weeks I answered that I took off my hat to Soviet efficiency. He seemed pleased, and on that note a somewhat trying interview closed.

No. 33.

Viscount Halifax to Sir W. Seeds (Moscow).

Foreign Office, May 9, 1939.

Sir,

THE Soviet Ambassador asked to see me this afternoon, and told me that he was speaking on instructions from his Government in seeking an elucidation of the formula which your Excellency had been instructed to submit to M. Molotov.

2. M. Maisky said that he had gathered from the conversation that he had had with me last week that it was our intention to identify the obligations to be incurred by the Soviet Government on the one hand and by France and Great Britain on the other, reciprocal in character but his Government felt great doubt whether our formula in fact did this, and it seemed to them that there was some possibility of the Soviet Government being involved either in advance of France and ourselves or alone.

3. I went through the draft with M. Maisky, and drew his particular attention to the words we had added to this formula in the event of Great Britain and France being involved in hostilities in fulfilment of their obligations. He had added these words for the express purpose of making it clear to the Soviet Government that we were not asking them to do anything that we were not *ex hypothesi* doing ourselves.

4. M. Maisky replied to this by saying that there were many ways in which the strategical position might develop and that I had not wholly succeeded in removing his doubts. I told him that, while I had never attempted to disguise from myself the particular difference of the approach to the problem that

had been made by the Soviet Government and ourselves. I did not think that on this particular point there was any room for doubt. I went on to assure him that, if his Government would set down precisely the point on which they felt misgiving, we would do our best to meet it, and I ventured to hope that if they put us in full possession of their doubts I could either show them that the draft in fact covered them, or I should hope that we could so amend it as to make our purpose indisputably plain.

5. He agreed that the purpose to which his observations were directed was to secure that, in the event of Russia being involved by her promise to render help to Poland and Roumania, she would not be rendering it alone. I repeated that I could not believe that there could be great difficulty in meeting this anxiety, always provided that the Soviet Government were not expecting us to travel outside the two conditions which we had attached to our guarantee, namely (1) that the independence of Poland or Roumania should be plainly threatened (his Excellency interjected: "direct or indirect?"); (2) that these countries were determined to resist with their national forces.

6. M. Maisky seemed gratified by my explanation and promised to submit a note of the actual point his Government might wish to raise.

7. I also drew the attention of the Ambassador to the concluding words of the formula, "on such terms as might be agreed." These words, I told him, we had also added to satisfy the Soviet Government that they would have some liberty of action in the discharge of the obligation that they might be willing to undertake; and that, while I fully recognised the undesirability of leaving all these discussions until the outbreak of war, we were, on the other hand, concerned to introduce the great steadying factor that would be made by such a Russian declaration as we had provided, and that it might be possible thereafter to develop the situation in greater detail.

No. 34.

Reply of the Prime Minister to Questions in the House of Commons on May 10, 1939.

The Prime Minister: I have seen the statement to which the right hon. gentleman refers and which seems to be based upon some misunderstanding of the suggestions actually put forward by His Majesty's Government to the Soviet Government. Though conversations are still in progress and the House will not, therefore, expect me to discuss the matters in detail, I think it right, in view of this statement, to place the House in possession of the general line on which the conversations have been hitherto proceeding.

As the House is aware, His Majesty's Government recently accepted a definite obligation in respect of certain Eastern European States. They did this in pursuance of their declared policy of assisting those States to resist any attempt, if such were made, to threaten their independence. His Majesty's Government undertook these obligations without inviting the Soviet Government to participate directly in them, in view of certain difficulties to which, as the House is well aware, any such suggestion would inevitably give rise. His Majesty's Government accordingly suggested to the Soviet Government that they should make, on their own behalf, a declaration of similar effect to that already made by His Majesty's Government, in the sense that in the event of Great Britain and France being involved in hostilities in discharge of their own obligations thus accepted the Soviet Government, on their side, would express their readiness also to lend assistance, if desired. Such a declaration, if the Soviet Government feel able to make it, seems to His Majesty's Government to be in accord with the recent pronouncement of M. Stalin, that it is the policy of the Soviet Government to support countries which might he victims of aggression and which were prepared to defend their own independence.

Almost simultaneously the Soviet Government suggested a scheme at once more comprehensive and more rigid which, whatever other advantages it might present, must in the view of His Majesty's Government inevitable raise the very difficulties which their own proposals had been designed to avoid. His Majesty's Government accordingly pointed out to the Soviet Government the existence of these difficulties. At the same time, they made certain modifications in their original proposals. In particular, they made it plain that it was no part of their intention that the Soviet Government should commit themselves to intervene, irrespective of whether Great Britain and France had already, in discharge of their obligations, done so. His Majesty's Government added that, if the Soviet Government wished to make their own intervention contingent all that of Great Britain and France, His Majesty's Government for their part would have no objection.

My noble friend yesterday saw the Soviet Ambassador, who explained to him that the Soviet Government were still not clear whether under the proposal of His Majesty's Government circumstances might not arise in which the Soviet Government would be committed to intervention unsupported by His Majesty's Government or France. My noble friend instructed the ambassador that this was definitely not the intention of the proposal made by His Majesty's Government and that, if there were any room for doubt on this point, my noble friend anticipated that it could without difficulty be removed. He accordingly invited the Soviet Ambassador to place His Majesty's Government in possession of the precise grounds all which these doubts of his Government were based, if they still existed, and this the Soviet Ambassador readily agreed to do.

I should add that the British Ambassador in Moscow had an interview two days ago with M. Molotov, at the conclusion of which M. Molotov promised that the Soviet Government would give careful consideration to our proposals, and we are now awaiting their reply.

Mr. Dalton: Would it not be a good thing in order to speed up these very slow negotiations, the slowness of which is causing grave apprehension in the country, that Lord Halifax should proceed to Moscow and have a straightforward discussion with M. Molotov?

The Prime Minister: I think we had better await the reply of the Soviet Government and then we shall see what further steps are required.

Mr. Mander: The Prime Minister has been good enough to explain to the House the policy put forward by His Majesty's Government to Russia, and will he be good enough at the same time to explain the so called rigid proposals of the Russian Government which the British Government have been unable to accept?

The Prime Minister: I do not think it is necessary for me to add anything to the statement I have made.

Mr. Attlee: May I take it from the Prime Minister that in these negotiations we are keeping in the closest touch with the French Government, in order that the views of all three Governments may be clear before the making, as we hope, of a firm agreement against aggression?

The Prime Minister: Yes, Sir, we are keeping in the closest touch with the French Government continuously.

Mr. Thurtle: Will the Prime Minister assure the House that the Government regard the conclusion of the negotiations as a matter of real urgency?

The Prime Minister: We regard it as of the greatest importance and of real urgency.

Mr. A. Henderson: Can the House take it that His Majesty's Government have not finally closed their minds to, if circumstances necessitate, the conclusion of a military alliance with Russia?

The Prime Minister: I cannot answer a hypothetical question. Discussions are going on on certain lines, and we are very hopeful that they will soon come to a satisfactory issue.

Mr. Benjamin Smith: Could the Prime Minister tell us whether the terms set out would include, if Great Britain found herself attacked by an aggressor, assistance by Russia to this country?

The Prime Minister: I made a careful and full statement, and I think it is very much better that I should not add to it.

Sir Archibald Sinclair: Do the Government's proposals contemplate only the contingency of war? Do they not also contemplate the contingency of peaceful negotiations, and is there any assurance to Russia that, if peaceful negotiations were entered into, Russia will be a party to those negotiations?

The Prime Minister: What the negotiations are contemplating is an act of aggression.

Mr. Noel Baker: Can the Prime Minister confirm the point that the guarantee given to Poland does not in any way preclude an alliance with Russia and that Colonel Beck gave express assurances on that point?

The Prime Minister: Does the hon. member mean an alliance between this country and Russia?

Mr. Noel-Baker: Yes.

The Prime Minister: No, that is not excluded.

Mr. Noel Baker: And did Colonel Beck raise no objection?

The Prime Minister: I did not say that at all. The question which the hon. member asked me was whether the arrangement with Poland excluded the possibility of an alliance between this country and Russia and to that I said "No."

No. 35.

Viscount Halifax to Sir W. Seeds (Moscow).

Foreign Office, May 11, 1939.

Sir,

DURING the course of a conversation with the Soviet Ambassador this morning I asked his Excellency whether he had any further information as yet from his Government in regard to what had seemed to be a misunderstanding of the British formula, to which we had referred in our last conversation. M. Maiskv said that he had received no instructions as yet, but again developed the insistence of his Government on the necessity for complete reciprocity. In the course of conversation he developed his meaning by saying that the Soviet Government might find itself involved in war in virtue of commitments undertaken by them in regard to Baltic States, towards whom His Majesty's Government had no obligation. In such a case the Soviet Government could count on no support from us. To this I replied that the proposal of the Soviet Government to build up a system of guarantees very much wider than we had ourselves suggested or undertaken might or might not be a good plan. But it did not seem to me to afford any evidence of lack of reciprocity in the proposals that we ourselves had put forward. Those proposals concerned only Poland and Roumania, and, in regard to those countries, it seemed to me quite plain that the obligations we were inviting the Soviet Government to undertake were identical with those we ourselves had assumed. It might, indeed, be our view that they were not so great, inasmuch as they were conditional and not absolute. In regard to the position of the Soviet Government in relation to other hypothetical commitments they might see fit to assume, the fact that in such circumstances we were not bound by our formula to give assistance to the Soviet Government might be reckoned as being exactly on all fours with the fact that the Soviet Government were not bound by our formula to give any assistance to us if we were involved with Germany, for example, in virtue of our guarantee to Belgium, or by any guarantee that we might give to any of the other smaller Western Powers. I still, therefore failed to see how there was any just ground for maintaining that our proposal denied the principle of reciprocity. It seemed to me, perhaps, that part of the difficulty in M. Maisky's thought consisted in the fact that he spoke of Russian assistance being rendered to France and Great Britain, whereas in fact what we contemplated was Soviet assistance being rendered to Poland and Roumania, who would already be assured of assistance from France and ourselves.

2. In connexion with his general argument, M. Maisky mentioned military conversations and sought to establish the case that under our proposal the date of Anglo-French intervention would be uncertain, inasmuch as this would depend on the decisions of the French and British General Staffs, and that, accordingly, again the Soviet Government would not

exactly know when such intervention would take place. To this I replied that our guarantee to Poland and Roumania involved us in coming immediately to their assistance if our conditions were fulfilled, and that, if words meant anything, it was impossible for us to give any assurance more complete. M. Maisky promised again to let me have a reasoned note from his Government on the points which, in their view, required elucidation, and said that he hoped it would be possible to clear up a good many of them before the postponed meeting of the Council at Geneva.

No. 36.

Sir W. Seeds to Viscount Halifax.

(Telegraphic.) *Moscow, May 14, 1939.*

YOUR telegram of 6th May. (No. 31)

M. Molotov handed me Soviet reply tonight as follows:-

"Soviet Government have given careful consideration to latest proposals of British Government, which were communicated to them on 8th May, and they have come to the conclusion that these proposals cannot serve as a
basis for organisation of a front of resistance against a further extension of aggression in Europe.

"This conclusion is based on the following considerations:-

"(1) The English proposals do not contain principle of reciprocity with regard to Union of Soviet Socialist Republics, and place the latter in a position of inequality, inasmuch as they do not contemplate an obligation by England and France to guarantee the Union of Soviet Socialist Republics in the event of a direct attack on the latter by aggressors, whereas England and France, as well as Poland, enjoy such a guarantee as a result of reciprocity which exists between them.

"(2) The English proposals only extend guarantee to Eastern European States bordering on Union of Soviet Socialist Republics to Poland and to Roumania, as a consequence of which northwestern frontier of "Union of Soviet Socialist Republics towards Finland, Estonia and Latvia remains uncovered.

"(3) On the one hand, absence of guarantee to Union Soviet Socialist Republics on the part of England and France in the event of a direct attack by aggressors and, on the other hand, fact that north-western frontier of Union of Soviet Socialist Republics remains uncovered may serve to provoke aggression in the direction of Soviet Union.

"Soviet Government consider there are at least three indispensable conditions for creation of an effective barrier by pacific States against a further extension of aggression in Europe; (1) The conclusion between England and France and Union of Soviet Socialist Republics of an effective pact of mutual assistance against aggression. (2) The guaranteeing by these three Great Powers of States of Central and Eastern Europe threatened by aggression, including also Latvia, Estonia and Finland. (3) The conclusion of a concrete agreement between England, France and Union of Soviet Socialist Republics as to forms and extent of assistance to be rendered materially to each other and to the guaranteed States, failing which (without such an agreement) there is a risk that, as experience of Czecho-Slovakia proved, pacts of mutual assistance may be ineffective."

2. I thought it well to express regret at specific mention of Finland, stating, *inter alia,* that we associated that country more with Scandinavia than with the Baltic States, quite apart from the fact that, on our side of the Anglo-Soviet conversations, we

had never considered undertaking any commitments with regard to the last mentioned. It was most important that Finland should maintain neutrality on the same lines as Norway and Sweden; this could he assured if Finland were not reminded of certain unpleasant historical associations with Russia; newspaper reports that Finland had been mentioned in Anglo-Soviet conversations had already caused some emotion in that country, and the whole situation needed delicate handling. M. Molotov listened attentively and only suggested that association of Great Britain and France with Soviet Union might weaken Finland's suspicions.

3. M. Molotov said that the main point of Soviet Government's reply was need for "reciprocity." When I asked whether we could assume that question of Baltic States was of less importance than that of laying down a more definite reciprocity in connexion with guarantees to Poland and Roumania, he answered that each point of reply followed logically from its predecessor.

4. As regards your Lordship's message about Geneva he thought he would not be able to go himself, but Soviet Government would be properly represented on 22nd May.

No. 37.

Extract from the Prime Minister's Speech in the House of Commons on May 19, 1939.

I TURN to the discussions with the Government of the Soviet Union. I cannot help thinking that there has been some misunderstanding, because the right hon. gentleman, the Leader of the Opposition, in the conclusion of his speech, put forward an idea which I have no doubt is held by many of his friends and supporters, namely, that the British Government were actuated in their conduct of these negotiations by mistrust of

Russian ideology. I have said before that that is not so. I want to repeat it now. We are not concerned at all with Russian internal political doctrine. We are concerned with the best method of building up what my right hon. friend the Member for Warwick and Leamington (Mr. Eden) has called a peace front. If we can evolve a method by which we can enlist the co-operation and assistance of the Soviet Union in building up that peace front, we welcome it; we want it; we attach value to it. The suggestion that we despise the assistance of the Soviet Union is without foundation. Without accepting any view of an unauthorised character as to the precise value of the Russian military forces, or the way in which they would best be deployed, no one would be so foolish as to suppose that that huge country, with its vast population and enormous resources, would be a negligible factor in such a situation as that with which we are confronted. I hope the right hon. gentleman will dismiss any idea that, because we do not agree with the internal system of government of the Soviet Union that has in any way affected our outlook in the present negotiations. or the way in which we are conducting them.

The House may remember a recent statement by M. Stalin that it was the policy of the Soviet Union "to support States which might be victims of aggression, provided that they were prepared to defend their independence." That is our own point of view, and it appeared to indicate that the Soviet Union might be prepared to collaborate in carrying this aim into effect. But we were also aware, and this is a point which has not been referred to at all up to the present, that the direct participation of the Soviet union in this matter might not be altogether in accordance with the wishes of some of the countries for whose benefit, or on whose behalf, these arrangements were being made. We would desire to have the collaboration of all these countries, and we do not want to have any division among them. Accordingly, we suggested to the Soviet Government that they should make a declaration with regard to Poland and

Roumania similar to the one which had been made by ourselves and France, namely, that if Great Britain and France should be involved in conflict in consequence of undertakings which we had given to these countries, or either of them, the Soviet Union should express its readiness to lend its assistance to Poland or Roumania, as the case might be, always provided, of course, that their assistance was desired. The Soviet Government, apparently, thought that this offer was not reciprocal. I want to say now that the British Government have never desired to ask the Soviet Government to do anything which they were not prepared to do themselves. They have always wanted the arrangement to be reciprocal, and I do really find it difficult to understand why it should be thought, or why it should ever have been thought, that the suggestion we made was lacking in reciprocity.

If it be argued that it did not provide for the case of a direct attack on the Soviet Union, agreed; but it did not provide for the case of a direct attack on this country. The hon. member said that it was not the same as the agreement with Turkey. If I may be allowed to say so, that is not the point. The point is, was it reciprocal? I am not saying it was the same as the agreement with Turkey, or with any country. What I want to examine is, was it unfair? Did it ask of the Soviet Union something more than we were prepared to do ourselves? It may be argued that it did not cover the case of certain States, other than Poland and Roumania which are neighbours of Russia, and through which perhaps they might be attacked. Again, I say, It is quite true that it did not cover that, but, on the other hand, it equally did not apply to certain Western States which, if attacked, might, cause us ultimately to be involved in war.

Again, I am not saying whether this was the same as any other treaty. What I am saying is that it is quite wrong to say that it was not reciprocal. I think I made it plain that our suggestion did not contemplate that the Soviet Government should intervene irrespective of whether Great Britain and France did so, although, as a matter of fact, our own commitments which follow upon the assurances we have given are irrespective of whether the Soviet Union come in. Therefore, if there be any inequality between the two states in the proposals which have been made, the inequality was in favour of the Soviet Union and not of this country. We rely on a matter of that kind because it is a question of fact, and, although I have given a little time to explaining our position, it is really because the Soviet Union really seemed to believe that we had tried to put an unfair proposal upon them, and because colour was given to that view by the intervention of the right hon. gentleman. It really is a misunderstanding, and whatever can be alleged against our proposal, I am sure that it cannot be alleged truly that it was unfair.

Nevertheless, since the proposal was not acceptable to the Soviet Union, we tried again. What we, above all were anxious for was, that we should be able to come to an agreement quickly, and it is always easy to come to an agreement quickly if you accept everything that the other side puts up. I do ask the House to remember that in this matter we are trying to build up, not an alliance between ourselves and other countries, but a peace front against aggression, and we should not be succeeding in that policy if, by ensuring the cooperation of one country, we rendered another country uneasy and unwilling to collaborate with us. Therefore, I suggest to the committee that in this matter, which is one of great difficulty and delicacy, a certain amount of caution is necessary, caution arising not out of ideological differences, not out of pure obstinacy, not even because we think that one course serves narrow British interests better than another, but because the object of our policy is to build up this peace front. We would rather delay for a few days longer than hastily taken step which might result in the work that we had already done crumbling before our very eyes.

We thought that perhaps the Soviet Government might have been willing to declare its agreement with us on those matters on which we could agree, and that it would be prepared to let us discuss further and at greater leisure the subjects on which difficulties still existed. That, in our view, would have been a wise course to take to show agreement, and I cannot help thinking that, if we agreed even on a part of the policy to be pursued, it would have made it easier to come to complete agreement on the rest. I cannot help saying how much I regret the decision of the Soviet Government not to let M. Potemkin go to Geneva. The Geneva Council was postponed for a week in order to allow him to go there, but after it had been postponed we heard that he could not go. My noble friend will, therefore, be deprived of the opportunity of discussing personally with him those matters which, I think, might have been valuable for both of us. No doubt the Soviet Government had good reasons for their action, but I only regret that it was not possible for this meeting to take place. This is one of the cases in which I cannot help feeling that there is a sort of veil, a sort of wall between the two Governments which it is extremely difficult to penetrate, and that if only that opportunity had been afforded us we might have, perhaps, managed to shake hands across the gap.

I am not going any further than I have gone already. The committee will realise that I must walk warily and I do not want to say anything which will make things more difficult than they are already. What I have said was, that we are not concerned merely with the Russian Government. We have other Governments to consider. There may be those who are out just to damage the Government or to make mischief, but those who want this policy to succeed, as His Majesty's Government do, will, I think, refrain from pressing us unduly to disclose the exact point where the difficulties arise, when I have already given them a general indication.

I have nothing more to say except this. Throughout this matter we have been in close touch with the Government of France, with whom we are happy to have collaboration and counsel. There is no difference between us, and my noble friend the Foreign Secretary will have the opportunity tomorrow for further discussions with the head of the French Government and with their Foreign Minister. I do trust that after this consultation, and with their help, it may be found possible to overcome those obstacles which have hitherto prevented us from reaching an agreement with the Government of the Soviet Union, and that we shall be able in due course to report to the House that we have at last made a final agreement with them.

No. 38.

British Delegation, Geneva, to Foreign Office.

(Telegraphic.) *Geneva, May 21, 1939.*

I (Viscount Halifax) had a conversation M. Maisky this morning, at which set myself to obtain as clear a statement as possible of his Government's views. He responded freely, but emphasised that although he could assure me that his observations were in accordance with the general line of his Government's views, they must be regarded as personal explanations.

2. I asked him why the Soviet Government had been unable to accept the British proposals. (No. 31)

3. He replied that the essential thing was to prevent war. The Soviet Government thought this could be done, but only by organising such a combination of forces that Germany would

not dare to attack. For this purpose a triple pact was necessary, and our proposals entirely ignored this element in the Soviet proposal.

4. In the second place, our proposals were not based on reciprocity. Under them Russia would be bound to assist Great Britain and France in the event of an attack on Poland or Roumania, but Great Britain would not be obliged to come to Russia's assistance in the event of an attack on the Baltic States.

5. The weakness of our plan was that it was based on a guarantee to Poland and Roumania alone. Supposing that Roumania should make friends with Germany or that Germany should, by intimidation or bribery, bring Roumania to allow German troops to pass freely across Roumania to attack Russia, Great Britain would not be obliged to intervene, though Russia would be forced to fight. He agreed with my reminder that under the Franco-Soviet Pact France might have to help Russia, but observed that this was not true of Great Britain.

6. So also if Poland's policy changed, the same thing might happen in Poland. The Baltic States, too, wished to be neutral at present, but they might equally be, intimidated or bribed into allowing German troops to pass through or German aerodromes to be established in their territory.

7. Then again Russia was being asked to give Poland a guarantee, but Poland was not being asked to give Russia a guarantee. Poland might therefore be neutral in a German-Russian war, and the caracter of her neutrality would be of importance to Russia.

8. I repeated to him our reasons for thinking that our proposals, whatever might be said about them, were fully reciprocal.

9. He admitted that from the logical or legalistic point of view this might be so, but in practice the position of the two countries would be quite different. Great Britain had a reciprocal agreement with Poland, while Russia had none. France had a reciprocal arrangement with Great Britain, while Russia had none. Russia was, therefore, exposed to far greater dangers than was Great Britain and might be left to fight alone.

10. I told him that if Russia was, in a situation of inequality, this was inherent in her treaty position. If we were not proposing any direct guarantee for Russia, neither were we asking any direct Russian guarantee for ourselves. Indeed, her position was made better not worse, than it was before, by the fact of our having guaranteed Poland and Roumania which were the only countries through which an effective German attack could be launched on Russia.

11. I then suggested that it would go some way to meet the Russian case if it was possible to introduce a provision by which the border States would undertake not to allow Germany to use their territory as a passage or base of operations against Russia. He doubted whether they would be willing to make such an arrangement or that they would be able to observe it if they made it.

12. M. Maisky explained that Russia had the choice of two positions. She could, on the one hand, take care of herself and enter into no obligations to other Powers. The advantage of this would be that, though she might have to defend herself single-handed, she would preserve her own liberty of action.

13. On the other hand, though she could in the long run win any war of defence single-handed, she could not single-handed prevent war in general. She was therefore ready to collaborate with other Powers for this purpose, and though she would thereby lose her freedom of action she would gain in

return the possibility of preventing war. If she accepted the British proposals she would lose her liberty of action without getting this result in return. She would, moreover, be undertaking heavy obligations, since owing to her geographical position she would have to bear the chief brunt of resisting an attack or the chief burden of assisting the Powers which she had guaranteed. It was for this reason that the Soviet Government thought a triple pact of mutual assistance to be essential.

14. I asked him how far it would meet the Soviet view if we could cover the Baltic States by our proposal. He replied that this would be all improvement, but it would not secure the main aim which was to prevent war in general.

15. He added, that if the triple pact could he arranged, the smaller States would no longer be shy about receiving Soviet assistance. Their hesitation arose from the fact that they saw a strong and well-organised aggressive block faced by an ill-organised and slow moving peace block. I told him that I thought he very much underestimated the difficulties in this respect and that their hesitation arose from quite other reasons.

16. I asked whether it would help to meet the Soviet view if it could be provided that, should any one of the three Powers become involved in hostilities through helping any other Power that requested their assistance (e.g., the Baltic States, Yugoslavia, Belgium or Holland, as well as Poland and Roumania), then all three would be in the war together.

17. He did not think that this would do, as it did not cover the case of a sudden collapse of States bordering on Russia or of their failure to resist.

18. I told him that, speaking frankly, I was greatly disappointed with the attitude of the Soviet Government throughout these negotiations. We had made very great efforts

to meet their point of view, whereas they had not changed their position at all had made little or no advance to meet us.

19. He observed that on the contrary whereas they had put forward eight points in their original proposal (No. 26) they had reduced these to three, and set aside the other five (No. 36). The Soviet Government might be able to compromise on secondary points, but they could not compromise on essentials. The triple pact was indispensable as a deterrent.

20. I asked whether I correctly interpreted his point of view as follows. The Soviet Government thought a triple pact of mutual assistance necessary, first, because by this means alone could Russia be protected against the collapse or intimidation by Germany of the buffer States, and secondly, because the Soviet Government felt that if they were to accept new and heavy obligations they could only do so as part of a system that in their view gave the best hope of preventing war.

21. He agreed with this statement of his Government's position. The Soviet Government were anxious that there should be no outbreak of war anywhere.

22. I asked him whether I should be right in stating the views of the Soviet somewhat as follows: In the event of any of the three Governments being involved in hostilities with a European Power, either as a result of its giving help to another European State which was a victim of aggression, or as a result of a direct attack on one of them, the other two would come to the assistance of that Government.

23. M. Maisky thought this was in keeping with the ideas of the Soviet Government.

24. I asked him whether it would be the intention of the Soviet Government to make the operation of such a pact

conditional upon the victim of aggression asking for assistance. He agreed that assistance could not be forced on those who did not desire it.

25. I finally asked him whether he thought the Soviet Government would be willing that such an agreement as they were pressing for should cover not only the Eastern European States (as in the Soviet proposal), but also the smaller Western European States. He replied that he could not answer this question with authority but did not see any insuperable difficulty, and was sure that it could be discussed.

26. I am afraid I was unable in the course of a long conversation to shake M. Maisky at all on his main point of insistence on a triple mutual guarantee against direct aggression as against only joint action in support of guarantees given the other States.

27. I thanked M. Maisky for information he had given me but told him that I could give him no indication of attitude of His Majesty's Government which would be decided as soon as possible in light of all the considerations of which they had to take account.

No. 39.

Statement by the Prime Minister in the House of Commons on May 24, 1939.

THE House is aware that my noble friend the Secretary of State for Foreign Affairs was able to have conversations with the French Ministers in Paris on his way to Geneva. He was also able to continue in Geneva the conversations which had been conducted with the Soviet Ambassador in London. As a result of these conversations all relevant points of view have now been made clear and I have every reason to hope that as a result of proposals which His Majesty's Government are now in a position to make on the main questions arising, it will be found possible to reach full agreement at an early date. There still remain some further points to be cleared up, but I do not anticipate that these are likely to give rise to any serious difficulty.

No. 40.

Viscount Halifax to Sir W. Seeds (Moscow).

(Telegraphic.) *Foreign Office, May 24, 1939.*

HIS Majesty's Government, after careful consideration, are now disposed to agree that effective co-operation between the Soviet, French and British Governments against aggression in Europe might be based on a system of mutual guarantees in general conformity with the principles of the League of Nations. This would have to cover both direct attack on any of the three Governments by a European State, and the case where any of them was engaged in hostilities with such a State in consequence of aggression by the latter upon another European country. The conditions of this last named eventuality will have to be carefully worked out.

2. Prime Minister made short statement in Parliament this afternoon indicating that he had every reason to hope that, as a result of proposals which His Majesty's Government are now in a position to make on main questions arising, it will be found possible to reach full agreement at an early date, though there remain some further points to be cleared up. Text of this statement was communicated to Soviet Embassy here before issue.

3. Please inform Soviet Government of above, and tell them

I hope to telegraph shortly outline of a formula which would give effect to principles indicated above.

No. 41.

Viscount Halifax to Sir W. Seeds (Moscow).

(Telegraphic.) *Foreign Office, May 25, 1939.*

MY telegram of 24th May. (No. 40)

1. My immediately following telegrams contain the text of a draft agreement (No. 42) and an explanatory memorandum (No. 43).

2. These are being communicated in the first instance to the French Government, with the suggestion that the agreement should be submitted to The Soviet Government jointly by yourself and your French colleague.

3. In the meantime the draft agreement and the memorandum are being sent to you only for your information and to save time in the event of my having to instruct you to act at short notice.

No. 42.

Viscount Halifax to Sir W. Seeds (Moscow).
Draft Agreement.

(Telegraphic.) *Foreign Office, May 25, 1939.*

THE Governments of the United Kingdom, France and the U.S.S.R., desiring to give effect, in their capacity of members of the League of Nations, to the principle of mutual support against aggression which is embodied in the Covenant of the League, have reached the following agreement:-

I.

If France and the United Kingdom are engaged in hostilities with a European Power, in consequence of either (1) aggression by that Power against another European State which they had, in conformity with the wishes of that State, undertaken to assist against such aggression; (2) assistance given by them to another European State which had requested such assistance in order to resist a violation of its neutrality; or (3) aggression by a European Power against either France or the United Kingdom, the U.S.S.R., acting in accordance with the principles of article 16, paragraphs 1 and 2, of the Covenant of the League of Nations, will give France and the United Kingdom all the support and assistance in its power.

II.

If the U.S.S.R is engaged in hostilities with a European Power, in consequence of either (1) aggression by that Power against another European State which they had, in conformity with the wishes of that State, undertaken to assist against such aggression; (2) assistance given by the U.S.S.R to another European State which had requested such assistance in order to resist a violation of its neutrality; or (3) aggression by a European Power against the U.S.S.R., France and the United Kingdom, acting in accordance with the principles of article 16, paragraphs 1 and 2, of the Covenant of the League of Nations, will give the U.S.S.R. all the support and assistance in their power.

III.

The three Governments will concert together as to the methods by which such mutual support and assistance could, in the case of need, be made effective.

IV.

In the event of circumstances arising which threaten to call their undertakings of mutual support and assistance into operation, the three Governments will immediately consult together upon the situation.

The methods and scope of such consultation will at once be the subject of further discussion between the three Governments.

V.

It is understood that the rendering of support and assistance in the above cases is without prejudice to the rights and position of other Powers.

VI.

The three Governments will communicate to each other the terms of any undertakings referred to in I(1) and II(1) above which they have already given. Any of them they may in future be considering the giving of such an undertaking will consult the other two Governments before doing so, and will communicate to them the terms of any undertaking so given.

VII.

This agreement will continue for a period of (five) years from to-day's date. Not less than (six months) before the expiry of the said period, the three Governments will consult together as to the desirability of renewing it, with or without modifications.

No. 43.

Viscount Halifax to Sir. W. Seeds (Moscow).

(Telegraphic.) *Foreign Office, May 25, 1939.*

Explanatory Memorandum.

HIS Majesty's Government consider it important from the point of view of public opinion in this country that the pact should be connected in some way with the position of the parties as members of the League of Nations. On the other hand, it is obviously impossible in existing circumstances to make the operation of the pact dependent on the application of article 16 by the League, especially as, Germany and Italy not being members of the League, the League machinery could only be set in motion by the application of article 17, a course which it might be impossible to follow. It is, moreover, important to prevent any fears on the part of other countries that an attempt is being made to involve them, either generally under article 16 or particularly under this provision in paragraph 8 of that article about affording passage through their territory to the forces of members of the League. For these reasons the Covenant is mentioned both in the preamble and in articles 1 and 2 only by a reference to its principles, and the references to article 16 of the Covenant mention only paragraphs 1 and 2 of that article.

2. Paragraphs 1 and 2 have been drafted in order to meet so far as possible the susceptibilities of Poland, Roumania and the Baltic States. The idea is that 1 in each of these articles covers the case (Poland, Roumania, Belgium, Greece, Turkey), where one of the parties had previously given an undertaking of assistance to the country concerned with its assent, while 2 covers the case (e.g., Baltic States, Holland, Switzerland), where

no such assurance had been previously given, but where the country concerned asked for assistance in resisting a violation of its neutrality. Paragraph 6 is intended, in conjunction with the words "in conformity with the wishes of that State" in paragraphs 1 and 2, to prevent fears that the Soviet Union might give guarantees to countries which do not desire them.

3. It will be observed that now that the pact has been made entirely reciprocal it makes no difference from the Franco-British point of view whether the Soviet Union give undertakings to Poland and Roumania or not, because in the event of France and Great Britain being engaged in hostilities in consequence of their undertakings to Poland or Roumania the Soviet Union would, under paragraph 1, be bound to come to their assistance.

4. The object of paragraph 5 is to indicate that the obligations of mutual assistance do not involve making use of the territory of other Powers without their consent.

No. 44.

Sir W. Seeds to Viscount Halifax.

(Telegraphic.) *Moscow, May 27, 1939.*

FRENCH Chargé d'Affaires and I saw M. Molotov this afternoon, who was accompanied by M. Potemkin.

2. M. Molotov said at once that he had already studied our proposal (No. 42) of which he had received the text from Paris, and that his personal reaction was in the negative. The impression produced on his mind was that Great Britain and France wanted to continue conversations ad infinitum, but were not interested in obtaining concrete results.

3. I said that His Majesty's Government, who had made so great an effort to meet - as they thought successfully - the wishes of the Soviet Government, would be as astounded as I was to hear this. On what did he base his impression? He said that our introducing references to the League of Nations was a clear indication that we were prepared to make effective cooperation dependent on the interminable delays of League of Nations procedure. Soviet Government wanted immediate guarantee of effective mutual assistance against aggressors, but Great Britain and France were apparently satisfied with a state of affairs where Russia would be bombed by the aggressor while Bolivia blocked all action at Geneva. I explained over and over again the reason for our allusion to the League Covenant in the terms of your Lordship's instructions, but my repeated emphasis on "the spirit," and "principles" of the Covenant was only met by repeated insistence on the League's procedure.

4. M. Molotov then used the astonishing argument why under point 5 we were proposing to safeguard the rights and position of an aggressor State. I explained that the point in question referred only to States to whom we were proposing to lend assistance, to which he retorted that this safeguarding of rights was typical of that reserve which he read into our proposals and which was calculated to ensure the maximum of talk and the minimum of results. He repeated that the Soviet Government wanted effective guarantee of action, not words and conversations.

5. We urged that point 3 covered effective action as regards the method and nature of assistance, i.e., military consultations, but he insisted that that point as well as point 4 referred vaguely to the future. He said that Soviet wishes in that respect had been clearly expressed, but we had not replied to them.

6. After more wrangling on the League of Nations question, he said he had been expressing his personal views, which were unchanged; he would report to his Government and give us the answer in due course. I suggested that the Soviet reply should be held up until I had communicated with your Lordship in the hope of finding means to clear up the misunderstanding, but he gave me no definite reply to this.

7. Assuming he was not merely manoeuvering to close negotiations, I can only suggest we should propose some formula which would provide for two simultaneous agreements, one being pact of mutual assistance, and the second a "concrete agreement as to the form and extent of assistance." But I see no possibility of meeting him on the League of Nations question, as presumably we could not lay down in our formula that we eliminate all League "procedure."

No. 45.

Viscount Halifax to *Sir W. Seeds (Moscow).*

(Telegraphic.) *Foreign Office, May 29, 1939.*

YOUR telegram of 27th May. (No. 44)

I approve your language. M. Molotov is evidently under a complete misunderstanding as to the scope and meaning of His Majesty's Government's proposals, which are sincerely intended to provide for effective and immediate mutual support.

There is not the slightest ground for the assumption that His Majesty's Government wish to adopt League procedure. They wish to act in accordance with League *principles,* and to this the Soviet Government, as a member of the League, surely cannot reasonably object. But His Majesty's Government are prepared to make it clear that the operation of the agreement shall not be made dependent on League procedure. M. Molotov is equally wrong in assuming that points 3 and 4 are intended to refer vaguely to the future or to defer conclusion of concrete arrangement. His Majesty's Government are ready to embark immediately on conversations to this end. It was felt, however, that it would be preferable, as in the case of the Polish and Turkish agreements, to lose no time in concluding an agreement in principle before elaborating the details. In this respect Soviet Government have no more reason to be suspicious than Polish or Turkish Governments who have shown no such anxiety in the matter.

Point 5 is intended to meet the susceptibilities of other Powers. These cannot be disregarded. But this does not mean that His Majesty's Government wish to qualify their undertaking to give immediate and effective support, and they are prepared to give Soviet Government every assurance on this point.

You should speak again to M. Molotov on above lines. His attitude is doubly disappointing in that I had understood that all the Soviet Government wanted was complete reciprocity and a guarantee of immediate effective support. This His Majesty's Government are ready to give and their proposals have no other aim.

No. 46.

Sir W. Seeds to Viscount Halifax.

(Telegraphic.) *Moscow, May 29, 1939.*

YOUR telegram of 29th May. (No. 45)

I have just (11.45 P.M.) returned from long conversation with M. Molotov.

2. I handed him practically the whole of paragraphs 2-4 of your admirably clear explanation of the intentions of His Majesty's Government in regard to League principles and military conversations. I think some success was achieved on former of these points and perhaps even on the latter, though he was most obstinate in insisting on what he considered lack of clearness in text of our draft, and on the fact that point 4 provided for nothing more than "consultations" at moment of danger. I urged that conclusions of military talks in June 1939, under point 8, might well be inapplicable to unforeseen conditions of an imminent aggression in June 1940, and that it was impossible in practice to do more than we were doing, namely, promising immediate effective support in general and immediate military in particular.

3. He insisted on taking me through the entire text of draft (except final two points), which involved wearisome reiteration of much that we had previously discussed but he also raised at great length the question of States who might on Czecho-Slovak precedent come to understanding with Germany. Did we mean not to cover German absorption of such States nominally with their consent? I said neither His Majesty's Government nor British public opinion would consider imposing on independent nations guarantees of protection against their will: such guarantees would amount to menaces, not protection against aggression. He retorted by asking whether His Majesty's Government and British public opinion would remain loftily unaffected were Belgium, for example, to compound with Germany.

No. 47.

Sir W. Seeds to Viscount Halifax.

HIS Majesty's Ambassador at Moscow presents his compliments to His Majesty's Principal Secretary of. State for Foreign Affairs, and has the honour to transmit to him a copy of a speech of M. Molotov, President of the Council of People's Commissars of the U.S.S.R. and People's Commissar for Foreign Affairs, made on the 31st May at the third session of the Supreme Council of the U.S.S.R.

Moscow, June 1, 1939.

Enclosure in No. 47.

Speech of the President of the Council of People's Commissars of the U.S.S.R. and the People's Commissar for Foreign Affairs, M. Molotov, made on May 31 at the Third Session of the Supreme Council of the U.S.S.R.

Comrade Deputies!

The proposal of the Deputies for a statement to be made by the People's Commissar for Foreign Affairs at the session of the Supreme Council is fully understandable. Important changes have occurred recently in the international situation. These changes have from the point of view of the peaceful Powers brought about a serious deterioration in the international situation.

We are now faced on the one hand, with certain results of the policy of the aggressor States, and, on the other hand, with the policy of non-intervention on the part of the democratic States. The representatives of the aggressor States are not averse at present to boasting of the results of the policy of aggression already achieved. Be that as it may, there is no evidence of lack of boasting (cheers in the hall). The representatives of the democratic States who had given up the policy of collective security and were pursuing a policy of non-resistance to aggression are endeavouring to minimise the significance of the deterioration which has occurred in the international situation. They are still occupied mainly in calming public opinion, and are acting as though nothing essential has happened recently.

The attitude of the Soviet Union in appraising current international events is different from both of these attitudes. The Soviet Union, as is clear to everybody, cannot be suspected of any sympathy with the aggressors. Any form of masking a real deterioration in the international situation is also alien to her. It is dear to us that attempts to conceal from public opinion the real changes which have occurred in the international situation must be met with facts. It will then become evident that "pacifying" speeches and articles are only necessary for those who do not wish to stop the further development of aggression in the hope that they may be able to direct aggression, so to speak, in a more or less acceptable direction. Not long ago authoritative representatives of England and France endeavored to pacify public opinion in their countries, and were glorying in the success of the ill-starred Munich Agreement. They said that the September agreement at Munich had prevented a European war at the cost of comparatively inconsiderable concessions on the part of Czecho-Slovakia. It seemed to many even then that the representatives of England and France went further at Munich than they had a right to do in their concessions at Czecho-Slovakia's expense. The Munich Agreement was, so to speak, the culminating point of the policy of non intervention, the culminating point of compromise with the aggressor Powers. To what results did this policy lead? Did the Munich Agreement put a stop to aggression? Not in the least. On the contrary, Germany did not restrict herself to the concessions received at Munich - that is to say, to the receipt of Sudeten areas inhabited by Germans. Germany went further and simply liquidated one of the huge Slavonic States- Czecho-Slovakia. Little time had passed from September 1938 when the Munich Conference took place when in March 1939 Germany put an end to the existence of Czecho-Slovakia. Germany succeeded in carrying this out without any opposition on the part of anybody. So smoothly did this happen that the question arises as to what was the real object of the conference at Munich.

In any case, the liquidation of Czecho-Slovakia, despite the Munich Agreement, demonstrated to the wide world whither led the policy of non-intervention which, it might be said, reached its culminating point at Munich. The breakdown of this policy became evident, and yet the aggressor States continued to adhere to their policy. Germany snatched from the Lithuanian Republic Memel and the Memel Province. As we know, Italy also did not remain idle. In April Italy put an end to an independent State - Albania.

Following upon this it is not surprising that the head of the German State cancelled two important international treaties in one of his speeches at the end of April - the Naval agreement between Germany and England and the Pact of Non-Aggression between Germany and Poland. At one time great international significance was ascribed to these agreements. Germany, however, disposed of these agreements very simply without taking account of any formalities. Such was Germany's reply to the proposals of the President of the United States of America, Roosevelt, which was permeated with the spirit of peacefulness.

The matter did not stop at the denunciation of two international treaties. Germany and Italy went further. During the last few days a military-political agreement concluded between them has been published. This agreement is basically of an aggressive character. According to this agreement, Germany and Italy are bound to support each other in any sort of hostilities undertaken by either of them, including any form of aggression and any form of offensive warfare. It is only quite recently that the rapprochement between Germany and Italy was masked by the alleged necessity of a joint struggle against communism. For this purpose not a little fuss was made about the so-called "Anti-Comintern Pact." The anti-Comintern noise played at one point its part in distracting attention. Now the aggressors do not see the necessity of hiding behind a mask. The military-political agreement between Germany and Italy does not contain a word about fighting the Comintern. On the contrary, the statesmen and the press of Germany and Italy are definitely saying that this agreement is directed specially against the chief European democratic States.

It seems to be clear that the facts adduced above testify to a serious deterioration in the international situation.

In this connexion certain changes in the direction of resistance to aggression are to be remarked in the policy of the non-aggressive States of Europe. It remains to be seen to what extent these changes are serious. At present one cannot even say whether these Powers have a real desire to refrain from the policy of non-intervention and from the policy of non-resistance to the further development of aggression. Will it not happen that the present tendency of these Powers to limit aggression to certain areas will fail to serve as a bar to the development of aggression in other areas? Questions of this nature are raised in certain organs of the *bourgeois* press abroad. Therefore we must be vigilant. We stand for the cause of peace and for the prevention of any sort of development of aggression. But we must remember the statement made by Stalin: "Care should be maintained not to allow our country to be drawn into conflicts by provocators of war who are accustomed to pull the chestnuts out of the fire with other people's hands." It is only by observing this that we shall be able to defend to the end the interests of our country and the interests of universal peace.

There seem, however, to be various signs that the democratic States of Europe are coming to realise more and more the breakdown of the policy of non-intervention and the necessity of more serious searches for ways and means to create a united front of peace-loving States against aggression. In such a country as England loud demands have come to be heard as to the necessity of an abrupt change in foreign policy. We, of course, understand the difference between a verbal declaration and actual policy. But it is appropriate to note that these demands have not been idle ones. Here are certain facts. No Pact of Mutual Assistance existed between England and Poland. Now the decision to create such a pact has been taken. The significance of this agreement is heightened by Germany's denunciation of the Pact of Non-Aggression with Poland. It would be idle to deny that the Pact of Mutual Assistance between England and Poland brings about a change in the European situation. Let us go further. There was no Pact of Mutual Assistance between England and Turkey, but recently a certain agreement of mutual assistance between England and Turkey has already come into being. This fact also makes for a change in the international situation.

In connexion with these new facts the endeavour of the non-aggressive European Powers to attract the U.S.S.R. into collaboration in the cause of resistance to aggression has to be acknowledged as one of the chief features of recent times. Naturally this endeavour merits attention. On this basis the Soviet Government accepted the proposal of England and France to enter into negotiations with the object of strengthening the political relations between the U.S.S.R., England and France and of forming a peace front against the further development of aggression.

How do we determine our problems in the present-day international situation? We consider that they follow the line of the interests of other non-aggressive States. They consist in stopping the further development of aggression and creating for this purpose a reliable and effective defensive front of the non-aggressive Powers.

In connexion with the proposals made to us by the English and French Governments, the Soviet Government entered into negotiations with these two Governments, having in view the necessary measures for fighting aggression. This was in the middle of April last. The negotiations which then began have not yet been terminated. However, it was possible then to see that if there were a desire to create an effective front of the peace-loving Powers against the advance of aggression, the following conditions would be a necessary minimum:-

The conclusion between England, France and the U.S.S.R. of an effective Pact of Mutual Assistance against aggression having a purely defensive character.

A guarantee on the part of England, France and the U.S.S.R. to the States of Central and Eastern Europe, including without exception all European States bordering on the U.S.S.R., from an attack by the aggressors.

The conclusion of a concrete agreement between England, France and the U.S.S.R. as to the forms and extent of immediate and effective assistance to be rendered to each other and to the guaranteed States in case of an attack by the aggressors.

This is our view which we impose on nobody, but for which we stand. We do not demand the acceptance of our point of view and do not ask this from anybody. We consider, however, that this point of view really corresponds to the security of the peaceful States.

This would be an agreement of a purely defensive character operative against an attack on the part of the aggressor, and radically different, from the military and offensive union which was recently concluded between Germany and Italy.

It is clear that the principle of reciprocity and equal obligations must form the basis of such an agreement.

It must be noted that a favourable attitude towards this elementary principle was not found in certain of the Anglo-French proposals. Having guaranteed themselves from a direct attack by aggressors by pacts of mutual assistance between themselves and Poland and having made sure of the help of the U.S.S.R. in case of an attack by aggressors on Poland and Roumania, the English and French left open the question whether the U.S.S.R. in its turn might reckon on assistance on their part in case of a direct attack on it by the aggressors. Another question was left open as well, namely, whether they could participate in a guarantee to the small neighbouring States which cover the north-western border of the U.S.S.R. should those States not be in a position to defend their neutrality from aggression. There arose in this way a position of inequality for the U.S.S.R.

During the last few days new Anglo-French offers have been received. In these offers the principle is already admitted of mutual assistance between England, France and the U.S.S.R. on a basis of reciprocity in the case of a direct attack by the aggressors. This is, of course, a step forward. One has to note, however, that it is hedged round with such reservations, including reservations connected with certain points of the statutes of the League of Nations, that it may prove to be a fictitious step forward. As to the question of a guarantee to the Powers of Central and Eastern Europe, the proposals referred to show no progress at all if one looks upon the question from the point of view of reciprocity. They provide for assistance to the U.S.S.R in regard to the five Powers to whom the English and French have already given a promise of guarantees, but they do not speak of their assistance to the three Powers on the north-western borders of the U.S.S.R., who may not be in a position to defend their neutrality in the case of attack by the aggressors.

The Soviet Union, however, cannot assume obligations in regard to the five Powers indicated should it not receive guarantees in regard to the three countries situated on its north-western frontier. This is the situation with regard to the negotiations with England and France.

While conducting negotiations with England and France we see no necessity for refusing commercial relations with such countries as Germany and Italy. As far back as the beginning of last year the German Government began negotiations for a trade agreement and new credits. At that time Germany offered to grant us a new credit of 200 million marks. Inasmuch as we did not come to terms about this new economic agreement the negotiations came to an end. At the end of 1938 the German Government again raised the question of economic negotiations and of the granting of a credit of 200 million marks. The German offer was accompanied by a readiness to make certain concessions. At the beginning of 1939 the People's Commissariat for Foreign Trade was informed that a special German representative, Herr Schnurre, was leaving for Moscow in connexion with these negotiations. Thereafter the negotiations were confided to the German Ambassador in Moscow, Count von der Schulenburg, in place of Herr Schnurre, and they were interrupted in view of differences of opinion. Now there are certain indications that the negotiations may be resumed.

I may add that we recently signed a mutually satisfactory trade agreement with Italy for 1939.

It is known that a special communiqué was published in February last confirming the development of good neighbourly relations between the U.S.S.R. and Poland. A certain general improvement is now noticeable in our relations with Poland. Furthermore, the trade agreement concluded in March with Poland may considerably increase the trade turnover between the U.S.S.R. and Poland.

Our relations with friendly Turkey are developing normally. The recent visit of Comrade Potemkin to Angora, which was undertaken for purposes of information, had a great positive effect.

Among international questions which have recently acquired great significance for the U.S.S.R. it is necessary to mention the problem of the Aland Islands. You know that these islands belonged to Russia for over a hundred years. As the result of the October revolution Finland received her independence. By agreement with our country Finland also received the Aland Islands. In 1921 ten Powers: Finland, Estonia, Latvia, Poland, Sweden, Denmark, Germany, England, France and Italy, signed a convention which prohibited, as had previously been the case, the fortification of the Aland Islands. The Governments of the capitalist States did this without the participation of Soviet representatives. In 1921 the Soviet Republic, which had been crippled by war and foreign intervention, was unable to protest against this illegal act in relation to the U.S.S.R. However, we then clearly and repeatedly stated that the Soviet Union could not ignore this question and that a change in the juridical status of the Aland Islands in violation of the interest of our country was impossible. The importance of the Aland Islands consists in their strategic position in the Baltic Sea. The fortification of the Aland Islands may be utilised for purposes hostile to the

U.S.S.R. Being situated not far from the entrance to the Finnish Gulf the fortified Aland Islands may serve to close to the U.S.S.R. the entrances and exits to the Finnish Gulf. For this reason, now that the Finnish Government, together with Sweden, wish to carry out a big scheme of fortification of the Aland Islands, the Soviet Government made enquiries of the Finnish Government as to the object and character of the proposed fortifications. Instead of meeting the very natural wishes of the Soviet Union the Finnish Government refused to give the requested information and explanations. The references made in this connection to military secrets are, as may be easily understood, entirely unconvincing. The Finnish Government did not mind communicating its plans of the fortification of the Aland Islands to another Government - the Swedish Government. It not only communicated its plans to this Government, but invited it to participate in putting into effect the whole of this plan of fortification. And yet, under the convention of 1921, Sweden enjoys no special rights in this connection. Moreover, the Soviet Union, which is interested in the question of the fortification of the Aland Islands, is not only not a smaller State than Sweden, but a larger one.

In consequence of the Finnish and Swedish Governments' proposal the question of the revision of the convention of 1921 was discussed at the League Council which has just closed. Without the Council's sanction this convention may not be revised, because the convention of the ten States was concluded on the basis of a decision of the League Council dated the 24th June, 1921. In view of objections on the part of the representative of the Soviet Union no unanimity, which was necessary for the decision of the League Council, was possible. The results of the discussion in the League Council are well known. The Council of the League did not ratify the proposal of Finland and Sweden. It did not give its sanction to the revision of the convention of 1921. One must assume that the Finnish Government will draw the necessary conclusions from this situation. In the light of recent international events the Aland question has acquired particularly serious significance for the Soviet Union. We do not consider it possible to become reconciled with the toleration of any attempt to ignore the interests of the U.S.S.R. in this question, which is of great significance for the defence of our country.

I will make quite a brief reference to questions in the Far East and to our relations with Japan.

The greatest significance during this year was attached to our negotiations with Japan on the fishing question. As you know, in the Primorye (the Far Eastern littoral province), in the Sea of Okhotsk, on Saghalien and on Kamchatka, the Japanese have a large number of fishing areas. At the end of last year 384 fishing areas were in their hands. The period of the convention, however, on the basis of which they had received these fishing areas had already expired. For many of the fishing areas the periods of lease established at an earlier date had also expired. In this connexion the Soviet Government entered into negotiations with Japan. It was stated on our part that, in view of strategical considerations, a certain number of areas, the leases of which had already expired, might not be granted in the future on lease to the Japanese. In spite of the obvious justice of our position the Japanese offered great resistance to the Soviet point of view. As the result of lengthy negotiations thirty-seven fishing areas were withdrawn from the Japanese and they were allotted ten new areas in other places. The operation of the convention was then extended for a further year. This agreement with Japan on the fisheries question is of great political significance, the more so as everything possible was done by reactionary circles in Japan to undermine the political aspect of this matter. They did not even stop at all kinds of threats. The Japanese reactionaries had another opportunity, however, of convincing themselves that threats in regard to the Soviet Union do not achieve their object (loud applause) and that the rights of the Soviet State are firmly defended. (Loud applause.)

Now about frontier questions. It would seem to be time for those whom it concerns to understand that the Soviet Government will not tolerate any provocative acts on the part of Japano-Manchurian military forces on its borders. It is necessary to recall this now in regard to the borders of the Mongolian National Republic as well. Under the agreement of mutual assistance existing between the U.S.S.R. and the Mongolian National Republic we consider it our duty to render the Mongolian National Republic the necessary help in the defence of its borders. Our attitude to such matters as a pact of mutual assistance signed by the Soviet Government is a serious one. I think it necessary to utter a warning that the borders of the Mongolian National Republic under the treaty of mutual assistance concluded between us will be defended by us with the same decision as our own frontiers. (Loud applause.) It is time that it should he understood that the accusations of aggression against Japan put forward by Japan against the Government of the Mongolian National Republic are laughable and nonsensical. It is also time to understand that there is a limit to all patience. (Applause.) It is therefore better to give up while there is still time the continual repetition of provocative violation by the Japano-Manchurian military forces of the borders of the U.S.S.R. and the Mongolian National Republic. A suitable warning has been delivered through the Japanese Ambassador in Moscow.

There is no necessity for me to speak of our relations with China. You are well aware of the statement of Comrade Stalin as regards support to people who have become the victims of aggression and who are fighting for the independence of their Fatherland. This applies in full measure to China and the struggle of that country for national independence. We are consistently applying this policy. It is in agreement with the problem which faces Europe, namely, with the problem of creating a united front of peace-loving Powers against further development of aggression. (Loud applause.)

The U.S.S.R. now is not what it was say in 1921 when it was only beginning its peaceful creative work. It is necessary to recall this, because, up to the present, none of our neighbours seem to be unable to understand this. (Laughter.) One must admit also that the U.S.S.R. is nor what it was, say, but five or ten years ago, and that the forces of the U.S.S.R have grown. (Applause). The foreign policy of the Soviet Union should reflect the existence of changes in the international situation and the grown might of the U.S.S.R., which is a mighty factor for peace. It is unnecessary to prove that the foreign policy of the Soviet Union is deeply peaceful and directed against aggression. This is known best of all to the aggressive Powers themselves. (Cheers.) Some democratic States are coming to the realisation of this simple truth after great delay and hesitation. (Cheers.) And yet the Soviet Union cannot fail to take its place in the foremost ranks of the united front of peaceful States who are really resisting aggression.

No. 48.

Sir W. Seeds to Viscount Halifax.

(Telegraphic.) *Moscow, June 2, 1939.*

M. MOLOTOV handed to the French Ambassador and myself this afternoon what he described as the text of the Anglo-French proposed agreement modified to meet the views of the Soviet Government as follows:-

"The Governments of Great Britain, France and U.S.S.R., with the object of making more effective the principles of mutual assistance against aggression adopted by the League of Nations, have come to the following agreement:-

"1. France, England and U.S.S.R. undertake to render to each other immediately all effective assistance should one of these States, become involved in hostilities with a European Power as a result either of (1) aggression by that Power against any one of these three States; (2) aggression by that Power against Belgium, Greece, Turkey, Roumania, Poland, Latvia, Estonia and Finland, whom England, France and U.S.S.R. have agreed to defend against aggression; (3) assistance rendered by one of these three States to another European State which has requested such assistance in order to resist violation at its neutrality .

"2. The three States will come to an agreement within the shortest possible time as to methods, forms and extent of assistance which is to be rendered by them in conformity with paragraph 1.

"3. In the event of circumstances arising which, in the opinion of one of the contracting parties, create a threat of aggression by a European Power, the three States will immediately consult together to examine the situation and, in case of necessity, to establish in common the moment for putting into immediate effect mechanism of mutual assistance and manner of its application independently of any procedure applied by the League of Nations to examination of questions.

"4. The three States will communicate to each other the texts of all their engagements assumed in the spirit of the obligations provided for under paragraph 1 in respect of European States. If one of these States contemplates in the future possibility of assuming new obligations of a similar character, it will first consult the other two States and communicate to them the contents (text) of agreement.

"5. In the event of commencement of joint operations against aggression in accordance with paragraph 1, the three States undertake only to conclude an armistice or peace by joint agreement.

"6. The present agreement enters into force simultaneously with agreement which is to be concluded in virtue of paragraph 2.

"7. The present agreement will continue in force for a period of five years from this date. Not less than six months before expiry of this period the three States will consider whether they wish to renew it with or without modification."

2. M. Molotov pointed out that, apart from consolidation of our articles 1 and 2 into one article with that additional precision which Soviet Government desired in regard to countries affected, main changes were *(a)* an attempt to deal with allusion to League of Nations in accordance with assurances your Lordship had instructed me to give; *(b)* omission of our article 5 (No. 42) which the Soviet Government considered unnecessary; and *(e)* insertion of provision (article 5) as regards conclusion of armistice or peace. He did not specifically mention new article 6, which is of considerable importance.

3. I made no comment and merely said that His Majesty's Government would give this text that friendly consideration which they were always ready to accord to the views of the Soviet Government.

No. 49.

Statement by the Prime Minister in the House of Commons on June 7, 1939.

The Prime Minister: For reasons which the House will

appreciate, it has not been possible to give day-to-day information as to the progress of the negotiations for an agreement between Great Britain, France and the Union of Soviet Socialist Republics. A stage has, however, now been reached which enables me to supplement the statement which I made on the 24th May.

It appears from the last exchange of views with the Soviet Government that there is general agreement as to the main objects to be attained. His Majesty's Government have, I think, been able to satisfy the Soviet Government that they are, in fact, prepared to conclude an agreement. on the basis of full reciprocity. They have also made it clear that they are ready, immediately and without any reserve to join with the French Government in giving the Union of Soviet Socialist Republics full military support in the event of any act of aggression against her involving her in hostilities with a European Power. It is not intended that the military support which the three Powers would agree to extend to one another should be confined to a case of actual aggression upon their own territory. It is possible to imagine various cases in which anyone of the three Governments might feel that its security was indirectly menaced by the action of another European Power. These cases have been reviewed in detail, and I hope that it may be possible now to suggest a formula acceptable to the three Governments which, while having regard to the rights and interests of other States, will assure co-operation between those Powers in resistance to aggression.

There remain one or two difficulties to be resolved, in particular the position of certain States, which do not want to receive a guarantee on the ground that it would compromise the strict neutrality which they desire to preserve. It is manifestly impossible to impose a guarantee on States which do not desire it, but I hope that some means may be found by which this difficulty, and any others which may arise in the adjustment of the general points on which there is now no difference between the three Governments, shall not stand in the way of giving the greatest effect to the principle of mutual support against aggression.

In order to accelerate the negotiations, it has been decided to send a representative of the Foreign Office to Moscow to convey to His Majesty's Ambassador there full information as to the attitude of His Majesty's Government on all outstanding points. I hope that by this method it will be possible more rapidly to complete the discussion that is still necessary to harmonise the views of the three Governments and so to reach final agreement.

Mr. Adams: Might I be allowed to thank the Prime Minister for that full statement and also to ask him whether it is not true to say that the final success of these negotiations will make defeat completely impossible and war itself unlikely?

Mr. Greenwood: Will the Prime Minister explain who is likely to go to Moscow and whether that visit will hinder the rapid conclusion of agreement on the principles of the treaty; whether the principles of the treaty cannot be settled by the Governments and only subsidiary matters left to be settled in Moscow?

The Prime Minister: I cannot say at the present time who will be the representative of the Foreign Office, because that is still under consideration.

Mr. Ellis Smith: Could not it be a Minister?

The Prime Minister: The object of sending a representative of the Foreign Office to Moscow is to facilitate and accelerate the negotiations, and not to delay them. I have every hope that that may be the result .

Mr. Greenwood: Is it not possible that a visit to Moscow might be interpreted as a delaying operation against the full completion of the treaty? While the principle might be agreed to now, could not the details be settled afterwards?

The Prime Minister: We are not in a position actually to conclude a treaty now, because of the points I have mentioned which are still to be resolved. It is in the hope of resolving them rapidly that this visit is to take place.

Mr. V. Adams: Can the Prime Minister say when the mission will go to Moscow?

The Prime Minister: At once.

Mr. Mander: Will the proposed agreement include an arrangement for immediate staff conversations?

The Prime Minister: I think we had better wait until we reach an agreement.

Mr. Sandys: Is the Prime Minister aware that his hopeful statement will be received as evidence of the Government's determination to reach this agreement as quickly as possible?

Mr. Cocks: Will the representative be a member of the Government, or a civil servant?

The Prime Minister: A civil servant.

Lieutenant-Commander Fletcher asked the Prime Minister, with - reference to the Anglo-Franco-Russian negotiations, whether His Majesty's Government have received any communication from the Governments of the Baltic indicating their wish to be guaranteed, or, on the contrary, not to be guaranteed?

The Prime Minister: His Majesty's Government have received several communications from the Finnish, Estonian and Latvian Governments indicating that, in view of their intention to maintain strict neutrality, they did not wish to receive a guarantee as a result of the present negotiations between Great Britain, France and Russia.

No. 50.

Viscount Halifax to Sir W. Seeds (Moscow).

Foreign Office, June 8, 1939.

Sir,

I ASKED the Soviet Ambassador to call on me this morning in order that I might explain to him the line of action which we were pursuing concerning the negotiations with his Government.

2. I expressed the hope to M. Maisky that he would have thought the statement made by the Prime Minister yesterday helpful. In that statement we had made it plain how very far we were prepared to go to meet the wishes of the Soviet Government by making it clear that the guarantee we would be willing to extend to them on a reciprocal basis was not confined only to a direct attack upon Soviet territory. I accordingly relied on what he had said to me at Geneva (No. 38) to the effect that, if we could meet his Government on this main point, we should not find them unduly difficult on others. M. Maisky recognised the importance of what had been said in the House of Commons yesterday and seemed on the whole fairly satisfied with it, adding, however, that he had never said anything at Geneva which precluded his Government from pressing their claim on other points to which they attached importance.

3. I told his Excellency that the principal matters in the draft

submitted by M. Molotov (No. 48) that caused us difficulty were, firstly, the recapitulation of States by name, irrespective of their own wishes in the matter. Incidentally, the list that the Soviet Government had submitted showed how far we had moved from the original conception of reciprocity. By this list we were to be bound to join Russia in the event of attack upon any of her neighbours that might be held to threaten her security, whereas the same obligation was not to be undertaken by Russia in the case of Great Britain thinking her security to be threatened by a German attack on other States not mentioned in the catalogue. M. Maisky admitted this, but said that we were, of course, fully entitled to raise such a point as this with his Government, and gave me the impression that they would not be unwilling to consider it. Secondly, we felt great difficulty about the article in M. Molotov's draft that made the conclusion of any agreement dependent upon the conclusion of military conversations. This, we thought, tended to make dangerous delay. Lastly, I myself felt considerable difficulty about the proposal of including at this stage an agreement, as suggested, in no case to make a separate armistice or peace. I well understood the desirability of such a provision, if and when we were launched into war and were all agreed as to the aims we sought to achieve. It seemed to me that the appropriate moment at which to give such a common undertaking would be when a decision as to the purpose of the war was reached.

4. I told M. Maisky that it had been our original intention to ask your Excellency to come from Moscow so that we might explain our point of view on all points fully to you, in order that, on return, you could have asked M. Molotov to give you the opportunity of going through the draft point by point so as to save delay by further exchange of notes. You had, unfortunately, succumbed to influenza; and we had, therefore, been obliged to adopt the alternative of sending a representative of the Foreign Office to Moscow. I had at one time though of suggesting to the Prime Minister that I should go myself, but it was really

impossible to get away, and, moreover, I felt that this kind of business was better handled by Ambassadors. M. Maisky seemed to think this a very reasonable proposal and spoke in terms of warm appreciation of Mr. Strang's ability, if he was the representative of the Foreign Office to be selected. He told me that Mr. Strang had been responsible with himself for drafting at the time of Mr. Eden's visit to Moscow, and said that he had considerable respect for his powers in this direction.

No. 51.

Memorandum of Instructions taken to Moscow by Mr. Strang on June 12, 1939.

HIS Majesty's Government have examined the draft agreement communicated to the British and French Ambassadors on the 2nd June. (No. 48)

2. His Majesty's Government are glad to note that a substantial measure of agreement has now been reached as to the general lines of the proposed agreement.

3. It is agreed:-

(1) That a treaty should be concluded between the three Powers on an equal footing, in which each of the three would undertake similar obligations towards the other two.

(2) That the three Powers would render each other immediate assistance:-
   a. In the event of one of them being the object of a direct attack by a European Power.
   b. In the event of one of the three Powers

going to the assistance of certain States which it had undertaken to assist against aggression.

(3) That the treaty should be in harmony with the principle of mutual assistance against aggression adopted by the League of Nations, but that assistance should be given under the treaty without it being necessary to await action by the League.

(4) That there should be immediate consultation between the three States with a view to settling the methods, forms and extent of the assistance to be tendered under the treaty.

(5) That in the event of threat of aggression by a European Power, there should be consultation between the three Powers and, should the necessity arise, a decision by them as to the moment and manner of application of the mechanism of mutual assistance.

(6) That the three States should communicate to each either the terms of the understandings given by them to other States, and contact each other before assuming further obligations.

4. His Majesty's Government hope, therefore, that it will be possible at an early date to settle the terms of a treaty based on these principles. The treaty should in, the view of His Majesty's Government, be as short and simple in its terms as possible.

5. There are, however, a number of points in the Soviet draft which causes His Majesty's Government some difficulty.

6. The chief of these relates to the States in whose case the guarantees referred to in paragraph 3 (2) (b) above are to apply. By sub-paragraph 2 of article 1 of the Soviet draft it is provided that the three countries would undertake to render assistance to each other should one of them become involved in hostilities with a European Power as the result of aggression by that Power against certain countries enumerated in the Soviet draft, whom the three countries would agree to defend against aggression. The countries mentioned in the Soviet draft are the five European countries to whom His Majesty's Government and the French Government, have given undertakings, namely, Belgium, Greece, Turkey, Roumania and Poland, together with the three States on the north-west frontier of Soviet Russia, namely, Latvia, Estonia and Finland, who have not received undertakings of assistance from Great Britain and France, nor, so far as His Majesty's Government are aware, from the Soviet Union.

7. His Majesty's Government think it undesirable that there should be any specific enumeration in the text of the treaty of the countries in whose defence the three Powers would collaborate. The three Baltic States, for example, are strongly opposed to being the object of a guarantee, or indeed, to being mentioned in the agreement at all. The Estonian Foreign Minister, in a recent public statement, has said that if a Great Power desired to assume the role of our defender, either as representing the collective system or to defend its own vital interests in the Baltic, such a system would be considered as aggression, against which the Baltic States are prepared to fight with all their forces. The Latvian and Finnish Governments take a similar view, and the Finnish Minister for Foreign Affairs has specifically stated that such a guarantee could not be accepted. Then again, although Poland has entered into reciprocal arrangements of mutual assistance with Great Britain and

France, and although Belgium and Roumania, for example, have received undertakings of assistance from Great Britain and France, it is clear that, for reasons which His Majesty's Government feel bound to respect; these States would prefer not to be made the subject of a treaty concluded by the three Great Powers. Indeed the Roumanian Foreign Minister has expressly requested that the name of his country should not be mentioned in any agreement which may be concluded by Great Britain, France and the Soviet Union.

8. But while His Majesty's Government are unable to accept this proposal in the Soviet draft, since they cannot agree to impose a guarantee on Powers which are unwilling to receive it, they fully sympathise with the desire of the Soviet Government that the military support which the three Powers would agree to extend to one another should not be confined to a case of actual aggression upon their own territory. They have already met the desire of the Soviet Government for a direct guarantee to cover the case of direct aggression, and they have given much thought to the question how best to devise means of dealing with a threat to the security of the contracting Powers caused by action other than direct aggression.

9. Part of this difficulty would be met if the treaty were to include a clause to the effect that the three Powers would undertake to assist each other in the event of one of them becoming involved in hostilities with a European Power as the result of aggression by that Power against another European State which had, with its own consent, received an undertaking of assistance from the contracting country. It would be unnecessary to mention these States by name - in the treaty, and by another article in the treaty it would be agreed, as indicated in paragraph 3 (6) above, that the three Governments would communicate to each other the terms

of any undertakings of this kind which they had given to other States.

10. There would still remain, however, the case of aggression against or through States which have not received any such guarantee, some of whom have declared that they would refuse to receive a guarantee. His Majesty's Government fully appreciate, for example, that the military occupation of one of the Soviet Union's north-west neighbours, whose resistance might be quickly over-borne or who might even acquiesce in the occupation, might be regarded by the Soviet Union as a menace to the security of the Soviet Union. A similar situation in Holland or Switzerland would be a menace to the security of Great Britain and France. His Majesty's Government have been giving much thought to the question how best to meet such a situation through common action by the three Powers, while at the same time not forcing a direct guarantee on the States concerned, or provoking undesirable reactions on the part of their Governments.

11. His Majesty's Government would be glad if the Commissar for Foreign Affairs would examine this question with His Majesty's Ambassador. His Majesty's Government are inclined to think that the best solution would be found by applying to this case the procedure which they understand to be contemplated in article 3 of M. Molotov's draft. They suggest accordingly that it should be agreed that the three Powers should immediately consult together if one of them considered that its security was menaced by a threat to the independence or neutrality of any other European Power. If the other two Powers agreed that such a menace existed, and if the contracting Power in question was involved in hostilities in consequence, the other two Powers would go to its assistance.

12. The foregoing suggestions seem to His Majesty's Government to cover the case of what might be called "indirect aggression" against the three contracting Powers through *(a)* other Powers who have already received a guarantee from the contracting Powers *(i.e.,* Belgium, Greece, Turkey, Roumania and Poland); *(b)* other Powers who have not received such a guarantee or do not wish to receive it (Latvia, Estonia, Finland, the Netherlands and Switzerland are the most obvious examples). The proposed provisions would thus take the place of sub-paragraphs 2 and 3 in article 1 of M. Molotov's draft.

13. There are three further points arising out of M. Molotov's draft to which His Majesty's Government wish to refer:-

14. Point 1. In article 2 of M. Molotov's draft it is provided that the three States will come to an agreement as soon as possible as to the methods, forms and extent of the assistance to be rendered by them. In article 6 of that draft it is further provided that the proposed treaty is not, to come into force until the conclusion of this proposed military agreement.

15. His Majesty's Government entirely agree that there should be immediate consultation between the three Governments as to the methods, forms and extent of the assistance, provided for in the treaty, since this furnishes the best means of making sure that such assistance shall be as effective as possible. They will accordingly be prepared that these conversations should be inaugurated at the earliest possible date and that they should be both frank and exhaustive. They doubt, however, whether it would he possible within any reasonably brief period to reach a concrete military agreement to cover every possible contingency. They are anxious to conclude an agreement

with the Soviet Government without any further delay, and they view with dismay the effect on the European situation which would be produced by the postponement of the entry into force of any such agreement until the conclusion of a military agreement. They think that the only practical course would be to make it clear in the treaty itself that the three States would concert together, immediately after the conclusion of the treaty, with a view to settling the methods, forms and extent of the assistance to be rendered, and it might indeed be understood between the three parties that the staff contacts would be inaugurated within a specified time from the conclusion of the treaty.

16. Point 2. Article 5 of M. Molotov's draft provides that the three States will undertake only to conclude an armistice or peace by joint agreement. His Majesty's Government see serious objection to such a provision. His Majesty's Government would of course loyally carry out the obligations of any treaty into which they entered, and they would count on the other two parties to do the same. But they doubt whether on practical grounds this kind of provision would in fact achieve its object. An essential condition of an undertaking not to conclude peace except on terms which had been jointly agreed is that agreement should have been reached as to the objects which the peace is to achieve, and no such agreement is possible before the circumstances which produced the war are known. His Majesty's Government would be prepared to consider some provision in this direction if agreement were reached on other points still outstanding.

17. Point 3. There is one further point which His Majesty's Government desire to consider in consultation with the Soviet Government; it is one rather of form than of substance. It will be noted that the drafts which His Majesty's Government and the Soviet Government have

been considering in the past have provided for a case in which the three contracting States become involved in hostilities with a European Power. Though they have of course had Germany in mind, no particular Power has been specified, nor indeed is it desirable to do so. The texts which have hitherto been under consideration, however, raise one difficulty, which is that His Majesty's Government and France will in effect be guaranteeing the Soviet Union against, for example, Poland. His Majesty's Government do not propose to guarantee Poland against the Soviet Union, a course to which the Soviet Government have stated that they object, and His Majesty's Government think it highly undesirable that the proposed treaty should be capable of being interpreted as involving a guarantee of the Soviet Union against Poland. Moreover, inasmuch as both France and the United Kingdom will have arrangements for mutual support with Poland, it would clearly be undesirable that the Soviet Union should appear to be guaranteeing them against that country. His Majesty's Government wish to draw the attention of the Soviet Government to this point and would be glad to consider with the Soviet Government the best method of excluding such a guarantee from the scope of the proposed treaty, it being understood of course that His Majesty's Government's guarantee would apply in the purely hypothetical case of Poland combining with Germany to attack the Soviet Union.
Foreign Office, June 12, 1939.

No. 52.

Anglo-French Draft of June 6, 1939, used by Sir W. Seeds as a Basis of Discussion in carrying out the Instructions contained in the Memorandum of June 12, 1939. (No. 51)

DRAFT ANGLO-FRANCO-SOVIET AGREEMENT.

The Governments of the United Kingdom, France and the U.S.S.R., with the object of making more effective the principles of mutual assistance against aggression adopted by the League of Nations, have reached the following agreement :-

1. The United Kingdom, France and the U.S.S.R. undertake to give to each other immediately all the support and assistance in their power should one of these countries become involved in hostilities with a European Power as a result either of-

   (1) Aggression by that Power against any one of these three countries.
   (2) Aggression by that Power against another European State which the contracting country concerned had, in conformity with the wishes of that State, undertaken to assist against such aggression.
   (3) Action by that Power which the three contracting Governments as a result of the consultation between them provided for in paragraph 3, considered to threaten the independence or neutrality of another European State in such a way as to constitute a menace to the security of the contracting country concerned.

Such support and assistance will be given in conformity with the principles of article 16, paragraphs 1 and 2, of the Covenant of the League of Nations, but without its being necessary to await action by the League.

2. The three States will immediately concert together as to the methods, forms and extent of the assistance to be rendered by them in conformity with paragraph 1, with the object of making such assistance as effective as possible in case of need.

3. Without prejudice to the immediate rendering of assistance on the outbreak of hostilities in accordance with

paragraph 1, in the event of circumstances arising which threaten to call into operation the undertakings of mutual assistance contained in paragraph 1, the three contracting Governments will, on the request of anyone of them, immediately consult together to examine the situation. Should the necessity arise, they will decide by common agreement the moment at which the mechanism of mutual assistance shall be put into operation and the manner of its application.

4. The three Governments will communicate to each other the terms of any undertakings referred to in 1 (2) above which they have already given. Any of them which may in future be considering the giving of such an undertaking will consult the other two Governments before doing so, and will communicate to them the terms of any undertaking so given.

5. It is understood that the rendering of support and assistance in the above cases is without prejudice to the rights and position of other Powers.

6. This agreement will continue for 1 period of (5) years from to-day's date. Not less than (6 months) before the expiry of the said period, the three Governments will consult together as to the desirability of renewing it, with or without modifications.

No. 53.

Sir W. Seeds to Viscount Halifax.

Moscow, June 20, 1939.

My Lord,

I HAVE the honour to report that Mr. Strang arrived in

Moscow during the morning of the 14th instant and handed me your Lordship's instructions on the subject of the negotiations with the Soviet Union. After examining them with Mr. Strang I invited M. Naggiar, the French Ambassador, to come to His Majesty's Embassy for a consultation the same evening. A further interview with M. Naggiar took place the next morning, the 15th, when he had had time to examine your Lordship's memorandum of instructions, of which we had given him a copy. To facilitate the conversations with M. Molotov and M. Potemkin, French translations of all the most important portions of your Lordship's memorandum were prepared. We agreed that it was most important that the Soviet Government should have the views of His Majesty's Government in your Lordship's own words on paper, having regard to the misunderstandings inevitably to be expected from the cumbrous procedure of a conversation in two languages.

2. At 5 o'clock the same afternoon M. Naggiar, Mr. Strang and myself proceeded to the Kremlin, where we were received by M. Molotov, with M. Potemkin as interpreter.

3. I began the conversation, as provided for by your Lordship's instructions, by stating the pleasure with which His Majesty's Government noted the great extent to which agreement had already been reached, as shown by the various points specified in paragraph 8 of your memorandum, which I proceeded to read. In most circumstances this should have formed a most promising gambit leading to an atmosphere of friendly understanding, but unfortunately M. Molotov was inclined to fear an attempt at compromising the Soviet position, and to examine with some distrust whether my allegation that we were basing this declared measure of agreement on the Soviet Government's own proposals was justified by the Russian text. This led to an exchange of questions and answers, with repeated assurances on our side that we were only talking on general lines and were not formulating a text.

4. I then proceeded to express the hope of His Majesty's Government that it would now be possible to reach an agreement on the whole question of a treaty with no undue delay, adding that such a treaty should, in our view, be as short and simple as possible. There were, of course, a number of points in the Soviet draft (No. 48) notably, articles 1 (2); 5 and 6 which caused His Majesty's Government some difficulty, and we proposed to examine these points round the table one by one, instead of the procedure hitherto followed of telegraphing between London and Moscow complete drafts of a treaty.

5. The most important point still at issue between us arose, I continued, out of sub-paragraph (2) of article 1 of the Soviet draft relating to aggressive action against certain countries therein specified by name. His Majesty's Government thought it undesirable that there should be any such specific enumeration of the countries in whose defence the three signatory powers would collaborate: I had discussed that point so fully in previous interviews with M. Molotov that it was unnecessary for me now to do more than remind him that the three Baltic States had strong objections not only to receiving guarantees under the treaty, but also to being mentioned in the treaty at all. I would also point out that Poland and Roumania had made it quite clear - especially the latter - that they did not wish to be cited in such a treaty.

6. At this stage of the interview it became clear that in order to facilitate translation of the views of His Majesty's Government the best procedure would be for M. Potemkin to take our French text of the relevant portions of the memorandum of instructions and to translate orally direct therefrom. I therefore handed him the French translation of paragraphs 8 to 12, inclusive, of the memorandum, but I made it clear that the English text (of which we also handed in a copy) was alone to be regarded as authoritative (copy enclosed,

Enclosure 1). I would add here that, to make the expression of our instructions complete, we subsequently gave M. Molotov the text of paragraphs 1 to 3 of the memorandum (copy enclosed, Enclosure 2).

7. When M. Potemkin had finished, M. Molotov said that he was disappointed at the tenor of our communication; he had expected from all he had seen in the British and French press that we would be the bearers of something much more positive and more in accordance with the views of the Soviet Government. We, in return, naturally deprecated undue reliance on unauthorised and ill-informed press comment, but M. Molotov said that his expectations had been, in fact, based to a considerable extent on other than press sources. He did not specify what these were.

8. M. Molotov then put a series of questions with a view to elucidating the exact implications of the suggestion contained in paragraph 11 of the memorandum. I need not enter into details of this part of the conversation beyond stating that we made the intention and the effect of the proposal absolutely clear. Eventually we handed him the text of articles 1 and 3 of the draft agreement dated the 6th June. I enclose copy herein (Enclosure 3).

9. M. Molotov then proceeded to put a number of questions about the international background of these negotiations.

10. His first question was whether His Majesty's Government and the French Government would be prepared to guarantee Finland, Estonia and Latvia if these three countries were willing to receive a guarantee. M. Naggiar and I replied that we had no instructions on this point; we had to deal with the situation as we found it, and the present attitude of these three Baltic States was well known.

11. M. Molotov asked how we thought the Polish Government would regard our present proposals. We told him that His Majesty's Government had understood, after enquiry in Warsaw, that the Polish Government would not be likely to raise objection to the system foreshadowed in the Anglo-French draft of the 25th May, and that the general idea of our present draft was the same as that of the earlier draft. We could not recall whether similar enquiries had been made in the Baltic Capitals. He then reverted to the attitude of the three Baltic States, and suggested that their respective views were by no means identical; the Latvian Foreign Minister had, for example, carefully refrained from associating himself with the violent statements recently made by the Finnish and Estonian Foreign Ministers. The drift of his remarks was that, since there were already shades of difference in the attitudes of the three Governments, the three Governments might be brought in time to change their views. We said that if there were shades of difference, the attitude of the three countries was still that they did not wish to be mentioned in the proposed treaty or to be made the object of a guarantee without their consent.

12. He then asked whether in the guarantees which we had given to other States (Belgium, Greece, Poland, Roumania and Turkey), we had made provision for joint assistance to third States. We gave him an outline of the arrangements so far made with those countries. He asked whether our arrangement with Poland dealt with the case of an attack on Lithuania. We repeated to him what the Polish Ambassador in London had said to the Soviet Ambassador on this point, namely, that when the Anglo-Polish declaration spoke of an indirect threat to the independence of Poland, what the two Governments had had in mind was possible action against Danzig, which was not, of course, Polish territory. The question of assistance to Lithuania had not been discussed with M. Beck. He then said that he understood that Poland would help Great Britain in the event of

an attack on the Netherlands. Was this so? Mr. Strang confined himself to saying that the question of dealing with an indirect threat to either country would no doubt have to he discussed during the negotiation of the formal treaty foreshadowed in the Anglo-Polish declaration, but that nothing definite had yet been settled.

13. It was somewhat irritating to be interrogated in this way, but we thought it well to reply as fully as we could, in order to convince M. Molotov of our frankness, and because His Majesty's Government would in any event be obliged in due course by the treaty itself, to inform the Soviet Government fully of the terms of their guarantees to other States. I would add that the entire burden of this part of the interview was borne by Mr. Strang alone, and I wish to put on record my appreciation of the skill and discretion with which he reinforced his knowledge and grasp of the various points involved.

14. I had thought of confining the interview to this question of the guarantees and other States, but M. Molotov expressed his desire to learn the views of His Majesty's Government on all other debatable points. We consequently read out to him, as before, a French rendering of paragraphs 14 to 16 inclusive of the memorandum of instructions and left with him a copy of the English text (copy enclosed - Enclosures 4 and 5). Paragraph 17 of the memorandum was only put verbally as a point of purely juristic or technical nature. M. Molotov asked a few questions but made no particular comment. Finally, he said he would study the material supplied to him and would summon us to another meeting in due course.

15. The next day, the 16th June, we were again summoned to the Kremlin, and M. Molotov handed us, in Russian, the text of the Soviet reply, of which I have the honour to enclose a translation (Enclosure 6). My telegram of the 16th June (No. 54) contained so full a summary of the conversation that I hope

I may be excused from repeating it now. But in view of the last sentence in paragraph 2 of your Lordship's telegram of the 19th June (No. 55), I would like to state that, amongst the points made by Mr. Strang, the argument that our guarantees to Poland and Roumania constitute a substantial protection to the Soviet Union, was most clearly brought out.

16. It is worth noting, as typical of the atmosphere with which we have to contend, that M. Molotov was most emphatic in his anxiety to make us understand that, in his view, the British and French Governments were treating them as simpletons ("naivny") and fools ("duraki"). It became necessary for M. Potemkin to assure him that he had well and truly rendered the word – "duraki") as "imbéciles."

17. On the other hand, when we brought up the question of issuing communiqués to the press (on the line that whereas our two embassies had maintained absolute silence here we had been somewhat surprised by a "Tass" communiqué stating that the impression produced in Soviet circles by the previous conversation had not been entirely satisfactory), M. Molotov had his own quite legitimate grievance in this matter of atmosphere. He pointed out that the Soviet Government had been continually shot at for weeks past by British and French journalists and also by parliamentary questioners, but that a remarkable reticence had on the whole been shown by Soviet organs of publicity. My French colleague and I are of opinion that, in fact, our interests have even more suffered from the publicity in question, but M. Molotov was technically in the right. We confined ourselves to repeating that we would continue to abstain from giving any impressions to journalists; and we were glad to note next day that the Soviet press published nothing beyond the bare announcement that a meeting had taken place.

18. Finally, I would pay tribute to the valuable assistance

rendered by the French Ambassador in both these conversations. His clear and logical mind, together with his ability to sum up a situation or a problem in concise and limpid terms, helped on many an occasion to dispel the mist of understanding and suspicion. I should add that M. Naggiar took occasion to lay stress on the earnest desire of his Government to bring the negotiations to an early and successful conclusion.

Enclosure 1 in No. 53.

Observations on Article 1 (2) of the Soviet Draft.

(Paragraphs 8-12 of the Memorandum of Instructions.)

WHILE His Majesty's Government are unable to accept the proposal in article 1 (2) of the Soviet draft, since they cannot agree to impose a guarantee on Powers which are unwilling to receive it, they fully sympathise with the desire of the Soviet Government that the military support which the three Powers would agree to extend to one another should not be confined to a case of actual aggression upon their own territory. They have already met the desire of the Soviet Government for a direct guarantee to cover the case of direct aggression, and they have given much thought to the question how best to devise means of dealing with a threat to the security of the contracting Powers caused by action other than direct aggression.

2. Part of this difficulty would be met it the treaty were to include a clause to the effect that the three Powers would undertake to assist each other in the event of one of them becoming involved in hostilities with a European Power as the result of aggression by that Power against another European State which had, with its own consent, received an undertaking of assistance from the contracting country. It would be unnecessary to mention these States by name in the treaty, and

by another article in the treaty it would be agreed as indicated in article 4 of the Soviet draft, that the three Governments would communicate to each other the terms of any undertakings of this kind which they had given to other States.

3. There would still remain, however, the case of aggression against or through States which have not received any such guarantee, some of whom have declared that they would refuse to receive a guarantee. His Majesty's Government fully appreciate, for example that the military occupation of one of the Soviet Union's north-west neighbours, whose resistance might be quickly overborne or who might even acquiesce in the occupation, might be regarded by the Soviet Union as a menace to the security of the Soviet Union. A similar situation in Holland or Switzerland would be a menace to the security of Great Britain and France. His Majesty's Government have been giving much thought to the question how best to meet such a situation through common action by the three Powers while at the same time not forcing a direct guarantee on the States concerned, or provoking undesirable reactions on the part of their Governments.

4. His Majesty's Government would be glad if the Commissar for Foreign Affairs would examine this question with His Majesty's Ambassador. His Majesty's Government are inclined to think that the best solution would be found by applying to this case the procedure which they understand to be contemplated in article 8 of M. Molotov's draft. They suggest accordingly that it should be agreed that the three Powers should immediately consult together if one of them considered that its security was menaced by a threat to the independence or neutrality of any other European Power. If the other two Powers agreed that such a menace existed, and if the contracting Power in question was involved in hostilities in consequence, the other two Powers would go to its assistance.

5. The foregoing suggestions seem to His Majesty's Government to cover the case of what might be called indirect aggression against the three contracting Powers through (a) other Powers who have already received a guarantee from one or other of the contracting Powers (i.e., Belgium, Greece, Turkey, Roumania and Poland), (b) other Powers who have not received such a guarantee or do not wish to receive it (Latvia, Estonia, Finland, The Netherlands and Switzerland are the most obvious examples). The proposed provisions would thus take the place of sub-paragraphs 2 and 3 in article 1 of M. Molotov's draft.

Enclosure 2 in No. 53.

Points on which there is Agreement.

(Paragraphs 1-3 of the Memorandum of Instructions.)

HIS Majesty's Government have examined the draft agreement communicated to the British and French Ambassadors on the 2nd June.

2. His Majesty's Government are glad to note that a substantial measure of agreement has now been reached as to the general lines of the proposed agreement.

3. It is agreed:-

(1) That a treaty should be concluded between the three Powers on an equal footing, in which each of the three would undertake similar obligations towards the other two.

(2) That the three Powers would render each other immediate assistance-
    (a) In the event of one of them being the object of a

       direct attack by a European Power.
- (b) In the event of one of the three Powers going to the assistance of certain European States which it had undertaken to assist against aggression.

(3) That the treaty should be in harmony with the principle of mutual assistance against aggression adopted by the League of Nations, but that assistance should be given under the treaty without it being necessary to await action by the League.

(4) That there should be immediate consultation between the three States with a view to settling the methods, forms and extent of the assistance to be rendered under the treaty.

(5) That in the event of a threat of aggression by a European Power, there should be consultation between the three-Powers, and, should the necessity arise, a decision by them as to the moment and manner of application of the mechanism of mutual assistance.

(6) That the three States should communicate to each other the terms of the undertaking given by them to other States and commit each other before assuming further obligations.

Enclosure 3 in No. 53.

Anglo-French Draft of June 6, 1939.

ARTICLE 1.

THE United Kingdom, France and the U.S.S.R. undertake to give to each other immediately all the support and assistance in their power should one of these countries become involved in hostilities with a European Power as a result either of -

(1) Aggression by that Power against anyone of these three countries.

(2) Aggression by that Power against another European State which the contracting country concerned had, in conformity with the wishes of that State, undertaken to assist against such aggression.

(3) Action by that Power which the three contracting Governments, as a result of the consultation between them provided for in article 3, considered to threaten the independence or neutrality of another European State in such a way as to constitute a menace to the security of the contracting country concerned. Such support and assistance will be given in conformity with the principles of article 16, paragraphs 1 and 2, of the Covenant of the League of Nations, but without its being necessary to await action by the League.

ARTICLE 3.

Without prejudice to the immediate rendering of assistance on the outbreak of hostilities in accordance with article 1, in the event of circumstances arising which threaten to call into operation the undertakings of mutual assistance contained in article 1, the three contracting Governments will on the request of any one of them, immediately consult together to examine the situation. Should the necessity arise, they will decide by common agreement the moment at which the mechanism of mutual assistance shall be put into operation and the manner of its application.

Enclosure 4 in No. 53.

Observation on Articles 2 and 6 of the Soviet Draft.

(Paragraphs 14 and 15 of the Memorandum of Instructions.)

IN article 2 of M. Molotov's draft it is provided that the three States will come to an agreement as soon as possible as to the methods, forms and extent of the assistance to be rendered by them. In article 6 of that draft it is further provided that the proposed treaty is not to come into force until the conclusion of this proposed military agreement.

2. His Majesty's Government entirely agree that there should be immediate consultation between the three Governments as to the methods, forms and extent of the assistance, provided for in the treaty, since this furnishes the best means of making sure that such assistance shall be as effective as possible. They will accordingly be prepared that these conversations should be inaugurated at the earliest possible date and that they should be both frank and exhaustive. They doubt, however, whether it would be possible within any reasonably brief period to reach a concrete military agreement to cover every possible contingency. They are anxious to conclude an agreement with the Soviet Government without any further delay, and they view with dismay the effect on the European situation which would be produced by the postponement of the entry into force of any such agreement until the conclusion of a military agreement. They think that the only practical course would be to make it clear in the treaty itself that the three States would concert together, immediately after the conclusion of the treaty with a view to settling the methods, forms and extent of the assistance to be rendered, and it might, indeed, be understood between the three parties that the staff contacts would be inaugurated within a specified time from the conclusion of the treaty.

Enclosure 5 in No. 53.

Observation on Article 5 of the Soviet Draft.

(Paragraph 16 of the Memorandum of Instructions.)

ARTICLE 5 of M. Molotov's draft provides that the three States will undertake only to conclude an armistice or peace by joint agreement. His Majesty's Government see serious objection to such a provision. His Majesty's Government would, of course, loyally carry out the obligations of any treaty into which they entered, and they would count on the other two parties to do the same. But they doubt whether on practical grounds this kind of provision would, in fact, achieve its object. An essential condition of an undertaking not to conclude peace except on terms which had been jointly agreed is that agreement should have been reached as to the objects which the peace is to achieve, and no such agreement is possible before the circumstances which produced the war are known. His Majesty's Government would be prepared to consider some provision in this direction if agreement were reached on other points still outstanding.

Enclosure 6 in No. 53.

Translation of Soviet Reply of June 16, 1939.

HAVING acquainted themselves with the Anglo-French formulas handed to Molotov on the 15th June, the Government of the Soviet Union have come to the following conclusion:-

1. As regards paragraph 1 of article 1 (Soviet Government's draft (No. 42), the attitude of the Soviet Government coincides with that of the English and French Governments.

2. As regards paragraph 2 of article 1 (Soviet Government's draft), the views of the Soviet Government are rejected by the English and French Governments.

The latter consider that the Soviet Union should render immediate assistance to Poland, Roumania, Belgium, Greece, and Turkey in the event of an attack on them by an aggressor and in the event of England and France being involved in hostilities in connection therewith, whereas England and France would not assume obligations to render immediate assistance to the Soviet Union in the event of the U.S.S.R. being involved in hostilities with an aggressor in connexion with an attack by the latter on Latvia, Estonia and Finland, which border on the U.S.S.R.

The Soviet Government cannot possibly agree to this inasmuch as they are unable to reconcile themselves to the position of inequality, humiliating for the Soviet Union, in which the Soviet Union would thereby be placed.

The Anglo-French proposals justify their refusal to guarantee Estonia, Latvia and Finland by the unwillingness of these countries to accept such a guarantee. If this argument is insurmountable, and if the Soviet Government, as already mentioned above, are unable to participate in assistance to Poland, Roumania, Belgium, Greece and. Turkey without the receipt of equivalent assistance in the defence of Estonia, Latvia and Finland from an aggressor, the Soviet Government are compelled to recognise that the whole question of a triple guarantee to all the eight States above named, as well as the question forming the subject of paragraph 3 of article 1, will have to be postponed as not being ripe for solution, and that paragraphs 2 and 3 of article 1 will have to be excluded from the agreement.

In this event article 1 would only consist of paragraph 1, and the obligations of England, France and the U.S.S.R. as regards mutual assistance would enter into force only in the case of direct attack by an aggressor on the territory of one or other of the contracting parties, but they would not extend to cases in which one of the contracting parties might be involved in hostilities as the result of having rendered assistance to any third Power which was not a party to the present agreement, but which was the object of an attack by an aggressor. In this connexion the drafting of paragraph 1 of article 1 would clearly have to be altered accordingly.

3. In view of the existence of differences of opinion, further discussion is necessary in the question of the simultaneous entry into force of the general agreement and the military agreement.

4. As regards the question of not concluding an armistice or peace except by general agreement, the Soviet Government maintain their attitude, inasmuch as they are unable to contemplate that any of the contracting parties should have the right, at the very height of defensive military operations against an aggressor, to conclude a separate agreement with the aggressor behind the back of and against its allies.

5. The Soviet Government consider the reference to article 16, paragraphs 1 and 2 of the Covenant of the League of Nations to be superfluous.

No. 54.

Sir W. Seeds to Viscount Halifax.

(Telegraphic.) *Moscow, June 16, 1939.*

M. MOLOTOV asked French Ambassador, myself, and Mr. Strang to see him again this afternoon. Meeting lasted an hour and a half. He handed us a paper containing the Soviet Government's reply to the representations we made to him yesterday. M Potemkin made for us an oral translation into French of M. Molotov's paper.

2. An English translation is contained in my immediately following telegram. (Enclosure 6 in No. 53)

3. M. Molotov then went on to say that the three Governments had several times tried to study in its widest aspect the question of proposed treaty. On each occasion the same difficulty had arisen and one of the Soviet conditions had been set aside. If His Majesty's Government and the French Government treated the Soviet Government as being naive or foolish people, he himself could afford to smile, but he could not guarantee that everyone would take so calm a view. Soviet Government had given an affirmative reply to suggestion of British and French Governments that they should undertake obligations in respect of the five guaranteed countries. Since then Great Britain and France had added Switzerland and Netherlands. When, however, the Soviet Government asked for similar guarantees from Great Britain and France in respect of the three border States which were weak and in need of assistance, they were met by a categorical refusal. This proposal would place Soviet Government in a humiliating position and they could not accept it. If the three Baltic States concerned did not want a Soviet guarantee, the Soviet Government were ready to postpone, as not being ripe for settlement, the whole question of assistance in respect of the States other than the three signatories. Soviet Government were ready to undertake obligations in respect of other States in which they had only a minor interest provided that the required guarantees could be secured for the Baltic States. As the Soviet Ambassador had observed to your Lordship, this was a *sine qua non*. It was clear from proposals that we had made that this question was not settled and that therefore it had better be postponed.

4. French Ambassador asked whether he could sum up the attitude of the Soviet Government as being that, if the two Western Powers could not create a system of guarantees which would be identical for the three Baltic States on the one hand and for the other five States on the other, the Soviet Government would prefer to postpone the whole question of guarantees in respect of non-signatory States and to confine treaty to an arrangement of mutual assistance among the three signatories to operate in the advent of direct aggression upon them. M. Molotov said this was so.

5. We asked him whether in this limited treaty it would be the intention to include such of the articles in the existing drafts as were still relevant. M. Molotov assented, but said that the question would, of course, have to be considered in detail if the time came.

6. We asked him whether, in the event of the scope of the proposed arrangement being limited in this way, the Soviet Government would contemplate the same kind of procedure as had been adopted in our conversations with Poland and Turkey, namely, negotiation of a preliminary declaration, to be followed by negotiation of a formal treaty. M. Molotov did not welcome this idea and said t.hat the immediate negotiation of a formal treaty would be preferable.

7. French Ambassador observed it was not enough to speak of the three Baltic States and five guaranteed States. Netherlands and Switzerland were just as important for Great Britain and France as the Baltic States for Soviet Russia.

8. We pointed out as matter of form that the statement about the Anglo-French proposals at the beginning of second sub-paragraph of paragraph 2 of M. Molotov's paper (Enclosure 6 in No. 53) was inaccurate, since His Majesty's Government and the French Government had not suggested that the Soviet

Government should render assistance to Poland and to other guaranteed States, but that the Soviet Union should render assistance to Great Britain and France if they became involved in hostilities on behalf of these States.

9. In view of thoroughness with which we had threshed out the whole question yesterday, we did not think it worth trying to argue M. Molotov out of his position especially as it was so categorically stated.

10. At one stage in the conversation M. Molotov reverted to the point about Poland dealt with in last paragraph of your memorandum of instructions. He seemed to take it amiss that His Majesty's Government would not be prepared in proposed treaty to support the U.S.S.R. against, for example, Poland; though at the same time he expressed surprise that possibility of an attack by Poland against the Soviet Union should even be thought conceivable, since in the same treaty the Soviet Government would be required to give a guarantee of assistance in respect of Poland. To his mind this purely technical point which we had raised apparently had sinister implications, the more so since, as he pointed out, Poland and Roumania were bound by a treaty which was directed against the Soviet Union.

No. 55.

Viscount Halifax to Sir W. Seeds (Moscow).

(Telegraphic.) *Foreign Office, June 19, 1939.*

YOUR telegram of 16th June. (No. 54)

To judge from the text of M. Molotov's aide-mémoire and of his remarks reported in your telegram of 16th June, it would seem that M. Molotov has not realised the extent to which we intended in our last draft to go in the direction of meeting the Soviet Government's wish that we would come to their assistance in the event of their security being threatened by aggression against any of the Baltic States. I had hoped that our intention in this respect had been made clear in paragraphs 8, 10, 11 and 12 of instructions brought to you by Mr. Strang. When M. Molotov states in his aide-mémoire that Britain and France would not assume obligation to render assistance to the Soviet Government in the event of their being involved in hostilities with an aggressor in connexion with an attack by the latter on one of the Baltic States, he appears to overlook completely the fact that our draft treaty was intended to provide precisely for this assistance if Russian security were menaced as a result of such aggression on a Baltic State.

2. Nor is it true that our proposals involve placing the Soviet Government in a position of inequality. The neighbouring countries whose integrity is important from the point of view of Russian security are Poland, Roumania and the Baltic States; in the case of France and ourselves the corresponding countries are Belgium, Holland and Switzerland. Under our proposals the cases of Poland and Roumania on the one side and Belgium on the other would be covered by the provision relating to countries which had received a guarantee. The Baltic States on the one side and Holland and Switzerland on the other would be covered by the provision in 1 (3) of our text of 6th June. There would be, therefore, complete equality of treatment, and the Soviet Union would receive the same assurances in respect of the Baltic States as would content us in the case of Holland and Switzerland. M. Molotov does not seem to appreciate that our guarantees to Poland and Roumania are, in effect, a substantial protection to the Soviet Union.

3. In fact, we are perfectly willing to meet the preoccupations of the Soviet Government about the Baltic States provided that this is done in a way which does not

involve naming them or thrusting upon them a guarantee which would be highly distasteful to them. It is because the only proposal which the Soviet Government have so far made is patently open to this objection that we are unable to accept it; but it does not follow that the result which the Soviet Government desire cannot be achieved in another way.

4. Although I do not want to involve you in fruitless argumentation with M. Molotov, our position, as stated above, should be fully understood by him, and unless you are satisfied that you have done all that is possible in this direction already, I would be glad if you would set forth the position to him on the lines I have indicated. In any ease you should impress upon M. Molotov that, in raising objections to his original draft, we are not trying to avoid dealing with points the importance of which for Russia we fully realise, and that, on the contrary, we are anxious to find a form of words which will remove his doubts, while at the same time taking account of the susceptibilities of the Baltic States, Holland and Switzerland. We should have hoped that after the exhaustive exchange of views, our respective positions were now sufficiently clarified to enable the two sides to proceed to the stage of putting into words the agreement which already exists in principle. In order, therefore, to lose no further time, you should try to bring M. Molotov to the point of discussing with you and your French colleague what form of words would meet his difficulties.

5. I have considered the suggestion contained in M. Molotov's aide-mémoire to the effect that the whole question of guarantees in respect of non-signatory States should be postponed, and that the Tripartite Treaty between Great Britain, France and Russia should be confined to the case of direct attack by an aggressor on the territory of one of the three contracting parties. Such a treaty would, however be a reversal of the idea with which we started and, which was to protect Poland and other States who, might find themselves in

immediate danger of aggression and would, in any case, be quite inadequate in present circumstances. I would not, therefore, be prepared to consider it except in the last resort. Incidentally, the effect of such a limited treaty would be that the Soviet Government would obtain the benefit of the guarantees we have given to Roumania and Poland without Great Britain and France receiving any reciprocal benefit on their side.

6. I attach the greatest importance to early and rapid progress, and as regards the subsidiary points mentioned in paragraphs 3 and 5 (No. 55), I would be prepared, in return for a prompt and satisfactory settlement, to agree (1) that staff conversations should start immediately on the signature of the agreement; (2) to the omission of the reference to the Covenant of the League in paragraph 1. I should also be ready to omit article 5 of 6th June draft regarding rights and position of other Power.

No. 56.

Sir W. Seeds to Viscount Halifax.

(Telegraphic.) *Moscow, June 21, 1939.*

YOUR telegram of 19th June. (No. 55)

We had another meeting with M. Molotov this afternoon, which lasted for two hours.

2. Although we felt that we had fully explained the views of the two Governments to M. Molotov, we thought it well to repeat the main points to him. We accordingly prepared a statement based on arguments contained in your telegram under reference, and this was translated orally by M. Potemkin to M. Molotov, and a copy of it was left with him. We then presented new draft of article 1. (No. 57)

3. We said as regards the subsidiary points mentioned in paragraphs 3 and 4 of the Soviet reply of the 16th June (Enclosure 6 in No. 53) that we agreed that further discussion was necessary on the question of staff conversations, and that we did not expect there would be any difficulty in coming to an agreement on the question of not concluding a separate peace.

4. M. Potemkin at once asked, with reference to paragraph 1 of our new draft of article 1, with whom would lie the decision on the question whether or not aggression on European State constituted a menace to the security of one of the contracting parties. To this we replied that nothing was said in our draft on this point. One course would be to leave the point undefined; another would be to try to find some definition. We asked whether M. Molotov had any views as to these alternatives. To this question we received no reply.

5. During the discussion we explained that the form of words in the second part of paragraph 1 of the new article 1 was designed to meet the views of the Soviet Government while at the same time avoiding an enumeration of other States and taking account of their susceptibilities. In spite of existing difficulties we thought that a way could be found to conclude a useful treaty, and it might well be that if the three Powers could reach an agreement such as we now proposed, the States which were now hesitating might in time come to take a. more positive attitude towards the arrangement reached by the three Powers.

6. M. Molotov said that he thought the Soviet Government must insist on the inclusion in the treaty of the names of the eight countries concerned, and we understood him also to say that the Soviet Government still maintained the view that all three signatories should undertake to defend these eight countries. If it was not possible to mention the names and if these countries could not take up a more positive attitude it

would be more logical to adopt the plan suggested in Soviet reply of the 16th June, namely, to conclude a treaty providing for direct aggression against the signatories only. He asked that view the British and French Governments took of that proposal. We told him that the two Governments would prefer to conclude a treaty on lines which they had already suggested, rather than a treaty of more limited scope.

7. M. Molotov said that the obligations we had asked the Soviet Government to assume in respect of the five guaranteed countries were very heavy. That being so it was essential that the guarantees which the Soviet Government would receive in return should be precisely stated and not left vague as in our draft.

8. The French Ambassador asked, as a personal suggestion, whether it would meet the Soviet view if the names of the countries concerned could be communicated in a separate document which need not be published. M. Molotov said that this point might be discussed. He asked what view I took of it. I said the question might be looked into.

9. French Ambassador enquired whether instead of enumerating the States it would be possible to name certain geographical areas. M. Molotov did not think this was a very useful suggestion.

10. Finally M. Molotov said that in his personal view the proposal we had made did not represent any progress. He would, however, submit it to the Soviet Government and let us have their reply. We said that we should be glad to see any counter-draft that the Soviet Government might wish to suggest. His only response was to reply that the proposals of the Soviet Government had already been embodied in the drafts already submitted to us.

No. 57.

Anglo-French Redraft of Article 1 handed to M. Molotov on June 21, 1939.

THE United Kingdom, France and the U.S.S.R undertake to give each other immediately all the support and assistance in their power should one of these countries become involved in hostilities with a European Power as a result of either:-

> (1) Aggression by that Power against any one of these three countries, or aggression by it which, being directed against another European State, thereby constituted a menace to the security of one of those countries; or
> (2) Aggression by that Power against another European State which the contracting country concerned had, with the approval of that State, undertaken to assist against such aggression.

Such support and assistance will be given in conformity with the principles of the Covenant of the League of Nations, but without its being necessary to await action by the League.

No. 58.

Sir W. Seeds to Viscount Halifax.

Moscow, June 21, 1939.

My Lord,

I HAVE the honour to transmit to you herewith the text of

the observations made to M. Molotov by the French Ambassador and myself at our interview this afternoon as reported in paragraph 2 of my telegram. (No. 56)

Enclosure in No. 58.

(Translation.)

Text of Observations made to M. Molotov by His Majesty's Ambassador and the French Ambassador at Moscow on June 22, 1939.

THE British and French Governments have carefully examined the reply handed by M. Molotov on the 16th June to the Ambassador of France and Great Britain. They appreciated the frankness with which the Soviet Government have expressed their point of view.

2. There are certain points in this reply which, in the opinion of the two Governments, would seem to call for rectification.

3. In particular, certain remarks in the second section of paragraph 2 of the Soviet reply of the 16th June (Enclosure 6 in No. 53) do not take account of the exact terms of articles 1 and 3 of the plan submitted on the 15th June for the consideration of the Soviet Government. These articles provide that France, Great Britain and the U.S.S.R. pledge themselves to give, in accordance with the conditions laid down by these articles, mutual assistance to each other, and not, as M. Molotov seems to believe, to the third Power which has been attacked.

4. Nor is it correct to say that the British and French Governments do not desire to contract an engagement to lend immediate assistance to the Soviet Government, were the U.S.S.R. to find itself engaged in hostilities with an aggressor as the result of an attack by this aggressor against Lithuania, Estonia or Finland. On the contrary, the purpose of the draft article handed on the 15th June to M. Molotov is expressly to provide for this assistance as a result of such an aggression upon the Baltic States.

5. There is therefore no doubt that the three Governments are completely in agreement as to the necessity of concluding a treaty on the basis of complete equality between the three contracting parties.

6. In this respect the two Governments wish to draw attention to the following considerations:-

Taking into account the point of view of the Soviet Government and the geographical situation, the neighbouring European countries whose integrity constitutes one of the elements of security of the U.S.S.R. are, if the opinion of the two Governments is correct, the Baltic States, Poland and Roumania. As far as France and Great Britain are concerned, the neighbouring European countries which have the same importance for the security of these two States as the other five have for that of Russia, are Belgium, Holland and Switzerland. According to the suggestions made on the 15th June by the French and British Governments, the cases of Poland and Roumania on the one hand and that of Belgium on the other were covered by the conditions of paragraph 2 of article 1 relating to the countries which have received a promise of assistance from one of the three contracting parties. Again, according to these Franco-British proposals, the cases of the Baltic States on the one hand and of Holland and Switzerland on the other were covered by the conditions of paragraph 3 of the same article 1. Thus, when considerations of proximity are taken into account the conditions laid down on the subject of the Baltic States do not differ from those applicable to Switzerland and Holland.

7. But the French and British Governments, having always desired to give the Soviet Government satisfaction on the subject of the Baltic States, have given careful consideration to the necessity for doing this in a way which takes account of the present political conditions. These conditions are not, however, peculiar to the Baltic States, but apply equally to the case of Holland and Switzerland, the maintenance of the independence of these countries being in equal measure for one or other of the three contracting parties an important element in their security.

8. In the light of the above considerations, the two Governments have examined the draft article laid before M. Molotov on the 15th June and have prepared a new draft which the two Ambassadors would be glad to have the opportunity of discussing with him.

No. 59.

Sir W. Seeds to Viscount Halifax.

(Telegraphic.) *Moscow, June 22, 1939.*

MY telegram of 21st June. (No. 56)

M. Molotov sent for us this afternoon to give us the reply of the Soviet Government to the proposals made to them in accordance with your instructions.

2. Reply is in the following terms:-

> "The Soviet Government have attentively examined the proposals of England and France handed to M. Molotov on the 21st June. In view of the fact that these proposals constitute a repetition of the previous proposals made by England and France, which, as already stated, have met with serious objections on the part of the Soviet Government, the latter have come to the conclusion that these proposals must be rejected as unacceptable."

3. We asked him whether he could give us any indication as to how the draft of article 1, submitted by the Soviet Government on the 2nd June (No. 48), which dealt with the fundamental point at issue, might be amended to meet our point of view. He replied that as His Majesty's Government and the French Government had not accepted the proposal made by Soviet Government on the 16th June (conclusion of limited treaty) (Enclosure No. 6 in No. 53), the Soviet Government reverted to their proposal of the 2nd June (No. 48) and maintained it.

4. We asked whether proposal of the 2nd June meant not only that there should be an enumeration of guaranteed States in the treaty itself, but also that treaty should provide for a common guarantee by the three signatories of the eight States mentioned in Soviet draft. M. Molotov replied that this was what the Soviet Government had proposed, and that this was what they insisted upon.

5. We asked whether the text of article 1 of their draft of the 2nd June was to be regarded as *ne varietur*. He replied that it had been submitted to the two Governments for discussion.

6. We asked whether pending settlement of fundamental question of article 1 we might proceed to settle the text of the

other article, which were unlikely to cause any difficulty. M. Molotov said it would be better to settle the main question first.

No. 60.

Viscount Halifax to Sir W. Seeds (Moscow).

(Telegraphic.) *Foreign Office, June 22, 1939.*

YOUR telegram of 21st June. (No. 56)

1. You are doubtless as bewildered as I am by the attitude of M. Molotov. The position as I see it is that we have declared ourselves ready to give him the substance of everything he requires, namely, a guarantee to come to the assistance of Russia should she be involved in hostilities owing to an act of aggression by Germany on any of the Baltic States. As regards the form, we have demurred to mentioning the Baltic States by name on the practical ground that these States do not wish it, and that their declarations show that, if we disregard their wishes, we shall alienate them and possibly even drive them into the arms of Germany. This eventuality is clearly in the interests neither of ourselves, nor, indeed of Russia. It is consequently not apparent why M. Molotov clings with such stubborn pertinacity to his original draft, in which the various States concerned are mentioned.

2. His Majesty's Government remain ready to meet the wishes of the Soviet Government fully so far as substance is concerned, but for the practical reason given above, they consider it against the joint interest of the contracting parties that mention should be made in the agreement itself of those States, namely, the Baltic States, Holland and Switzerland, which do not wish to receive a public guarantee.

3. It is difficult for me to instruct you without some further indication of what is in M. Molotov's mind. Is he merely afraid that, if the States are not mentioned, some undefined loop-hole will be left, such us that mentioned in paragraph 4 of your telegram? If so, the suggestion embodied in paragraph 8 of your telegram under reply ought to reassure him.

4. But I would not propose that you should put forward any further text until by means of further conversations you have been able to find out what is really at the back of M. Molotov's mind and what he is really holding out far. I should be grateful for any comment you can make on his general attitude, and on what you consider now to be the best line of approach.

5. Whatever suggestion I may eventually instruct you to put forward, you should, in doing so, try again to make M. Molotov realise that the independence of Holland and Switzerland is as essential to Great Britain and France as that of the Baltic States to Russia. No guarantee has been given to these two States because for obvious reasons they do not wish to receive one, but, if complete reciprocity is to be accorded they should be treated naturally on the same footing as the Baltic States.

6. I may observe parenthetically that M Molotov appears to regard the guarantees to Poland and Roumania as a purely Franco-British interest. But in point of fact a threat to these countries would constitute an indirect threat to Russia and our guarantee is thus an important contribution to Russian security.

No. 61.

Sir W. Seeds to Viscount Halifax.

(Telegraphic.) *Moscow, June 23, 1939.*

YOUR telegram of 22nd June. (No. 60)

You will since have received my telegram of 22nd June (No. 59) reporting on the outcome of yesterday's conversation. We think we are now sufficiently aware of what is in M. Molotov's mind without having recourse to further interview with him.

2. The conclusion I had reached after that conversation was that we now appeared to have exhausted all means of arriving at a settlement on the crucial point of guarantees to other States on the lines of the drafts which we had ourselves submitted. It seemed to me that we had now to decide definitely whether to accept the principle embodied in article 1 of the Soviet draft of 2nd June (No. 48) or to conclude a simple treaty of mutual guarantee against direct aggression.

3. I will try in the present telegram to recapitulate what, seems to me to be M. Molotov's reasons for holding that there is a fundamental difference between the Soviet draft of 2nd June and the two drafts we have recently submitted to him.

4. Paragraph 2 of article 1 of the Soviet draft of 2nd June not only names certain States, but also provides for a common undertaking by the three Powers to defend those States against aggression. We understood from M. Molotov yesterday that the Soviet Government stand fully by both these principles though they are perhaps not wedded to the precise expression given to them in their draft.

5. There are two reasons why the Soviet Government

insist on an enumeration. The first is that, being suspicious by nature and having little confidence in the good faith and resolution of the Western Powers in the light of past experience, they wish the obligations to be assumed by the three Powers to be set down in black and white and to be clear beyond dispute.

6. The second reason is one which applies equally to their desire for a common guarantee by the three Powers of the States named. It is, I think, that they wish to have some international warrant for going to the assistance of the Baltic States, even perhaps without the assent or contrary to the wishes of the Governments concerned.

7. They are intensely suspicious of the Governments of the Baltic States. They seem to feel that the Baltic States may voluntarily, or under pressure, move into the German orbit and accept a degree of German domination which the Soviet Government would regard as a menace to their security. They therefore have it in mind to secure our assistance, or at the least apparent connivance, should they ever find it expedient to intervene in the Baltic States (not necessarily in case of a major conflagration, but in conditions which we would not regard as threatening peace of Europe) on plea that Governments and ruling classes as distinct from rest of population of those countries were about to compound with Germany.

8. A further reason why they propose a common undertaking by the three Powers to defend the States named in their draft may be that they wish as a matter of pride to place themselves on the same footing with Great Britain and France, and they have accordingly offered to add their own guarantee to those already given by Great Britain and France to Belgium, Poland, Turkey, Roumania and Greece, asking in return a similar undertaking in respect of the Baltic States.

9. In the light of the above considerations, I would

suggest the following reasons for M. Molotov's objection to the redraft of article 1 communicated to M. Molotov on 21st June (No. 57):-

10. Paragraph 1 of that draft did not make it clear beyond question that the Baltic States would be fully covered. It did not specify who was to judge whether an act of aggression against the Baltic States constituted a menace to the security of the Soviet Union. This was a loophole through which Great Britain and France might evade their obligation to assist the Soviet Union. No such loophole for the Soviet Government seemed to exist in paragraph 2 of our draft, since the mere fact of Great Britain and France becoming engaged in hostilities on behalf of a country to whom they had given a guarantee would apparently of itself bring into play the obligation of the Soviet Union to come to their assistance, and the Soviet Government would have little voice in the matter. There was here again the consideration of national pride, since the introduction of a special paragraph to deal with the guaranteed States stressed the fact that the guarantees in question had all been given by Great Britain and France, and that the Soviet Union had not been considered acceptable as a guarantor.

11. There is the further objection that our draft only creates obligations for the signatory Powers towards each other and does not create new obligations for the signatories to assist other States. Molotov asked us how in the event of an attack on Poland Russia could possibly help Great Britain and France if she were not to help Poland.

No. 62.

Viscount Halifax to Sir W. Seeds (Moscow).

Foreign Office, June 23, 1939.

Sir,

I ASKED the Soviet Ambassador to come to see me to-day in order to discuss with him the present position of the Anglo-Soviet negotiations now proceeding in Moscow. I showed the Ambassador our last draft of article 1 (No. 57). The Ambassador had evidently not seen it and studied it with great attention. I told him that it seemed to us to meet all M. Molotov's requirements, but we were now told that M. Molotov had rejected it in a note in which he gave no reasons. I asked if M Maisky could explain exactly in what respect our draft was unsatisfactory, but M. Maisky declined to commit himself, and merely said that this was surely a matter which Sir William Seeds would be able to ascertain in Moscow. I replied that I should naturally have hoped that this would have been the case, but, as a matter of fact, it seemed impossible to obtain much enlightenment from M. Molotov on the subject. I, of course, was aware of the fact that he attached importance to the treaty containing a list of the countries whose independence the signatories had undertaken to defend, but I could not make out why he attached particular importance to this naming of the States.

2. I then asked M. Maisky point-blank whether the Soviet Government wanted a treaty at all; to which M. Maisky said that of course they did, and why did I ask the question? Because, I replied, throughout the negotiations the Soviet Government had not budged a single inch and we had made all the advances and concessions.

3. M. Maisky's only answer to this was that his Government had probably made a mistake in frankly stating at the outset what was their irreducible minimum. Perhaps they ought to have asked for more than they wanted so as to be able subsequently to make concessions. In any case, he could not understand why we were so reluctant to agree to a list of countries to be defended. To this I said that saying "No" to everything was not my idea of negotiation, and that it had a striking resemblance to Nazi methods of dealing with international questions.

4. In spite of a good deal of sparring on M. Maisky's part, the conversation was carried on in a most friendly spirit, and I concluded it by asking the Ambassador to tell his Government that we wanted a treaty, and that if they wanted one too, we ought to be able to reach a settlement without further difficulty.

No. 63.

Viscount Halifax to Sir W. Seeds (Moscow).

(Telegraphic.) *Foreign Office, June 27, 1939.*

YOUR telegram of 23rd June. (No. 61)

I am grateful for this full and clear statement of Soviet point of view.

2. It seems certain that M. Molotov will make difficulty about any draft which differentiates in any way between guaranteed and non-guaranteed States.

3. It is plain also that he wishes obligations of Powers to be clearly defined.

4. It may be that he also feels that this cannot be secured without nominal roll of States figuring in treaty, though I should hope that this difficulty might be avoided if we could convince him that we are not attempting to restrict his liberty, at his discretion, to intervene against aggression designed to threaten or undermine independence or neutrality of Baltic States.

5. I should accordingly hope that agreement might be reached on following formula:-

> "The United Kingdom, France and the U.S.S.R. undertake to give to each other immediately all effective assistance should one of these countries become involved in hostilities with a European Power as a result of aggression by that Power against anyone of these three countries, or aggression by it against another European State whose independence or neutrality the contracting country concerned felt obliged to defend against such aggression."

6. You will observe that this brings together in one grouping all States to whom assistance might be given. It also gives the Soviet Government the right to decide whether any aggression against a Baltic State constitutes a threat to the independence or neutrality of that State, such that the Soviet Government feels obliged to assist the victim of aggression by engaging in hostilities with the aggressor. Once engaged in such hostilities, the Soviet Government would be entitled to assistance from France and Great Britain. This is surely giving the Soviet Government all they ask.

7. I hope this will show M. Molotov that our intentions are sincere and that our aim is the same. If he can be convinced of this, we have a right to ask him to meet us on a matter of form and to have some regard for the considerations we have

urged against public mention of States in question. He may not share our apprehensions as to the embarrassment and disadvantage that is to be expected from a public announcement of what amounts to a guarantee of States who are reluctant to accept or receive such, but we feel them to be very real. Roumania has expressly indicated her desire not to be mentioned by name; Finland and Estonia have publicly stated their objections to receiving a guarantee involving the Soviet Government, and have declared that any assistance from any Great Power without their invitation would be regarded by them as an act of aggression. Latvia has made it clear that she is in full sympathy with the attitude of Finland and Estonia. Nor can we predict the reaction in the Netherlands. And if the published list of States to be assisted figures in, or is attached to, the Anglo-French-Soviet Agreement, it is to be expected that Germany will at once ask all the countries mentioned whether they welcome such undertakings, and will quite likely elicit the response that they did not. The result of such replies must be one of extreme embarrassment to all of us and very prejudicial to the solidarity of the peace front.

8. For these reasons, if you can satisfy M. Molotov that my draft formula gives him what he wants, I wish to avoid any mention of States. If, however, it is necessary to have a nominal roll of States, I should infinitely prefer to supplement the formula in paragraph 5 above by a private agreement between the contracting Governments, which it should be definitely understood should not be made public as to the States to which it should in any case apply. This might be subject to periodical revision or addition by agreement between the three contracting Governments.

9. We trust you will impress very strongly on M. Molotov how far His Majesty's Government have been willing to go in desire to meet Soviet Government. We have not been met by corresponding concessions by Soviet Government, and as we

have now given M. Molotov substance of all he has asked, we do expect agreement to be reached without further obstacles being raised from the other side.

No. 64.

Sir W. Seeds to Viscount Halifax.

Moscow, June 30, 1939.

HIS Majesty's Ambassador at Moscow presents his compliments to His Majesty's Principal Secretary of State for Foreign Affairs, and has the honour to transmit translation of an article by M. Zhdanov on the Anglo-Franco-Soviet negotiations for the conclusion of an effective pact of mutual assistance against aggression, from the *Pravda* of the 29th June, 1939.

Enclosure in No. 64.

Translation of an Article by M. Zhdanov in Pravda *of June 29, 1939.*

"The English and French Governments do not want an Agreement on Terms of Equality with the U.S.S.R."

THE Anglo-Franco-Soviet negotiations for the conclusion of an effective pact of mutual assistance against aggression have reached an *impasse*. In spite of the extreme clarity of the attitude of the Soviet Government and in spite of all their efforts to reach a speedy conclusion of a mutual assistance pact, no real progress can be observed in the course of the negotiations. In the present international situation this fact cannot be without serious significance. It gives wings to the hopes of the aggressors and all enemies of peace - hopes for a possible breakdown of the agreement of the democratic Powers against aggression; and it drives the aggressors on to further acts of aggression.

In this connexion the following question arises: what is causing the delay in these negotiations, the successful outcome of which is impatiently and hopefully awaited by all peace loving nations and all friends of peace? I will venture to express my personal opinion on the subject although my friends do not agree with it. They still think that the English and French Governments began negotiations for a mutual assistance pact with the U.S.S.R. with the intention of creating a powerful barrier against aggression in Europe. My opinion is, and I will endeavour to prove it by facts, that the English and French Governments do not want an agreement on terms of equality with the U.S.S.R., by which I mean the only form of agreement that any self-respecting State could conclude, and I consider this to be the cause of the state of stagnation which the negotiations have now reached.

What is the nature of these facts? The Anglo-Soviet negotiations, I use that word in its most literal sense, i.e., reckoning from the 15th April, the date on which we received the first English proposals, have now lasted for seventy-five days. Of this period, the Soviet Government only required sixteen days for the preparation of their replies to the various English drafts and proposals, the remaining fifty-nine days were wasted in procrastination and delay on the part of the English and French. Who, one may ask, is responsible in this case for the slow progress of the negotiations, if not the English and French?

It is a matter of common knowledge from practical experience of the conclusion of international agreements similar to the Anglo-Franco-Soviet one that this self-same England concluded pacts of mutual assistance with Turkey and Poland within a very brief period: which only goes to show that when England wished to conclude the agreements with Turkey and Poland she found the means of ensuring the necessary tempo in the negotiations. The inadmissible delays and endless procrastination in the negotiations with the Soviet Union must raise doubts as to the sincerity of the real intentions of England and France, and make us wonder what, in point of fact, is behind such a policy: Is it a serious endeavour to form a peace front or is it their desire to make use of the negotiations, and of the delay attending them, for some ulterior objects which have nothing in common with the creation of a front of the peace-loving Powers?

Such a question becomes all the more insistent in view of the position of the English and French Governments in piling up artificial difficulties in the course of the negotiations, and making it look as if serious differences of opinion existed between England and France on the one hand and the U.S.S.R. on the other, on questions which, given goodwill and sincere intentions on the part of England and France, could have been settled without a hitch. The well-known example of this sort of artificially created stumbling blocks in the negotiations is provided by the question of a tripartite guarantee of immediate assistance to Latvia, Estonia and Finland in case of a violation of their neutrality by the aggressors. There is clearly no foundation for statements that the said Baltic States do not want these guarantees, and that it is this consideration which prevents England and France from accepting the Soviet proposals. Such statements can only be inspired by one motive, namely, the desire to complicate the negotiations and to bring them to a dead end. In any case we all know of instances which prove that when, for instance, England considers it to be in her interest to guarantee this or that country, she can find ways and means of doing so without waiting for the countries concerned to ask for guarantees for themselves.

The English newspaper, *Sunday Times*, states in its issue of the 4th June that, "should Great Britain be involved in hostilities as a result of an attack on Holland, Poland has agreed to come to her assistance." The *Sunday Times* continues: "On the other hand, if Poland is involved in hostilities as the result of an attack on Danzig or Lithuania, Great Britain has agreed that she will come to the assistance of Poland." Hence it follows that Poland and Great Britain simultaneously guarantee both Lithuania and Holland, and we do not know whether Lithuania and Holland were asked about this bilateral guarantee. In any case, there is nothing clear on the subject in the press. Moreover, both Holland and Lithuania, so far as I am aware, deny the existence of such a guarantee. An agreement for the bilateral guarantee of these two countries has, however, already been concluded in principle, according to the *Sunday Times*, and it is no secret to anybody that the statement in the *Sunday Times* has not been denied anywhere.

Not long ago the Polish Minister for Foreign Affairs, Beck, in an interview given to a French journalist, stated amongst other things quite unequivocally that Poland had no demands or requests to make as regards the granting to her of any guarantees by the U.S.S.R. and he also stated that she was perfectly well satisfied with the recently concluded trade agreement between herself and the Soviet Union. What difference is there in the present case between the attitude of Poland and that of Government circles in the three Baltic States? Absolutely none. This, however, does not prevent England and France from asking the Soviet Union to guarantee not only Poland and four other countries (of whose desire to receive guarantees from the U.S.S.R. we know nothing), but also Holland and Switzerland, with whom the U.S.S.R. is not even in ordinary diplomatic relations.

All this argues that the English and French do not want an agreement with the U.S.S.R. based on the principles of equality and reciprocity, in spite of their daily protestations of their desire for "equality." What they want is an agreement in which the Soviet Union would play the part of a hired labourer and bear the whole weight of responsibility on its shoulders. No self-respecting country will conclude such an agreement unless she wants to be a plaything in the hands of people whose habit it is to allow others to pull the chestnuts out of the fire for them. Still less can such an agreement be acceptable to the Soviet Union, the power, might and dignity of which are known to the whole world. It seems to me that the English and French do not want a real agreement or one acceptable to the U.S.S.R.; the only thing they really want is to talk about an agreement and, by making play with the obstinacy of the Soviet Union to prepare their own public opinion for an eventual deal with the aggressors.

The next few days must show whether this is the case or not.
Deputy of the Supreme Council of the U.S.S.R.:
A.ZHDANOV.

No. 65.

Sir W. Seeds to Viscount Halifax.

(Telegraphic.) *Moscow, July 1, 1939.*

FRENCH Ambassador and I took action this morning on your telegram of 27th June. (No. 63)

2. We submitted to M. Molotov draft of article 1 contained in paragraph 5 of your telegram. M. Potemkin asked whether the phrase "felt obliged" was to be interpreted as covering only a treaty obligation or whether it covered also an obligation dictated by vital interests. We told him that it covered both.

3. M. Molotov made it clear that in the view of the Soviet Government this draft as it stood was too vague and that it would be necessary to give it precision by adding

a nominal roll. We suggested that the list of States might be embodied in an unpublished annex to the treaty. He said that he thought that the Soviet Government would be willing to agree to this.

4. We submitted to him a draft for this purpose, the text, of which is given in my immediately succeeding telegram. (No. 66)

5. M. Molotov at once said that the inclusion of the Netherlands, Luxemburg and Switzerland introduced a new element into the negotiations. He reverted to his arithmetical arguments, which are now familiar enough not to require repetition. He thought it would be difficult if not impossible for the Soviet Government to accept obligations in respect of the Netherlands and Switzerland (he did not mention Luxemburg). In the first place the Soviet Government had no diplomatic relations with these two countries and it would therefore be juridically and politically objectionable for the Soviet Government to undertake obligations in respect of them. (We here pointed out that the obligation would not be to them but to us.) In the second place such obligations would represent a serious addition to those to be assumed by the Soviet Government. The fact that His Majesty's Government and the French Government had in this way extended the scope of the treaty would make it necessary for the Soviet Government in their turn to consider the situation afresh. There were two questions which they would have to study:-

    A. The possibility of establishing normal relations between the Soviet Union on the one side and the Netherlands and Switzerland on the other.

B. The possibility of obtaining compensation elsewhere for the increased obligation which the inclusion of these two countries in the list would involve for the Soviet Union. He noted, for example, that Poland and Turkey had made agreements of mutual assistance with both Great Britain and France. The Soviet Union would have to consider whether she could not make similar arrangements with Poland and Turkey so that the assistance which Poland and Turkey would undertake to afford to the Soviet Union might compensate for the assistance which the Soviet Union were now being asked to undertake to afford in respect of the Netherlands and Switzerland.

6. We asked whether this meant that the Soviet Government wished the present negotiations to be interrupted until these two questions could be settled. M Molotov replied that the two questions he had mentioned were logically and politically bound up with our proposal for an extension of Soviet obligations to cover the Netherlands and Switzerland. The Soviet Government must therefore study them carefully.

7. We asked whether this represented the official reply of the Soviet Government. M. Molotov said that what he had given was a preliminary expression of his personal reactions. He would submit our proposals to the Soviet Government and let us have a reply.

8. We left him in no doubt that the inclusion of the Netherlands and Switzerland was a matter of vital importance for Great Britain and France. The two Governments were ready to accept obligations in respect of all the States covering the Western border of the Soviet Union. It was essential to them as a matter of reciprocity that the Soviet Government should assume

corresponding obligations in respect of the Netherlands and Switzerland which were as important for Great Britain and France as were the Baltic States to the Soviet Union. The aim of the treaty being the establishment of security in Europe, the treaty must cover countries in Western European as well as in Eastern Europe.

9. During the conversation M. Molotov raised one other point in connexion with our new draft of article 1. Our draft provided for cases of direct aggression against one of the three contracting countries or against one of the states mentioned in the list. It did not make provision for cases of "indirect aggression." This would be particularly important in the case of the States mentioned in the list. He had in mind circumstances such as President Hacha's surrender last March. We told him that this was a new point. There was nothing about such "indirect aggression" in the Soviet draft of 2nd June (No. 48) and, indeed, our new draft gave the Soviet Government everything that they had asked for in their own draft. He replied that the question of "indirect aggression" had been discussed during the conversations and that the Soviet Government were as much entitled as were His Majesty's Government and the French Government to raise new points during the discussions. He suggested that the point might be met if the words direct or indirect could be inserted after the word "aggression" in the second place in which that word appears in our new draft article 1. We told him that we should have to refer this suggestion to our Governments.

No. 66.

Sir W. Seeds to Viscount Halifax.

(Telegraphic.) *Moscow, July 1, 1939.*

FOLLOWING is text referred to in paragraph 4 of my immediately preceding telegram: (No. 65)

"It is understood between the three contracting Governments that article 1 of the treaty between them signed to-day will apply to the following European States:-

"Estonia, Finland, Latvia, Poland, Roumania, Turkey, Greece, Belgium, Luxemburg, Netherlands and Switzerland.

"The foregoing list of countries is subject to revision by agreement between the three contracting Governments.

"The present understanding between the three Governments will not be made public."

No. 67.

Sir W. Seeds to Viscount Halifax.

(Telegraphic.) *Moscow, July 8, 1939.*

MY telegram of 1st July. (No. 65)

M. Molotov sent for us this afternoon to give us reply of the Soviet Government to our latest proposals.

2. He said that the Soviet Government (a) agreed to inclusion of the list of States in an unpublished protocol; (b)

could agree to include in the list only the eight States mentioned in article 1 (2) of their draft of 2nd June; (c) wished to suggest certain amendments to our drafts of article 1, the unpublished protocol and article 3.

3. He handed us revised Russian texts of these three drafts which M. Potemkin translated for us into French. For English translations please see my immediately following telegram (No. 68). The principal changes suggested by Soviet Government are:-

A mention of "direct and indirect" aggression in article 1; a definition of "indirect aggression" in the unpublished protocol; and reference to periodical exchange of view and mutual diplomatic support in article 3.

No. 68.

Sir W. Seeds to Viscount Halifax.

(Telegraphic.) *Moscow, July 3, 1939.*

MY immediately preceding telegram. (No. 67)

The following are the texts proposed by Soviet Government for article 1, for the unpublished protocol and for article 3:-

Article 1. - The United Kingdom, France and the U.S.S.R. undertake to give each other immediately all effective assistance if one of these three countries becomes involved in hostilities with any European Power as a result either of aggression aimed by that power against one of the three countries, or of aggression, *direct or indirect,* aimed by that Power against any European State whose independence or neutrality one of the three countries concerned feels obliged to defend against such aggression.

The assistance provided for in the present article will be given in uniformity with the principles of the League of Nations, but without it being necessary to follow the procedure of or to await action by the League.

Unpublished Protocol.

"It is understood between the three contracting Governments that article 1 of agreement between them signed today will apply to the following European States in the event either of direct aggression *or of "indirect aggression," under which latter term is to be understood an internal coup d'état or a reversal of policy in the interest of the aggressor:-*

"Estonia, Finland, Latvia, Poland, Roumania, Turkey, Greece, Belgium.

"The foregoing list of countries is subject to revision by agreement between the three contracting Governments.

"The present supplementary understanding will not be made public."

Article 3 to read as follows:-

"Without prejudice to the immediate rendering of assistance in accordance with article 1 and with a view to securing its more effective organisation, the three contracting Governments will exchange information periodically about the international situation and will lay down the lines of mutual diplomatic support in the interests of peace, and in the event of circumstances arising which threaten to call into operation the undertakings of mutual assistance contained in article 1, they will, on the request of any one of them, immediately consult together to examine the situation and to determine jointly the moment at which the mechanism of mutual assistance shall be put into immediate operation and manner of its application, independently of any procedure of the League of Nations."

No. 69.

Sir W. Seeds to Viscount Halifax.

(Telegraphic.) *Moscow, July 5, 1939.*

MY telegram of 3rd July. (No. 67)

We did not make much progress in regard to Holland and Switzerland.

2. When M. Molotov said that his Government could only accept secret list with omission of those two countries, I said we had reached a remarkable situation inasmuch as Soviet Government, which had always harped on our alleged lack of sincerity and on the unfairness of our proposals were now, after all our concessions, expecting British and French assistance in the event of direct or "indirect aggression" against any part of their European frontiers, while an aggressor had only to attack us through Holland or Switzerland in order to make sure that, under existing draft, Soviet Union would not be bound to come to our assistance.

3. M. Molotov said that Holland and Switzerland were a new extension of Soviet liabilities proposed by us after meeting of the Supreme Council, when he had mentioned (and obtained approval of the People's representatives) five countries plus Baltic States; no more countries could therefore be added. But later on he suggested that if Poland and Turkey made pacts of mutual assistance with Soviet Union those two countries could be dropped out of number of third party States and their names

replaced in list by those of Holland and Switzerland.

4. As regards alleged extension of Soviet Government's liabilities, French Ambassador pointed out that Soviet Government had originally offered more than they were doing now. By the present omission of article 1 (3) of the Soviet draft of 2nd June we were being, in fact, penalised for our concessions in regard to Baltic States. M. Molotov answered that acceptance of secret list was a concession on part of Soviet Government, and that it must be balanced by dropping provision about countries which might request assistance. He would not accept my argument that secret instead of published list was only a matter of form, while loss of a provision which might cover countries like Holland was one of substance.

5. He pointed out that Soviet Government were not objecting in principle to considering an extension or their liabilities in respect of those two countries, but they must have compensation in the form of treaties of mutual assistance with Poland and Turkey.

6. He only mentioned absence of diplomatic relations, with two countries as a technical difficulty, but we feel we cannot be sure that that obstacle will not be raised later.

No. 70.

Viscount Halifax to Sir W. Seeds (Moscow).

(Telegraphic.) *Foreign Office, July 6, 1939.*

YOUR telegrams of 3rd July. (Nos. 67, 68, 69)

1. The French Government are anxious that a further effort should be made to secure the inclusion of Holland, Switzerland and Luxemburg, and they are telegraphing

arguments to be employed in further discussion with M. Molotov. I concur, and you may concert with your French colleague in exhausting every possible means of securing inclusion of these three countries, but if, as I anticipate, M. Molotov remains adamant you may inform him that His Majesty's Government agree, though very reluctantly, to omission of Holland, Switzerland and Luxemburg, but only on condition that satisfactory solution is found of question of "indirect aggression."

2. The definition of "indirect aggression" which the Soviet Government now proposes is completely unacceptable. We could not possibly defend it either to the countries concerned or to public opinion here. Questions as to the meaning of "indirect aggression," if this term is employed in the published agreement, are bound to be raised, and, if so, we should either have to reply in the sense of the definition in the unpublished protocol, or give an untrue statement of the position.

3. It must be remembered that this phrase, and the secret definition of it, have not previously appeared in the discussions, and are now suggested for the first time. The use of the term "indirect aggression" would confirm the worst suspicions of the Baltic States, whose objection to the proposed treaty rests largely on their fear of Russian interference in their internal affairs. M. Molotov seems impervious to the argument that it is undesirable to drive the Baltic States gratuitously into the arms of Germany, but we cannot overlook this consideration.

4. Nevertheless we would be prepared to meet fully M. Molotov's demand that Russia should be covered not, only in the case of "direct aggression," but of "indirect aggression," such as that practised against Czecho-Slovakia on 15th March last (the case to which he seems constantly to be referring). We should accordingly propose that the first paragraph of the unpublished protocol should be altered to read as follows:-

"It is understood between the three contracting Governments that article 1 of the agreement between them signed to-day will apply to the following European States, and that *the word "aggression" is to be understood as covering action accepted by the state in question under threat of force by another Power and involving the abandonment by it of its independence or neutrality.*"

5. It is understood that for the reason stated in paragraph 3, article 1 of the agreement should speak only of aggression omitting words "direct or indirect."

6. Although prepared in the last resort to agree to the omission of Holland, Switzerland and Luxemburg subject to agreement on the point about "indirect aggression" on lines indicated above, I am anxious that some provision should be made in the treaty for dealing with German aggression on these three countries. You should, therefore, try to induce M. Molotov to agree to include in the unpublished protocol a provision for immediate consultation between the three Governments at the request of any one of them in the event of aggression against Holland, Switzerland or Luxemburg. Such a provision should also not figure in the agreement itself, but would have to be inserted in the unpublished protocol.

7. We would be prepared to accept the above solution outlined in preceding paragraphs, provided that it secures a rapid settlement and that the other outstanding points are disposed of according to the instructions which you already have.

No. 71.

Viscount Halifax to Sir W. Seeds (Moscow).

Foreign Office, July 6, 1939.

Sir,

I ASKED the Soviet Ambassador to call on the 6th July to discuss recent developments in our negotiations with the Soviet Government. I said that I was glad to note that agreement had been reached on certain important points. We had informed M. Molotov that we were willing to agree to a list being drawn up and he had agreed that this list should not be published. Although we did not expect the list would remain a secret, we thought this procedure preferable.

2. Unfortunately, two further difficulties had arisen during the last exchange of views at Moscow. In the first place, the Soviet Government had objected to the inclusion of the Netherlands and Switzerland in the list. This caused us very great difficulty as we had always supposed that the Soviet Government were in favour of complete reciprocity. As we had now agreed to guarantee the east of Europe we expected that the Soviet Government would be prepared to give similar guarantee for Western Europe. M Molotov had taken the line that he only had authority to guarantee eight States - Poland, Turkey, Roumania, Greece, Belgium, Finland, Estonia and Latvia. Therefore, unless two of the States were left out, he was not in a position to include two additional States, He had therefore suggested that his difficulties might be removed if the Soviet Government were to negotiate pacts of mutual assistance with Poland and Turkey. This seemed to us a curious argument and did not meet our difficulty regarding the question of reciprocity. M. Molotov's attitude also seemed to us to be a departure from what we had understood to be the general aims of Soviet policy as defined by M. Stalin on the 10th March.

3. Our second difficulty was that M. Molotov now desired the words "indirect aggression" to he added in the text of the

published treaty and a definition of the meaning of these words to be included in the unpublished annex. The suggested Soviet definition was quite unacceptable to us since it could be represented as authorising almost unlimited interference in the affairs of the Baltic States. We had gone as far as we possibly can in dealing with the Baltic States and we could not accept a formula of this nature. We had therefore redrafted it in such a way as to meet the sort of case which M. Molotov seemed to have in mind, *e.g.*, conduct such as that of Dr. Hacha and the Czecho-Slovak Government in submitting to a threat of force last March. We hoped it would be possible to reach agreement on the basis of our redraft. I intended to send fresh instructions to Moscow tonight if the French Government agreed, but I could not conceal from M. Maisky that it would be difficult for us if M. Molotov still felt unable to include the Netherlands and Switzerland in the list.

4. M. Maisky thanked me for my information and said that although he was kept informed by his own Government, it was helpful to have the views of both sides. He reminded me, however, that the negotiations were being conducted in Moscow, and that it was therefore difficult for him to say anything definite. He saw the difficulties but did not think they were insurmountable.

5. I then asked M. Maisky for his personal advice on the following question. I thought all delay was most regrettable and I had no doubt we were in agreement that it was important to get something settled quickly. I therefore wanted, if the French Government agreed, to send a telegram to Moscow laying down the limits within which a settlement could be reached and giving a certain latitude to our negotiators to reach agreement within these limits, thus putting an end to the perpetual exchange of telegrams and delays. If, however, there were still further difficulties, I wondered whether it might not be better to fall back upon a purely tripartite agreement as an immediate

possibility and then pursue our discussions afterwards with regard to the questions concerning other States.

6. M. Maisky replied that he could only express his personal opinion on this point but it occurred to him that M. Molotov had suggested such a solution on the 16th June. If we wanted to reach a quick result, he thought we might, however, include in the treaty the eight States about which we were already agreed. This would give a far wider basis than the purely tripartite agreement and other questions could be left over for discussion. I pointed out that there would still remain the difficulty about the definition of "indirect aggression" and that it might take considerable time to find a formula to meet this difficulty.

7. I asked M. Maisky some questions regarding the method of negotiation in Moscow, but could only elicit from him that M. Molotov had to refer back to a Committee of the People's Commissars, similar to our own Foreign Policy Committee, although he himself had the usual authority of a Foreign Minister in conducting negotiations.

No. 72.

Sir W. Seeds to Viscount Halifax.

(Telegraphic.) *Moscow, July 9, 1939.*

WE spent nearly three hours with M. Molotov this evening and went over the whole ground again.

2. Soviet Government insist on inclusion of the words "direct or indirect" in article 1. We said that we were not authorised to agree to this.

3. M. Molotov submitted a completely new draft of the protocol which he now calls a "supplementary letter." For

translation of this draft please see my immediately following telegram. (No. 73)

4. We asked him what kind of case the phrase "without any such threat" was designed to cover. M. Molotov made an obscure reference to Danzig, and added that Latvia or Estonia might, for example, make an agreement with Germany which would be inconsistent with their independence or neutrality without there being any threat of force on Germany's part. We also asked him what was meant by the term "use of the forces of the State in question." The example he gave was the employment of German officers or instructors by the Estonian or Latvian army and the consequent transformation of those armies into instruments of aggression against the Soviet Union.

5. You will see from paragraph 2 of M. Molotov's new draft of the protocol that Holland and Switzerland are included in the list, but that it is stated that the agreement will only apply to them when Turkey and Poland have concluded pacts of mutual assistance with the Soviet Union. M. Molotov added during our conversation that it would be necessary also that Holland and Switzerland should be in diplomatic relations with the Soviet Union before article 1 could apply to them. He declined to include Luxemburg in the list.

6. A long discussion took place on article 6 (relation between the political agreement and military agreement). M. Molotov said that it was absolutely essential in the view of the Soviet Government that these two agreements should not merely enter into force but also he signed simultaneously. There were differences of opinion among members of the Soviet Government on some points connected with the agreement, but on this point they were unanimous. As the result of persistent questioning we were able to discover that the procedure which M. Molotov would accept is the following. As soon as agreement has been reached on the text of the seven articles of

the political agreement, the text of each article in three languages would be initialled. Conversations between the General Staffs would then immediately begin, and on the conclusion of the negotiations for a military agreement the texts of the political and military agreements would be signed at the same time and come into force simultaneously. Although the text of the political agreement would have been settled this agreement would exist only as a series of articles and not as a diplomatic instrument until such time as signature of the two instruments could take place. The articles of the political agreement would not be published before signature, although as soon as the text had been agreed upon announcements could be made by the three Governments outlining the contents of the various articles.

7. We expressed our astonishment and pointed out to M. Molotov with the greatest emphasis our objections to this course but he was quite immovable. He said that without a military agreement the political agreement would he a mere empty declaration and the Soviet Government were not prepared to sign any political agreement unless they could at the same time sign a military agreement which would form an organic whole with the political agreement. The only suggestion he was apparently prepared to make was that a date should be fixed in article 6 for the conclusion of the military agreement.

8. In these circumstances my French colleague and I think we can carry the negotiations no further without further instructions.

No. 73.

Sir W. Seeds to Viscount Halifax.

(Telegraphic.) *Moscow, July 9, 1939.*

FOLLOWING is translation of draft referred to in paragraph 8 of my immediately preceding telegram. (No. 72)

"Supplementary letter:
"The three contracting Governments have agreed as follows:-

"Article 1 of the agreement signed by them to-day will apply to the following European States: Turkey, Greece, Roumania, Poland, Belgium, Estonia, Latvia, Finland, Switzerland, Netherlands.

2. "As regards the two last-named States (Switzerland and Netherlands) the agreement will only enter into force if and when Poland and Turkey conclude pacts of mutual assistance with the U.S.S.R.

3. *"The expression 'indirect aggression', covers action accepted by any of the above mentioned states under threat of force by another Power, or without such threat, involving the use of the territory and forces of the State in question for purposes of aggression against that State or against one of the contracting parties, and consequently involving the loss by that State of its independence or the violation of its neutrality.*

"The foregoing list of States is subject to revision by agreement between the three contracting Governments.

"The present supplementary agreement will not be made public."

No. 74.

Viscount Halifax to Sir W. Seeds (Moscow).

(Telegraphic.) *Foreign Office, July 12, 1939.*

YOUR telegrams of 9th July. (Nos. 72 and 73)

I fear that we cannot possibly accept M. Molotov's formula as given in paragraph 3 of your telegram. (No. 73) Our concern throughout has been to avoid anything which might give the impression that the signatories claimed the right to intervene in the internal affairs of the countries with whose independence and neutrality they are interested. It was for this reason that in trying to describe "indirect aggression" we have always applied two tests: (1) that the Government of the country concerned should be acting against its will under threat of force by another Power; and (2) that the action should involve the abandonment by that State of its independence or neutrality. To carry definition of indirect aggression beyond this point is to defeat our own ends, for the methods by which a country can be coerced so as to abandon its independence or neutrality are so manifold that it is impossible in the scope of any formula to cover all eventualities, and to try to do so is bound to lead to nothing but suspicions and misunderstandings, both between the signatories themselves and among the other countries concerned. This not only would not serve the purposes which we and the Soviet Government have at heart, but would most certainly undermine our whole moral position in Europe generally, and give the German Government invaluable opportunity for setting the smaller countries against us.

2. But it is precisely such over-definition that the Russian Government appear to be aiming at, and the result is a formula which I am convinced would fill the States concerned with most profound suspicions as to our intentions.

3. The words "or without any such threat" would, as you have realised, allow each signatory to decide whether any voluntary arrangement which the State in question might make with a potential aggressor was to be interpreted as being "for purposes of aggression" even though no aggression had taken

place. Such a claim to interpret and pass judgment upon the actions of an independent State is one to which His Majesty's Government could not possibly be a party.

4. The insertion in M. Molotov's formula of the words "and forces" after territory would similarly be open to abuse and is therefore likewise objectionable.

5. Again the words "for purposes of aggression" would seem to give each signatory the right to judge whether the "use" to which the territory and forces of the State concerned were being put were "for purposes of aggression" or not. The signatory having decided that even though no aggression had occurred the ulterior object was aggression, might on the strength of this unilateral decision proceed to hostilities and thereby claim to bring the whole guarantee system of the agreement into play. Similarly, the word "consequently" would imply that each signatory was the judge whether something short of complete subservience to a foreign State was to be considered as constituting the loss of independence or neutrality.

6. Lastly, I see grave objections to the provision which is made in M. Molotov's formula with reference to aggression against the State in question in addition to aggression against one of the contracting parties. This no doubt is intended to cover the case of a civil war or coup d'état in which foreign forces were participating, but I do not think that this eventuality can be safely covered by any form of words and it ought not to be attempted. In fact, I am not prepared to accept the view that changes of Government, even if brought about by civil wars or coups d'état in the countries concerned, must necessarily threaten the interests of one or other of the signatory Powers and must on that account be prevented. The test still remains whether or not the country concerned has lost its independence or neutrality, and that is provided for in our formula. It would

be highly unwise to proceed on the assumption that a coup d'état or civil war must necessarily deprive the country of its independence or neutrality merely because at some stage or other another State had "used" the territory of the State in question.

7. In short, any attempt to amend M. Molotov's formula can only be satisfactory if it is reduced in effect to the substance of our original formula as set forth in paragraph 4 of my telegram of 6th July. (No. 70)

8. I am not clear whether when you presented our formula to M. Molotov he rejected it outright, and if so gave any reasons for this rejection; or whether he merely offered his own formula as an alternative. In any case you should now tell him that for the reasons given in the preceding paragraphs you are unable to accept his formula of 9th July, and urge him as strongly as you possibly can to study our formula with the utmost care, since in substance it represents the utmost limit that we are prepared to go in the direction of a definition of "indirect aggression." I do not insist upon preserving every word in the present text, but the general sense is essential to our purpose. If he is prepared to examine it without prejudice and without unwarranted suspicions, he will realise that it covers all the possible cases which would justify the Soviet Government in calling upon their allies to join them in going to war with Germany over events occurring in one of the limitrophe States. You will also realise that whereas our definition should not unduly offend the susceptibilities or arouse the fears of the limitrophe States any further definition would most certainly do so.

9. Incidentally, we should prefer, if our formula is accepted, to embody it in article 1 of the Agreement instead of relegating it to the unpublished annex. In that case any reference to "direct or indirect" aggression in article 1 would be unnecessary but we

would be ready to agree to the retention of the phrase if M. Molotov attaches importance to it.

10. I will now turn to, the new difficulty which M. Molotov has raised in insisting that the political agreement must wait upon a military agreement, which will only be signed simultaneously. We most strongly object to this completely abnormal procedure. The fact that M. Molotov should make this demand reveals a suspicion of our sincerity and *bona fides* which is most offensive and quite unjustifiable, more especially as we are prepared immediately on signature to start military conversations. The natural course in all agreements of mutual assistance is for the political agreement to precede the military arrangements. The insistence of the Soviet Government that the political shall be dependent on the military agreement suggests that unpleasant suspicion that the Soviet Government hope by this means to force us to accept military condition which would be against our better judgment. Otherwise it is difficult to see what the Soviet Government stand to gain by withholding their signature to the political agreement until the military arrangements have been completed. With the best will in the world the latter may take considerable time, and during the period the absence of any political agreement will naturally be exploited by the German Government's evidence that the negotiations with the Soviet Government have broken down. We are sure that the Soviet Government will not wish to produce this impression any more than we do. You should therefore urge M. Molotov most strongly to persuade his Government not to insist upon this condition.

11. I appreciate the fact that I am setting you an arduous task in instructing you to reject the two chief proposals which M. Molotov made to you at your last interview. But we are nearing the point where we clearly cannot continue the process of conceding each fresh demand put forward by the Soviet Government. In order to meet M. Molotov we have made the

following concessions: (1) We have met the Soviet Government's demand that the treaty should cover the case of the Baltic States; (2) We have abandoned our demand that the Netherlands, Switzerland and Luxemburg should be included among the countries to be covered by the agreement; (3) we have agreed to provide for the case of "indirect aggression"; (4) we have, against our better judgment, undertaken to define it; (5) we are prepared to insert this definition in the agreement itself; (6) We have accepted M. Molotov's proposal that the agreement should contain a provision prohibiting the signatories from concluding a separate armistice or peace.

12. If, in return for all these concessions, the Soviet Government are unwilling to meet us on the two points now at issue His Majesty's Government may have to reconsider their whole position. I do not suggest that you should actually say this to M. Molotov at the present stage, but it would be useful if you could find means of giving him to understand that our patience is well-nigh exhausted, and that he will do well not to presume any further on our readiness to yield to the Soviet Government each time they put forward a new demand.

No. 75.

Sir W. Seeds to Viscount Halifax.

(Telegraphic.) *Moscow, July 17, 1939.*

WE had a meeting to-day as M. Molotov was unable to receive us yesterday.

2. After telling M. Molotov that we proposed as a concession to the Soviet Government's general views to put definition of "indirect aggression" into text of article 1 and even

to retaining words "direct and indirect," I said that His Majesty's Government regarded it as of greatest, and even decisive, importance that definition should be such as not to arouse suspicions of independent and neutral States and that I had received most precise instructions as to limits beyond which His Majesty's Government were not prepared to go in this matter. I said we were in agreement with the Soviet Government regarding, the case where a Government under threat of force from an aggressor took action against its will in sense which entailed loss of independence or neutrality, but we must avoid anything capable of being interpreted as an intention of interfering in another country's internal affairs. Formula must provide for a case where there existed a threat of force and where independence or neutrality was thereby imperilled, but nothing vaguer or more far reaching could be accepted. For these reasons His Majesty's Government could not agree to latest Soviet formula and I was instructed to press the Soviet Government urgently to accept our definition, which, if carefully and impartially examined, would be seen to cover all that was required and all that was legitimate.

3. M. Molotov said that our formula was inacceptable; it was too vague and too restricted. In reply to question, he said that he must insist on the inclusion of the words "without threat of force" (because otherwise formula would not cover case like that of President Hacha, who would have denied that he was acting under threat) and of words "use of territory and forces." After vainly protesting that his formula could be interpreted as empowering one signatory to drag other signatories into hostilities if a third Government exercised its right to decide its own policy, I suggested that we were prepared to consider verbal changes in our formula so long as substance was maintained. But he was not to be moved. Soviet definition represented official decision of his Government and he kept on pressing us to pass on to the next item on agenda.

4. We then submitted a new draft of the protocol omitting the Netherlands and Switzerland from the lists of States, but adding a general formula providing for consultation "in the event of aggression or threat of aggression by a European Power against a European State not named in the foregoing list." M. Molotov said that he noted with satisfaction that the two Governments were disposed to omit the Netherlands and Switzerland from the list and that he would consider the formula for consultation which they had submitted, though at first sight it raised doubts in his mind.

5. M. Molotov then asked whether we had any further remarks to make on other points. We turned to article 6 (No. 48) and put to him the arguments contained in paragraph 10 of your telegram of 12th July (No. 74). M. Molotov made it clear at once that the Soviet Government must insist upon the simultaneous entry into force of the political and military agreements. He said indeed that in the Soviet conception there would not be two agreements (a political and a military agreement), but a single politico-military agreement. The political part would have no existence without the military part. The Soviet Government wished to have the military obligations and contributions on each side clearly settled. On this point there should be no misunderstanding. Unless His Majesty's Government and the French Government could agree that the political and military parts of the agreement between the three countries should form one organic and inseparable whole, there was no point in pursuing the present conversations. He begged us to put this point to our Governments, and proposed that further discussion should be adjourned until an understanding on this point had been reached. He alleged that it had been throughout the idea of the Soviet Government that there should be a single politico-military agreement, and that the idea of separating the two agreements had been introduced into the discussions at a later stage. In the circumstances we did not think any useful purpose would be served by arguing about this

extremely debatable assertion.

6. He said that, if this point of fundamental principle could be settled, the question of how agreement on the text of the political articles was to be recorded was a technical matter of secondary importance. We reminded him that he had agreed at our last meeting that the political articles might be initialled when agreement had been reached on them, and that statements might he made in public by the Governments concerned giving the substance of the articles on which agreement had been reached. M. Molotov did not, however, commit himself definitely to agree to this procedure.

7. He put the definite question whether or not His Majesty's Government and French Government were really willing to open military conversations. We assured him that they were, and the French Ambassador said that he thought the French Government would be willing to begin military conversations at once without waiting for the signature on the political agreement. M Molotov asked me my opinion, and I told him that we should be ready without further delay to start technical conversations, but only if agreement had been reached on the articles now under discussion. French Ambassador asked whether the idea of the Soviet Government was to open military conversation at once before conclusion of discussion on the political articles and parallel with those discussions. M. Molotov said that if the two Governments made an official proposal in this sense he thought that the Soviet Government might agree.

8. He repeated that the question to which he asked us to obtain a definite answer was whether the two Governments were prepared to agree that political and military parts of the agreement should form one organic whole.

9. M. Molotov then started to rise with the remark that

our two Governments' decision on this question was the crucial point and nothing else mattered much. I stopped him and begged to remind him of what I had said on the question of "indirect aggression," which was of supreme importance to His Majesty's Government. I said frankly that my reports on our latest conversations had produced a painful impression in London, where it was felt that we were making fruitless concessions. Our stock of goodwill was not yet exhausted, and His Majesty's Government would give full consideration to Soviet views regarding article 6; in return we hoped for similar goodwill in regard to definition of indirect aggression. In reply he gave me no encouragement beyond general assurance of goodwill.

No. 76.

Sir W. Seeds to Viscount Halifax.

(Telegraphic.) *Moscow, July 23, 1939.*

WE saw M. Molotov this afternoon.

2. I opened the proceedings by saying that I had faithfully reported to your Lordship the capital importance attached by the Soviet Government to the simultaneous entry into force of the political and military agreements. His Majesty's Government's objection to this course had been mainly of a practical character, since they feared that the existence of an interval between the conclusion of the political agreement and its entry into force would encourage an aggressor. I was happy to inform him that His Majesty's Government, with the goodwill they had always shown in these negotiations, and after consultation with the French Government, now accepted article

6 as it appeared in the Soviet draft and agreed to the simultaneous entry into force of the two agreements. M. Molotov expressed his keen satisfaction.

3. I observed that two points now remained outstanding, the chief of which was the definition of "indirect aggression" in article 1. I recalled that at our last conversation I had assured M. Molotov that His Majesty's Government would examine the question of article 6 with complete goodwill, and had expressed the hope that the Soviet Government would study with the same sympathy the question of the definition of "indirect aggression," which was a question of principle for us. We had submitted to him revised drafts of article 1 and of the protocol. We hoped that M. Molotov was in a position to say that the Soviet Government accepted them.

4. In reply to a question by M. Molotov, the French Ambassador said that the French Government were in full agreement with what I had said.

5. M. Molotov said that he had already explained the point of view of the Soviet Government as regards the definition of "indirect aggression" in article 1 and as regards the protocol. He did not now think, however, that these questions would raise insuperable difficulties, and he was convinced that the three Governments could find a formula, which could satisfy them. The important point from the Soviet point of view was to define the form and extent of military engagements of the contracting parties. Was he right in taking our reply to mean that, in our view the three Governments had reached a basis for an agreement, and that the engagements to be undertaken by the three Governments should now be concretely defined? I asked him whether he meant by this question that military conversations should be started. He said that he did. I said that His Majesty's Government were ready to start military conversations, but they wished first to reach agreement on the

outstanding political points; as M. Molotov had said that there would be no insuperable difficulty about this I thought it preferable that the outstanding political points should be settled at once so that there might be a political basis on which the military conversations could be conducted.

6. M. Molotov repeated that he did not foresee any insuperable difficulty about article 1 and the protocol, and for that reason it was necessary to start military conversations immediately. Since His Majesty's Government and the French Government had now agreed to the simultaneous entry into force of the two parts of the agreement, it was essential that there should be no further delay about the opening of military conversations.

7. The French Ambassador observed that in order to study the military problems it was necessary that the main political basis should be settled. It was, therefore, desirable to try to reach agreement at once on the two outstanding points since if there was no agreement on these, a study of the military problems would not be possible.

8. M. Molotov replied that although the definition of "indirect aggression" would not present insuperable difficulties, it was a delicate question on which there was still a slight difference of view. If we now pursued discussions on this subject and put off the military conversations, we should lose more time. The international situation was such as to impose on the three Governments the duty of making concrete arrangements with the least possible delay. The French Ambassador said that he understood the Soviet proposal to be that military conversations should start at once. M. Molotov agreed. The French Ambassador repeated that French military experts, before they started conversations, would have to be informed of the political basis which had been agreed upon for the military conversations. M. Molotov thought the political

basis was already clear enough to permit of the opening of military conversations. It would be a needless waste of time to put off military conversations until the last remaining details were settled. The fact that the three countries were engaged in settling the concrete details of their obligations would be of great interest to possible aggressors.

9. I said that His Majesty's Government had no intention of wasting time. I was ready to report by telegram at once what he had said, but, pending a reply to his proposals, could we not get to work on settling the two outstanding points? M. Molotov asked why it was thought necessary to waste time upon points of detail and delay the consideration of the essential problem, *i.e.*, the military conversations, without which the treaty would have no substance. I repeated that I thought it would be useful to go on discussing article 1 and the protocol pending a reply from His Majesty's Government and the French Government. I felt bound to insist also that the question of the definition of "indirect aggression" was, for His Majesty's Government, not a point of detail, but a question of principle.

10. M. Molotov repeated that once the military experts had started their indispensible work of defining the military obligations of contracting parties, the two outstanding political points could easily be settled. I asked him whether the Soviet Government were ready to accept the two principles which formed the basis of our proposed definition of "indirect aggression," namely, that the State in question should be acting under threat of force, and that its action should involve the abandonment of its independence and neutrality. Could I report to His Majesty's Government that Soviet Government accepted these two principles? M. Molotov gave no reply to this question beyond repeating once again, this time in the name of the Soviet Government that, during military conversations, the outstanding political points could easily be settled.

11. He then asked whether His Majesty's Government and the French Government had any objection to the immediate opening of military conversations or whether they still had some doubts on the subject.

12. The French Ambassador repeated that military conversations must have a political basis. He recited the articles of draft treaty on which agreement had been reached and the two points which were still outstanding. Even if His Majesty's Government and the French Government were ready to start military conversations immediately, it would be necessary for the three Governments to record that they had reached an agreement on such and such articles and that there were still differences of view on two outstanding points. I said that I saw no obstacle to the immediate opening of military conversations except for the two points still outstanding.

13. M. Molotov asked whether he was to take it that His Majesty's Government and the French Government would be unwilling to open military conversations until these two points had been settled.

14. The French Ambassador replied that proposal made by M. Molotov was a new one, and that, until he had reported it to the French Government and learned their views he could not give an official answer to M. Molotov's question. I said that this was also my position. He said he was not sure whether we were right in saying that his proposal was a new one. At our last interview he had spoken about the immediate opening of military conversations. The French Ambassador and I said that we thought he had spoken chiefly about the simultaneous entry into force of the two parts of the agreement.

15. I asked whether M. Molotov's idea was that the military conversations and the political discussions on the two outstanding points should be carried on concurrently. He

replied that it was. I asked him whether he had thought where military conversations would take place. He said he hoped that, if His Majesty's Government and the French Government saw no objection, they might be held in Moscow and that they might open immediately. He hoped that the two Governments would be able to give their reply very soon.

16. French Ambassador thought that, if it was decided to start military conversations, it would be desirable to issue a joint communiqué announcing that such a decision had been taken. I agreed and suggested that declarations might also be made by the Governments concerned. I said that our public opinion would wish to be assured that we had not been wasting our time in Moscow and that progress had been made on the main points. French Ambassador thought announcement might be to the effect that the three Governments considered political conversations to be sufficiently advanced for military conversations to be opened.

17. M. Molotov promised to study this suggestion.

18. French Ambassador thought it was true to say that, if the three Governments started military conversations, this in itself would imply that they had reached agreement on the main political questions and that they took a common view in regard to international affairs and had the same objects. M. Molotov agreed with this statement, but said the military part of the agreement was more important than the political part, and, since the political part would have no existence without the military part, he was not quite sure whether any preliminary declaration by the Governments concerned about the political articles would be necessary.

19. French Ambassador and I observed that French and British Ministers would certainly be questioned in Parliament and would have to say something to the effect that the three

Governments had reached agreement on the main political questions and that they were now passing on to military conversations. I said that I agreed with M Molotov that the political treaty would not be effective without the military treaty, but, from the point of view of public opinion, this was not the point. The public would ask what the two ambassadors had been doing in Moscow all these months, and it would be necessary to give them some information.

20. M. Molotov observed in conclusion that the mere fact that the military conversations were starting would have a much greater effect in the world than an announcement that could be made about the political articles. It would be a powerful demonstration on the part of the three Governments.

No. 77.

Viscount Halifax to Sir W. Seeds (Moscow).

(Telegraphic.) *Foreign Office, July 25, 1939.*

YOU should now inform M. Molotov that His Majesty's Government are ready to agree to immediate initiation of military conversations at Moscow without waiting for final agreement on article 1 and protocol, or any other outstanding points in agreement. I hope in a few days to give you names of our representatives and the probable date of their arrival. For your information on purely material grounds some little time must elapse before the members of the military mission can be selected from the three services and supplied with the necessary data and authority. This will be done with the utmost urgency.

2. Meanwhile, you should make it clear to M. Molotov, when informing him that we will start military conversations, that,

whilst he may attach capital importance to them, we attach capital importance also to a satisfactory settlement of article 1. We shall accordingly expect that present discussions will be resumed forthwith, with a view to settlement of outstanding questions in political agreement in particular article 1, and we hope that M. Molotov will, in a similar spirit, meet us on the points to which, as expressed above, we attach such capital importance so that they may now be brought to a speedy and satisfactory conclusion at the earliest possible moment.

3. From what you report of M. Molotov's attitude there would appear to be some prospect now that Soviet Government may not be rigid over article 1 and that the moment in which we announce our readiness to start military conversations immediately may be the most favourable one for inducing them to meet us over article 1.

No. 78.

Viscount Halifax to Sir W. Seeds (Moscow).

Foreign Office, July 25, 1939.

Sir,

THE Soviet Ambassador called on the 25th July, and I informed him of the result of your Excellency's latest conversation with the Soviet Minister for Foreign Affairs.

2. I told M. Maisky that you had informed M. Molotov that we understood that the Soviet Government regarded article 6 to be the most important point at issue, and that you had been authorised to meet the Soviet Government by agreeing to the simultaneous conclusion of military and political conversations. We continued, however, to attach great importance to the question of "indirect aggression" dealt with in article 1, and we hoped that agreement might be reached on this point. M

Molotov had replied expressing appreciation of our attitude regarding article 1, and had suggested that it should not be too difficult to reach agreement on article 1.

3. M. Molotov had asked whether we would agree to the immediate opening of military conversations, his idea being that this would avoid any further delay and would have a good effect on the general situation. I went on to inform M. Maisky that you had referred M. Molotov's question to me, and that we were now instructing you to agree to military conversations being opened as soon as a suitable military mission could he collected. The French Government were following the same course.

4. We thought that it would take at least a week or ten days to appoint a suitable military mission, and to provide its members with the necessary instructions. We had originally thought that Paris would be the best place for these conversations, but, in view of M. Molotov's insistence, we were now prepared to agree to them being held at Moscow.

5. I emphasised to M. Maisky that we continued to attach capital importance to reaching agreement on the political articles, and that we hoped that, as we had met M. Molotov on the question of Staff conversations, he would now he prepared to meet us over the question of "indirect aggression." As M. Maisky knew, we thought that our formula fully covered the case of Czecho-Slovakia. but if any other case should arise which was not covered by our formula, we were prepared for immediate consultation just as we, on our part, expected the Soviet Government to agree to similar consultation in the case of the Netherlands and Switzerland.

6. We agreed with M. Molotov that the opening of military conversations would have a real value as regards world public opinion and we hoped it would also remove any doubts that might exist in the minds of the Soviet Government. We

should therefore be disappointed if real progress could not now be made.

7. M. Maisky thought that the arrangement which I had outlined to him was a good one, and that the deterrent value of Staff conversations would be very great and impress the outside world more than any other step could have done. Meanwhile we could proceed with the elaboration of the outstanding political points. I said that I hoped there would be no delay over this, and that instructions were being sent to you to see M. Molotov to try to reach an agreement on these points without waiting for the arrival of our military mission in Moscow. I asked M. Maisky whether be had any indication of the views of his Government about the most recent developments. He replied that they considered real progress had been made. They welcomed this fact and hoped that we were now approaching the end of our negotiations.

8. M. Maisky then enquired what detailed arrangements we had in mind and whether the members Staff mission had yet been selected. I told him that I had already approached Lord Chatfield and that I could assure him that there would be no unnecessary delay. We should require to consult the Soviet Government shortly about the terms of a statement which we should have to make in Parliament probably at the beginning of next week. This would be no more than a general statement to the effect that certain political points were still outstanding, but that the three Governments were engaging at once in military conversations. Finally, I impressed upon M. Maisky that this information must be kept confidential for the present.

No. 79.

Sir W. Seeds to Viscount Halifax.

(Telegraphic.) *Moscow, July 27, 1939.*

AT our meeting with M. Molotov this afternoon I spoke to him in the sense of your telegram of 25th July (No. 77) informing him of the agreement of His Majesty's Government to the immediate initiation of military conversations in Moscow, and of their expectation that discussions on outstanding political points would be resumed forthwith. The French Ambassador spoke in the same sense and hoped Soviet Government would help the two military missions to find convenient accommodation in Moscow. This M. Molotov promised to do. M. Molotov was unable, in reply to question by French Ambassador, to give any information as to the composition of Soviet delegation.

In reply to my observation about the settlement of outstanding political points, M. Molotov said that Soviet Government were studying the question of "indirect aggression."

2. I asked him whether the definition could be discussed at an early meeting without waiting for the arrival of the military mission. It was important for His Majesty's Government that this question should be settled without delay.

3. M. Molotov enquired whether the attitude of His Majesty's Government and French Government on this point was immovable. Would they refuse any modification in their formula? If so, solution would be difficult to reach.

4. I replied that as I had told him before, we were ready to

admit changes of wording, but the substance must be preserved. The basis of our definition was: (a) that there should be threat of force; (b) that there should be abandonment of independence and neutrality. Our formula was wide enough to cover any legitimate case that might arise. If we tried to make the definition wider, we should find ourselves countenancing interference in internal affairs of third States; and this His Majesty's Government were not prepared to do. I hoped that, before our next meeting, he would look at our formula again, and see if he could suggest some alternative which, though it might change the words, would maintain substance.

5. M. Molotov said that he thought our formula could be improved. It ought to be amended so as to cover the case of President Hacha, and also the case of Danzig, *i.e.*, the case of all internal movement which modified the external position of another State. He hoped that His Majesty's Government and the French Government would have alternative drafts to propose as well as the Soviet Government; if so, he was convinced that a satisfactory formula could be found.

6. French Ambassador said that the definition of "indirect aggression" was important and that all three Governments were agreed in trying to find a means of dealing with a new form of aggression. But His Majesty's Government and the French Government wished to avoid using expressions which implied that the three Governments would interfere in internal affairs of other States.

7. I said that in the view of His Majesty's Government the case of President Hacha was fully covered by our draft. There had been an evident threat of force. What President Hacha might say about it was not evidence.

8. French Ambassador suggested certain historical examples might be quoted in the protocol to illustrate meaning

of the term "indirect aggression." M. Molotov asked with a smile, whether it would not be as well to quote future cases also. He again asked that the two Governments should try to find a compromise formula. My French colleague and I said that we would do so and compare our results with his. I asked him whether we might have an interview for this purpose at an early date, and he said he had no objection.

No. 80.

Statement by the Prime Minister in the House of Commons on July 31, 1939, about Military Missions.

THE Soviet Government has proposed that at the present state of the negotiations it would be an advantage to begin military conversations forthwith. His Majesty's Government and the French Government have concurred, and arrangements are being made to send British and French military representatives to Moscow as soon as possible. It is proposed that, concurrently with the military conversations, political discussions should continue with a view to reaching final conclusion on the terms of the political agreement. The British delegation will be headed by Admiral the Hon. Sir Reginald Plunkett Ernle-Erle-Drax, and will include Air-Marshal Sir Charles Burnett and Major-General Heywood.

No. 81.

Extracts from Speeches by the Prime Minister and the Parliamentary Under-Secretary of State for Foreign Affairs in the House of Commons on July 31, 1939.

The Prime Minister: The hon. member and the right hon. gentleman opposite both devoted a large part of their speeches to the negotiations with Russia. Both of them suggested, though they did not actually say so, that the delay in coming to an agreement was entirely the fault of this Government. I do not know whether the French Government were also included. Both of them said that they had been kept in the dark although the hon. member opposite afterwards professed to give a time-table, I think he called it, of the negotiations to illustrate his thesis that the delay had all been on the side of the British Government.

He said it in such a way as to convey the impression, the deliberate impression, that though he did not seek to allocate the blame, meaning to say that he could not prove it he wished the House to understand that the blame did lie, and lie entirely, with the Government. The hon. member opposite has been very proud of his persistence in asking questions about the course of these negotiations for a long period of time, and, in fact, he has tried for a long time to goad me into recriminations against the Soviet Government by seeking to put the blame for the delay upon this Government. If I have restrained myself, if I have refused to enter into discussion as to the, differences which prevented the completion of the agreement between ourselves and the Soviet Government, if I have done that all this time, that is the measure of the sincerity of my desire to come to an agreement. I can assure the committee that it has required some self-control to abstain from refuting the false impressions which the hon. gentleman has sought to convey.

No, Sir, I am not going to-day to give a historical summary of the negotiations between the British and the French Governments on the one hand and the Soviet Government on the other, for that very reason. I know perfectly well that there are people in other countries who are watching very jealously the progress of these negotiations, and who would be exceedingly glad for any ammunition which they could use in order to divide the Soviet Government and ourselves. I do not propose to give them that ammunition. Of course, there is no secret about the fact that the Soviet Government and the British and French Governments combined have not hitherto been able to agree upon a definition satisfactory to all parties of the term "indirect aggression," although all three of us realise that "indirect aggression" may be just as dangerous as "direct aggression" and all three of us desire to find a satisfactory method of providing against it. At the same time - I have the agreement of the right hon. gentleman - we are extremely anxious not even to appear to be desirous of encroaching upon the independence of other States. And if we have not agreed so far with the Soviet Government upon this definition of "indirect aggression," it is because the formula which they favoured appeared to us to carry that precise signification.

I have not the slightest doubt that if you were to make out an accurate time table you would find that much more time had been consumed by the British Government and the French Government in making their answers to the Soviet Government than has been consumed by the Soviet Government in making their answers to us. Is not that natural and, indeed, inevitable? M. Molotov was conducting these negotiations on the spot. If he wished to refer to his own Government he had only to drive a short distance through the city and he was in their presence. The British and French Ambassadors had to refer to their respective Governments and to report on each stage of the negotiations. We had to communicate with one another and agree upon the answer before we could reply. Therefore, when the hon. member opposite talks about this dawdling diplomacy, without precedent, I wonder whether he has looked up the precedents or whether it was just one of those phrases that he throws off in order to denigrate the Government.

I have looked up one or two precedents, just to see whether, in fact, these negotiations provide an outrageous exception to the general rule of expedition in conducting negotiations which involve more than two parties. The Anglo-Japanese Alliance, which was a bilateral arrangement, took six months to negotiate.

The Anglo-French *Entente* of 1904 took nine months. The Anglo-Russian Convention of 1907 took fifteen months, and the negotiations which led up to the Treaty of Locarno took eight months before they arrived at a conclusion. It would have been possible, perhaps, to make a provisional agreement at an early date with the Soviet Government, referring to a later date the conclusion of a detailed treaty. That was the course that we pursued with Poland and with Turkey, and we and the French Government would have been quite ready to have followed that course in this case, but the Soviet Government thought otherwise. They preferred to sign nothing, to initial nothing until we had got to a complete agreement, and as a result of that we were not able to present the world, as I would have liked to do, with even a provisional agreement at an earlier stage.

The announcement which I made to-day at question time shows that we have done something that must, I think, be almost without precedent in history in negotiations of this kind. We have agreed and the French Government have agreed to send military missions to Moscow to engage upon staff conversations with the corresponding officers appointed by the Russian Government, before we have come to a political agreement.

Here is a country which is a long way off and with which we had not had close relations for a very long time. We are showing a great amount of trust and a really strong intention to bring these negotiations to a successful issue when we can agree to send our sailors, soldiers and airmen to Russia to discuss how we can make our military plans together before we have an assurance that, we shall yet be able to come to an agreement upon political matters. The Russian Minister for Foreign Affairs, in the course of conversation, expressed the view that if we once began these military conversations, to which he attached very great importance, the political difficulties should not prove insuperable. It was that expression of views which weighed with us in taking this very unusual decision, and it certainly is the sincere hope of the French Government and ourselves that this anticipation of M. Molotov will be realised, and that we shall find it possible to agree not only in substance but also in form upon the remaining outstanding political difficulties.

Mr. Butler (summing up the Debate): It would be wrong if, in the last minute or two at my disposal, I did not make some reference to Russia. I can add very little to what the Prime Minister has said on this subject. My right hon friend the Member for Warwick and Leamington (Mr. Eden) said that the agreement was rather like Rochefoucauld's reference to ghosts and love; everyone had heard of them, but no one had seen them: All I would say is, instead of ghosts and love, do not let us have bogies and suspicions about Russia. There is no reason whatever for the sort of remarks that were made by the hon. gentleman opposite. We have proceeded with the utmost vigour to discuss with Russia our outstanding difficulties, and, as was rightly observed by the right hon. Baronet, the main question has been whether we should encroach on the independence of the Baltic States. We are in agreement with the right hon. Baronet that we should not do so, and the difficulty of reaching a formula on this point is one of the main reasons why there has been delay in these negotiations. We are, therefore, in agreement with him on this point, and I trust that now, with what we have achieved over the last few months with the growing strength of this country, with the determination we have shown, and with the success of our diplomatic efforts, we can at any rate, face the summer ready for anything.

No. 82.

Extract from the Speech by the Secretary of State for Foreign Affairs in the House of Lords on August 3, 1939.

The Secretary of State for Foreign Affairs (Viscount Halifax): Now I must say something about Russia. His Majesty's Government have, I suppose, taken the lead in endeavouring to organise a combination of resistance against aggression, and the fact that the principal portion of blame for every difficulty or delay falls on them shows indeed that their leading role is generally acknowledged. If the world were just, His Majesty's Government would receive, of course, the lion's share of credit for whatever has been achieved, but as the world, or the people in it, is or are not always just, His Majesty's Government make no complaint at all of shouldering the greater part of the blame for real or imaginary failures. The basis of British policy has been, as your Lordships are aware, close co-operation with France in defence of interests that are common, as was explicitly laid down in the declaration made so long ago as the beginning of February by my right honourable friend the Prime Minister in another place. It was starting from that point that His Majesty's Government offered their guarantee to Poland and Roumania, and undoubtedly by doing that they made a substantial contribution to the security of Russia and it was in view of the fact that they felt obliged at that time to act promptly, with, I think I can say, the approval of the overwhelming mass of opinion in this country - not in the presence of Lord Ponsonby clearly unanimous, but I think the overwhelming mass of opinion - that they did not make their action dependent on receiving any counterpart then and there from the Soviet Government.

The present negotiations with Russia have as we all know, as their object, the strengthening of the forces against possible aggression, and noble Lords will no doubt realise that to provide an instrument which will cover every possible contingency is a very complicated task which must inevitably give rise to certain divergencies of view. Moreover, as we also know very well, the problem is further complicated by the necessity of trying to provide for the new technique of "indirect aggression." His Majesty's Government and the French Government and the

Soviet Government are in full agreement on the necessity of trying to make such provision, but the differences which have arisen relate to the precise form in which this elusive shadow of "indirect aggression" can be brought to definition. Our common object is to find a formula which may cover what may rightly be regarded as indirect aggression without in any way encroaching on the independence and the neutrality of other States and it is no secret that the proposals that the British and French Governments have made have appeared to the Soviet Government insufficiently comprehensive, whilst the formula favoured by the Soviet Government has seemed to His Majesty's Government and the French Government to go too far in the other direction. The delays - and I confess, although I am naturally restrained in judgment, I am not so pessimistic as Lord Ponsonby who talks in terms of years - which have occurred have not only arisen from the complexity of the problem in hand which affects the rights and interests of a very large number of States.

I rather doubt whether even noble Lords, and I am quite sure still more of the general public outside, fully realise all that is involved in negotiations of this character. It is quite true that an interim agreement such as those made with Poland and with Turkey can be concluded relatively quickly; in the case of both these countries, the formal agreements are still under discussion. The noble Lord, Lord Davies, asked me whether our agreement with Poland included a definition of "indirect aggression" and, if it did, why it was not possible to transplant that definition into the Russian Agreement. Well, the answer is that the formal agreement with Poland is still being agreed, it is still not concluded, and the arrangement on which we have been working and are working, with Poland does not, I think, refer to "indirect aggression" in the form that he has in his mind, and for the simple reason that will be at once apparent to the noble Lord if he casts his mind back, that our guarantee to Poland rested upon a perfectly simple, precise, but rather different basis. Our guarantee to Poland, he will remember, was made operative in the event of Polish independence being clearly threatened and the Polish Government feeling it necessary to resist and so on. However, that is rather by way of parenthesis.

The Soviet Government, in contradistinction from what we were able to do with Turkey and Poland, preferred to proceed without any intermediate stage to the conclusion of a formal agreement, and the terms of that formal agreement naturally have required careful consideration, and it was inevitable that there was a great deal of discussion to be done on the drafting and so on. I was very glad to hear the noble Lord, Lord Davies, acknowledge, as he very fairly did, that the fact that we had to agree any modifications and alterations with the French Government necessarily and inevitably involved a certain measure of additional time expenditure. It has been assumed in some quarters, and I rather think that Lord Davies assumed it today attributing, indeed, I think to me a certain role that seemed to him appropriate that had His Majesty's Government been represented by a Cabinet Minister instead of an Ambassador a quick agreement would have been secured. Well, I do not really know what warrant he can certainly feel to have for any such surmise, and I do not think experience supports him. He will remember, as I remember, the Washington Naval Conference, for example, in 1921 when His Majesty's Government was represented by a most distinguished Minister, the late Lord Balfour. Although the ground for that conference had been prepared with the utmost diligence through diplomatic channels it took no less than three months there to secure agreement. In the present case, I understand, M. Molotov is obliged at every stage to consult his Government, and the same would, have applied to any British representative, whether in the Cabinet or out of the Cabinet, who had been on our behalf conducting the negotiations for His Majesty's Government in Moscow. The fact that His Majesty's Government and the French Government have decided to despatch military missions to Moscow - I think they leave, if I am rightly informed, the day after tomorrow - before full agreement has been reached on the political issues may be held, I hope to be the best evidence of the *bona fides* and determination of His Majesty's Government, and concrete evidence not only of our interest to bring these negotiations to an early and successful conclusion but of our belief that that step will facilitate outstanding discussions on political issues which will proceed simultaneously with the military discussions.

No. 83.

Sir W. Seeds to Viscount Halifax.

(Telegraphic.) *Moscow, August 2, 1939.*

FOLLOWING is translation of Tass communiqué from *Izvestiya* of 2nd August: -

"In his speech in the House of Commons on 31st July, Parliamentary Under-Secretary for Foreign Affairs, Mr. Butler said, according to the press, that the British Government were doing all they could with a view to hastening the removal of existing differences of opinion between U.S.S.R. and England, the chief of which is the question whether we should infringe the independence of the Baltic States or not.

"I agree," said Mr. Butler, "That we should not do this, and it is in this difference of opinion that chief reason for delay in the negotiations is to be found."

"Tass are authorised to state that, if Mr. Butler really made the foregoing statement he misrepresented the attitude of the Soviet Government. In actual fact, the differences of opinion do not lie in question of infringement or non-infringement of the independence of Baltic States, since both parties are in favour of guaranteeing that independence, but in question not leaving in the formula about "indirect aggression" any loophole for an aggressor who is making an attempt on the independence of the Baltic States. One of the reasons for the delay in the negotiation lies in the fact that the British formula leaves such a loophole for an aggressor."

No. 84.

Sir W. Seeds to Viscount Halifax.

(Telegraphic.) *Moscow, August 2, 1939.*

M. MOLOTOV received us this afternoon.

2. I informed him of the composition of our military mission and said that, they would probably leave at the end of this week. M. Molotov said that this would be convenient and that he would shortly be in a position to give us the names of Soviet delegation. He asked whether our mission would be furnished with full powers to negotiate. I said, that I could not answer this question as I have not had to deal with military conversations before. In reply to a question from the French Ambassador as to procedure for conversations, M. Molotov suggested that the three heads of the delegations might meet to draw up a programme.

3. M. Molotov then said that he wished to state the views of Soviet Government about remarks made by Mr. Butler in House of Commons on 31st July, which were the subject of a communiqué in Soviet press this morning (my telegram of 2nd August – No. 83). Mr. Butler had grossly misrepresented the Soviet attitude as regards the Baltic States. I asked M. Molotov

whether he had the full text of Mr. Butler's remarks. I had not myself seen it. He replied he had the full text from Tass Agency. I suggested that much would depend upon the exact words used. I was convinced, however, that there had been no intention on the part of Mr. Butler to say anything wounding to Soviet Government. In fact, I was sure that the contrary was the case.

4. M. Molotov said that Mr. Butler had represented the Soviet formula as meaning that the Soviet Government wished to infringe the independence of Baltic States. Attitude which Soviet Government had taken up was one which contemplated the defence of independence and neutrality of the Baltic States.

5. I repeated that I did not know exactly what Mr. Butler had said or what he had been reported as saying. In the course of our conversations we had made no such accusation against Soviet Government. What we had said was that it was in our view essential to avoid using any word or any phrase in the treaty which would give cause for suspicion in Baltic States or give a handle for hostile propaganda against us, and that we had in particular to avoid giving the impression that we considered it possible that any of the parties should intervene in the internal affairs of other States. This was a danger which we felt it essential to avoid. Our objection to that Soviet formula was that it might be interpreted in this sense by suspicious or hostile opinion. We had accepted the Soviet Government's request for inclusion of the term "indirect aggression" in the treaty, and when the Soviet Government had further pressed for a definition we had felt some hesitation about agreeing, precisely because we feared that hostile opinion might interpret the definition in the wrong sense. I felt sure that this must be what Mr. Butler had in mind, namely, the importance of not giving cause for suspicion to the Baltic States or a handle for hostile propaganda.

6. My general conclusion was that what had happened showed how important question of "indirect aggression" was and how necessary it was to come to an agreement about it soon. Could M. Molotov give us a favourable opinion on the formula we had presented to him? M. Molotov said that he had himself no new proposal to make and he asked whether I had any solution.

7. I said that His Majesty's Government had considered the matter again. As I had already told M. Molotov His Majesty's Government thought that their formula covered all the cases that it was legitimate to cover and they could go no further. They were, however, prepared to agree that cases which might not be covered by their formula should be made the subject of consultation. I then submitted text of our original formula together with additional sentence about consultation as approved. M. Potemkin made an oral translation into Russian from the French text of draft.

8. M. Molotov said that additional sentence did not improve the definition. Consultation was not sufficient to meet cases which he had in view. French Ambassador asked why M. Molotov took this view. M. Molotov replied that the sentence about consultation did not provide for immediate assistance in cases contemplated.

9. I said I understood M. Molotov thought our formula was too narrow and did not cover the cases which he had in mind. I admitted that technique of aggression had recently been developed and was difficult to deal with but I thought that if we tried to give too precise a definition we might run the risk of excluding (by that very precision) new or unforeseen cases which might arise in the future. That was one reason why we thought that consultation might be useful.

10. M. Molotov agreed that consultation might

sometimes be necessary but observed that in the cases he had in mind it was a question of giving immediate assistance. The objection to our new sentence was that it weakened the play of the article as regards immediate assistance. The draft definition which he had himself submitted did not cover all cases of "indirect aggression" and those which it did not cover might be made the subject of consultation. The idea of consultation was already present in article 3. He therefore begged us to continue our search for a solution, and said that he would do his best to help us. He thought his own draft was a very modest one. It was designed to cover at least the case of President Hacha and the case of Danzig, this was all that he had set out to do. I replied that our draft of article 1 covered both these cases. M. Molotov observed that President Hacha had accepted the German demands of his own free will and would not admit that be had acted under threat of force. To this I replied that everybody knew that he had been acting under threat. As regards Danzig, I had been in communication with your Lordship, and you had confirmed my impression that the case of Danzig was covered by words "indirect aggression" in paragraph 2 of article 1.

11. I observed that our formula covered not only the case of the victim who resisted or protested, but also the victim who not only did not protest, but pretended to act willingly even though it was clear that he was acting under threat of force.

12. The French Ambassador asked whether M. Molotov would give us the results of his study of the various formulae. The two Governments had done their best and had made a fresh suggestion. M. Molotov replied that he had as yet no concrete proposal to make. If he should later on have anything to suggest he would let us know.

13. In reply to a question by Mr. Strang whether it was now quite clear what was the nature of the difference between the three Governments, M. Molotov said that he thought that

the words "under threat of force" unduly restricted the scope of the Anglo-French definition. He recalled that the Soviet Government had originally proposed a formula which His Majesty's Government and the French Government had rejected, proposing a counter-formula of their own. Soviet Government had then tried their hand at a further draft. The views of the Soviet Government were clearly expressed in terms of that draft.

14. I said that we saw great danger in the use of words "without any such threat" in the Soviet formula. They would arouse suspicions in third States and give a handle to hostile propaganda. There was also the danger that if we claimed to invoke the treaty in respect of action freely taken by independent States we should give the impression of wishing to interfere in their internal affairs.

15. M. Molotov repeated that in his view the case of President Hacha was not covered by the Anglo-French formula. I repeated the conviction of His Majesty's Government that it was. If it was for this reason alone that he wished to insert the words "without any such threats," I begged him not to overlook the danger which I had already pointed out to him of using these words. Our point was not that we thought that the Soviet Government wished to interfere with internal affairs of third States, but that other Governments would proclaim that this was what the treaty meant.

16. M. Molotov asked why, if that were so, Mr. Butler himself had placed this interpretation on the Soviet formula. I repeated that I could not admit that Mr. Butler had given this as his own interpretation. I believed that what he had tried to do was to show that the Soviet formula was capable of this interpretation.

Annex to No. 84.

Draft Definition of "Indirect Aggression." Handed to M. Molotov, August 2, 1939.

(3) It is agreed between the three contracting Governments that the expression "indirect aggression" in paragraph 2 above is to be understood as including action accepted by the State in question under threat of force by another Power and involving the abandonment by it of its independence or neutrality.

In the event of circumstances arising which fall outside the framework of the foregoing definition, but which, in the view of one of the contracting Governments, involve a threat to the independence or neutrality of the State in question, the contracting Governments will immediately consult together at the request of any one of them with a view to such action as may be mutually agreed upon.

No. 85.

Viscount Halifax to Sir W. Seeds (Moscow).

(Telegraphic.) *Foreign Office, August 4, 1939.*

MR. Butler explained to the Soviet Ambassador on 4th August that he had not intended in his speech on 31st July to convey the impression that there was any difference of opinion between His Majesty's Government and the Soviet Government on the question whether we wished to permit any encroachment upon the independence and neutrality of the Baltic States.

2. M. Maisky replied that he had listened to Mr. Butler's speech and realised that he had been left very little time to deal with the Moscow negotiations at the end of the debate. Mr.

Butler drew the Ambassador's attention to the Prime Minister's earlier references to the question of "indirect aggression" and he agreed that these accurately represented the position. His Excellency undertook to communicate with his Government and to inform them that any misunderstanding that had arisen was due partly to the incorrect Tass version of Mr. Butler's remarks and partly to the fact that these had been rather elliptical in view of the fact that they were introduced at the very end of a speech.

No. 86.

English Text of the proposed Anglo-Franco-Soviet Agreement as it stood after the last meeting with M. Molotov on August 2, 1939, before the Military Conversations opened.

PREAMBLE

[Agreed.]

THE Governments of the United Kingdom, France and the U.S.S.R., with the object of making more effective the principle of mutual assistance against aggression adopted by the League of Nations have reached the following agreement:-

ARTICLE 1.

[Agreed in part.]

The United Kingdom, France and the U.S.S.R. undertake to give to each other immediately all effective assistance should one of these three countries become involved in hostilities with a European Power as a result either-

(1) Of aggression aimed by that Power against one of these three countries, or

(2) Of aggression, "direct or indirect," aimed by that Power against any European State whose independence or neutrality, the contracting country concerned felt obliged to defend against such aggression.

[N.B.-*A formula defining "indirect aggression" had still to be agreed. The final Anglo-French and Soviet drafts were respectively as follows:-*

Anglo-French Draft.
  (3) It is agreed between the three contracting Governments that the expression "indirect aggression" in paragraph 2 above is to be understood as including action accepted by the State in question under threat of force by another Power and involving the abandonment by it of its independence or neutrality.

  In the event of circumstances arising which fall outside the framework of the foregoing definition, but which, in the view of one of the contracting Governments, involve a threat to the independence or neutrality of the State in question, the contracting Governments will immediately consult together at the request of any one of them with a view to such action as may be mutually agreed upon.

Soviet Draft.
  (3) The expression "indirect aggression" covers action accepted by any at the above mentioned States under threat of force by another Power, or without any such threat, involving the use of the territory and forces of the State in question for purposes of aggression against that State or against one of the contracting parties and consequently involving the loss by that State of its independence or the violation of its neutrality.]

The assistance provided for in the present article will be given in conformity with the principles of the League of Nations, but without its being necessary to follow the procedure of, or to await action by, the League.

ARTICLE 2.

[Agreed.]

The three contracting Governments will concert together as soon as possible as to the methods, forms and extent of the assistance to be rendered by them in conformity with article 1, with the object of making such assistance as effective as possible.

ARTICLE 3.

[Agreed, subject to agreement on words in brackets.]

The three contracting Governments will exchange information periodically about the international situation and will lay down the lines of mutual diplomatic support in the interests of peace. Without prejudice to the immediate rendering of assistance in accordance with article 1, and with a view to securing its better preparation, in the event of circumstances arising which threaten to call into operation the undertakings of mutual assistance contained in article 1 the three contracting Governments will, at the request of anyone of them, immediately consult together to examine the situation and [in case of necessity] to decide by common agreement the moment at which the mechanism of mutual assistance shall be put into immediate operation and the manner of its application, independently of any procedure of the League of Nations.

ARTICLE 4.

[Agreed.]

The three contracting Governments will communicate to one

another the terms of any undertakings of assistance which they have already given to other European States. Any of the three Governments which may in future be considering giving any fresh undertaking of the same character will consult the other two Governments before doing so, and will communicate to them the terms of any undertaking so given.

ARTICLE 5.

[Agreed.]

In the event of joint operations against aggression being begun in accordance with article 1, the three contracting Governments undertake only to conclude an armistice or peace by common agreement.

ARTICLE 6.

[Agreed.]

The present agreement enters into force simultaneously with the agreement which is to be concluded in accordance with article 2.

ARTICLE 7.

[Agreed.]

The present agreement will continue for a period of five years from today's date. Not less than six months before the expiry of the said period, the three contracting Governments will consult together as to the desirability of renewing it, with or without modification.

PROTOCOL.

[Agreed except for paragraph 3.]

The three contracting Governments have agreed as follows:-

1. Article 1 (2) of the agreement signed by them to-day will apply to the following European States :

    Turkey, Greece, Romania, Poland, Belgium, Estonia, Latvia, Finland.

2. The foregoing list of States is subject to revision by agreement between the three contracting Governments.

[Anglo-French Draft.]

3. *In the event of aggression or threat of aggression by a European State not mentioned in the foregoing list, the three contracting Governments will, without prejudice to the immediate action which any of them may feel obliged to take, immediately consult together at the request of any one of them with a view to such action as may be mutually agreed upon.*

[Soviet Draft.]

3. *As regards the two last-named States (Switzerland and Netherlands), the agreement will only come into force if and when Poland and Turkey conclude pacts of mutual assistance with the U.S.S.R.*

4. The present supplementary agreement will not be made public.

No. 87.

Explanatory Memorandum prepared on December 12, 1939, summarising Reports on the Anglo-Franco-Soviet Military conversations in Moscow: August 11 to August 25, 1939.

THE Prime Minister announced in the House of Commons on the 31st July the decision to send British and French Military Missions to Moscow for conversations with the Soviet General Staff. The British Mission was headed by Admiral the Honourable Sir R.A. R. Plunkett-Ernle-Erle-Drax, K.C.B., D.S.O., and its other members were Major-General T. G. G. Heywood, O.B.E., and Air Marshal Sir C. S. Burnett, K.C.B., C.B.E., D.S.O. The French Mission was headed by General Doumenc, and also included General Valin. On the 3rd August His Majesty's Ambassador in Moscow was informed that the Soviet delegation would be presided over by Marshal Voroshilov, the People's Commissar of Defence, and would also include Army Commander of the First Rank B. M. Shaposhnikov, Chief of the General Staff; Flagman Flotta of Second Rank, H. G. Kuznetsov, People's Commissar of the Navy; Army Commander, Second Rank A. D. Lokhtionov, Chief of the Air Force; and Corps Commander I.V. Smorodinov, Deputy Chief of the General Staff.

Arrangements were immediately made for the British and French Military Missions to leave for Moscow at the earliest possible date, but, as their instructions covered a very wide field, a few days were necessary to enable them to familiarise themselves with these instructions before their departure.

The British and French Missions left England on the 5th

August by the steamship *City of Exeter*, which had been specially chartered for the voyage, and arrived at Leningrad on the 10th August. They at once proceeded to Moscow, and conversations opened on the 11th August. The British and French delegations were given instructions to examine, in conjunction with the High Command of the Armed Forces of the Soviet Socialist Republics, all questions regarding the collaboration needed between the armed forces of the Soviet Union and those of the United Kingdom of Great Britain and Northern Ireland and of France.

(Note: On the proof copy of the original Blue Book used to create this edition, in the previous paragraph, the words "instruction to examine, in conjunction" *were crossed through by hand and in the margin, to the side of them, were the handwritten words* "full powers to negotiate." *Editor)*

The Allied Missions were given a friendly welcome in Moscow. The conversations opened in a favourable atmosphere and meetings were held on five successive days from the 11th August to the 16th August. In view of the seriousness of the international situation, every effort was made by the allied missions to dispose of outstanding difficulties and reach an early agreement.

Two main difficulties, however, arose at an early stage in the conversations. The first concerned naval operations in the Baltic, and the second land operations in support of Poland or Roumania.

As regards the Baltic, the Soviet delegation intimated that they desired His Majesty's Government and the French Government to make arrangements whereby British and French naval forces should be able to use bases on the coast of Finland, Latvia and Estonia, on the Aland Islands and on the islands at the mouth of the Gulf of Riga. It was also the intention of the

Soviet delegation that, once this had been satisfactorily managed, these bases should be available to Soviet naval forces who would collaborate with Allied naval detachments in the Baltic. As His Majesty's Government and the French Government had made it plain during the earlier political conversations in Moscow that they could not countenance any action which might be regarded by the Governments of Finland, Estonia, or Latvia as an infringement of their neutrality, the Soviet demands obviously raised a fundamental difficulty. Their significance has been clearly revealed by later events.

The second difficulty concerned the question raised by the Soviet military authorities as to whether the Polish and Roumanian Governments would allow Soviet troops to operate in their territory in the event of German aggression against their countries. The Soviet authorities made it clear that the successful conclusion of the Staff conversations depended on the readiness of these two Governments to agree in advance to their demand and to draw up at an early date the plans necessary to provide for this eventuality. The Soviet Government did not apparently consider that they were in a position to approach the Polish or Roumanian Governments directly on this issue, and the Soviet delegation therefore suggested that this approach should be made by His Majesty's Government and the French Government. As Poland was at that time in more immediate danger from German aggression than Roumania, the case of Poland was considered first. His Majesty's Government and the French Government had, however, to take account of the fact that the Polish Government were determined to avoid anything which might have the effect of provoking an immediate German attack, and a Polish-Soviet agreement to permit the passage of Soviet troops through Poland might well have had such an effect, and have precipitated the hostilities which it was the object of the Anglo-French-Soviet negotiations to avoid.

These were questions with which the British and French

missions at Moscow were not empowered to deal, as they concerned the territorial integrity of third powers not taking part in the Moscow negotiations. The conversations were therefore adjourned on the 17th August with a view to the question being reconsidered by His Majesty's Government and the French Government in consultation with the Polish Government. Conversations took place in Warsaw from the 17th August onwards, from which it appeared that the Polish Government were still unable to agree to any action which in their opinion was calculated to accelerate German aggression; but that they did not exclude collaboration between Poland and the U.S.S.R. in the event of common action being taken against German aggression.

When the military conversations were resumed in Moscow on the 21st August, a statement had already appeared regarding the conclusion of a Soviet-German economic agreement. This was followed on the 22nd August by the announcement of the decision to conclude a Soviet-German Non-Aggression Pact and by the news of Herr von Ribbentrop's impending visit to Moscow. No further progress could therefore be made in the military conversations.

On the 25th August Admiral Drax and General Doumenc saw Marshal Voroshilov and asked him whether, in the changed political situation, he thought it likely that the Soviet Government would desire the military missions to continue their conversations. Marshal Voroshilov replied that, in the new political situation, there would be no sense in continuing those conversations. The British and French Missions left Moscow shortly after this interview.

No. 88.

Sir W. Seeds to Viscount Halifax.

(Telegraphic.) *Moscow, August 21, 1939.*

TASS communiqué announced in Soviet press of 21st August conclusion of a commercial credit agreement between U.S.S.R. and Germany, as follows:-

"On 19th August, after prolonged conversations which eventually reached a successful conclusion, a commercial credit agreement was signed in Berlin between U.S.S.R. and Germany.

Agreement was signed on behalf of the U.S.S.R. by deputy trade representative Comrade E. Babarin, and on behalf of Germany by Herr Schmidt.

"Commercial credit agreement provides for granting by Germany to U.S.S.R. of a credit of 200 million German marks for a period of seven years at 5 per cent for purchase of German goods over a period or two years from date of signature of agreement.

"Agreement similarly provides for supply of goods to Germany by U.S.S.R. during the same period, that is to say during, the course of two years to the value of 180 million German marks."

Further details of agreement given in leading articles in *Pravda* and *Izvestiya*, full translations of which follow by air mail are:-

1. The 200 million marks credit by Germany to U.S.S.R. is to be used principally for Soviet purchases in Germany of machine tools and mechanical equipment.

2. German Government will assist Soviet trade delegation to place order with individual German firms; to obtain favourable delivery dates for these orders; and to ensure that machinery and equipment is of high quality.

3. German Government guarantees in full the 200 million marks credit opened for the Soviet Government, so as to enable the Soviet Trade Delegation to pay on the spot for goods supplied.

4. Interest is fixed at 5 per cent per annum, which is lower than in the case of previous German credits to the U.S.S.R.

5. New credits are for longer period than in the past, average period for new credit being seven years; 30 per cent being repayable within six years; 40 per cent within seven years and remaining 30 per cent within seven and a half years.

Izvestiya states that these substantial improvements in conditions of loan were an essential prerequisite for surmounting obstacles in the way of an agreement.

No. 89.

Sir W. Seeds to Viscount Halifax.

(Telegraphic.) *Moscow, August 22, 1939.*

FOLLOWING is translation of Tass communiqué in press this morning:-

"After the conclusion of the Soviet-German Trade and Credit Agreement, the question arose of the improvement of political relations between Germany and the U.S.S.R. An exchange of views on this question took place between the German and Soviet Governments, which has established the existence of a desire of both parties to relieve the tension in the political relations between them, to avert the danger of war; and to conclude a pact of non-aggression. In connexion with this matter the German Minister for Foreign Affairs, Herr von Ribbentrop, will visit Moscow in a few days for the necessary conversations."

No. 90.

Viscount Halifax to Sir W. Seeds (Moscow).

(Telegraphic.) *Foreign Office, August 22, 1939.*

HIS Majesty's Government have noted a statement issued by the German official news agency to the effect that the German Government and the Soviet Government have come to an understanding with regard to the conclusion of a non-aggression pact, and that the German Foreign Minister will arrive in Moscow on 23rd August to bring the negotiations to a conclusion. They have also noted a statement by the Tass agency to the effect that, after the conclusion of the Soviet-German Trade and Credit Agreement, the Governments of Germany and the Soviet Union desire to relieve the tension in their political relations, eliminate the war menace and conclude a non-aggression pact, and that, consequently the German Foreign Minister will arrive in Moscow in a few days for corresponding negotiations. These negotiations are further reported to have been proceeding for some months.

2. You should seek an immediate interview with M. Molotov and say that, in view of the negotiations which have been proceeding between Great Britain, France and the Soviet Union and which have gone far towards a successful conclusion, His Majesty's Government find it hard to credit this report. If confirmed, it would seem to render nugatory the results already achieved during the negotiations between the three Powers and to constitute an act of bad faith on the part of the Soviet Government. It would, indeed, be incredible that

the Soviet Government should have been carrying on, let alone concluding, such negotiations without a single word to His Majesty's Government or the French Government, with whom the Soviet Union is already in treaty relations. That being so, His Majesty's Government prefer to suspend judgment upon this report until they can obtain official confirmation from the Soviet Government.

3. You should therefore ask M. Molotov for an immediate reply and report to me at once.

No. 91.

Sir W. Seeds to *Viscount Halifax.*

(Telegraphic.) *Moscow, August 22, 1939.*

YOUR telegram of 2nd August. (No. 90)

I saw M. Molotov at 8 PM and spoke to him textually in accordance with paragraph 2 of your telegram.

2. He said that Tass communiqué represented the exact facts, but he rejected the accusation of bad faith; he would not admit the right of His Majesty's Government to employ that expression or to stand in judgment on the Soviet Government. In answer to my suggestion that at least we should have received a warning, he retorted that His Majesty's Government did not inform Soviet Government of modifications in their policy. I said that I was not talking of changes in general policy in normal times, but of a change such as this in the very height of negotiations.

3. He wished to say that he had, as I knew, constantly and rightly reproached us during all these negotiations with a lack of

sincerity. Height of this insincerity had been reached when military missions arrived in Moscow empty handed and, above all, quite unprepared to deal with fundamental points on which whole question of reciprocal assistance depended, namely, the passage of Soviet troops through Polish and Roumanian territory. That showed that we were only "playing" with the Soviet Union. The Soviet delegation had again and again asked questions and had repeatedly been put off; finally (either yesterday or the day before), the Soviet Government had made up their mind that they were being played with and "had accepted proposal made to them by the German Government."

4. I denied that mission had arrived empty handed. They were prepared to deal with questions concerning British and French military assistance, &c., but a question of passage of troops through the territory of a third sovereign State was clearly not within their competence.

5. A considerable portion of the interview was taken up with reiterations by M. Molotov of statements contained in foregoing two paragraphs.

6. I asked what exactly the German proposal amounted to. He only pointed to Tass communiqué. I said that there were various forms of non-aggression treaties, and asked whether the treaty now proposed would enable the Soviet Union to pursue what we had always understood to be her policy, namely, the protection of the victims of aggression. Would it, for example, mean that the Soviet would stand still with arms crossed and allow Poland to be overrun? He clearly did not like this questioning and could only say that we must wait and see how negotiations would work out.

7. I persisted that I wanted to know whether all we had achieved in the way of arranging a system of general defence against aggression was rendered null. Would it not be possible

to continue this good work? Finally, he said that it all depended on the German negotiations, but perhaps, after a bit, say a week, we might see.

8. I said that I regretted report which I would now have to send to His Majesty's Government but I, above all, regretted his aspersions on our sincerity and on military missions. As regards the former it was sufficient to point to the fact that starting from, say the 2nd June, when the Soviet Government presented their draft, our negotiations were one long series of concession after concession on our part to meet the Soviet point of view ending up with unexampled concession in agreeing to send military missions before the political discussions had been concluded. He said that he was not so much interested in the comparatively distant past as in the immediate crowning display of insincerity, *i.e.*, failure to answer the question of the passage of troops.

9. I said that I regretted and contested this. It would be understandable for the Soviet negotiators to complain had our mission either asked for an amount of assistance which it was beyond Soviet power to give or else offered a derisory amount of assistance on the part, of Great Britain and France. In actual fact our mission's suggestions had been that the Soviet troops should line up along their own frontier for action if necessary: in other words we had asked for less than the Soviet Union was prepared to give.

10. Our missions had, I said, done their utmost to get an answer to Marshal Voroshilov's question: indeed, I rather thought that the French general was giving some reply to marshal at that moment. Reminding him of what he had said about "seeing in a week's time" I expected assurance that we would most probably know the answer by then. He said "we will see" and on this vague note the interview terminated.

No. 92.

Extract from the Speech by the Secretary of State for Foreign Affairs in the House of Lords on August 24, 1939.

THE Secretary of State for Foreign Affairs (Viscount Halifax):-

That, in outline, was the situation when on the 22nd August, the day before yesterday, it was officially stated in Berlin and Moscow that negotiations had been in progress, and were to be at once continued, for the signature of a non-aggression pact between the Soviet Union and Germany. I do not conceal the fact that this announcement came as a surprise to His Majesty's Government.

For some time past there had been rumours of a change in the relations between the German and Soviet Governments, but no hint of such a change was conveyed by the Soviet Government to His Majesty's Government or the French Government, with whom they were in negotiation; and on the 31st July last the Prime Minister remarked in another place that His Majesty's Government were showing a great degree of trust, and a strong desire to bring their negotiations with the Soviet Government to a successful issue, when, before any agreement had been finally reached on political matters, they agreed to send a Military Mission to Moscow to discuss military plans. The Military Missions of France and this country reached Moscow on the 11th August, and the conversations were proceeding, to all appearance on a basis of mutual confidence, and it is, I do not conceal from your Lordships, certainly disturbing to learn that while these conversations were taking place the Soviet Government were secretly negotiating a pact with Germany for purposes which, on the face of it, were inconsistent with the objects, as we had understood them, of their foreign policy.

I would not now pass any final judgment on this matter. That would be premature until we have had time to consult with the French Government as to the meaning and the consequences of the agreement, the actual text of which has been published this morning, but one matter forces itself upon the immediate attention of His Majesty's Government. They had to consider what effect this changed situation should have on their policy. In Berlin the agreement was somewhat cynically welcomed as a great diplomatic victory which removed the danger of war, since, so it was alleged Great Britain and France would no longer fulfil their obligations to Poland, and His Majesty's Government felt it their first duty to remove this dangerous illusion. It should be recalled, if it is not in mind, that our guarantee to Poland was given before any agreement with Russia was in prospect, and without condition that such agreement should be reached. His Majesty's Government, therefore, at once issued a statement that their obligations to Poland and other countries remained unaffected; and throughout these days, as noble Lords will imagine, we have been in close and constant contact with the French Government, whose attitude is identical with our own. Our obligations rest on the agreed statements which were made in this House and in another place, and which are binding. Effect is being given to them in treaties, which are in an advanced stage of negotiation, and these treaties will formally define the mutual obligations of the parties, but they neither add to nor subtract from the obligations of mutual assistance which have been already accepted.

No. 93.

German-Soviet Friendship and Frontier Agreement.
September 28, 1939.

THE Government of the U.S.S.R. and the German Government, following the collapse of the former Polish State, consider it as exclusively their own task to restore peace and order in this territory and to assure to the peoples inhabiting it a peaceful existence which will correspond to their national characteristics. With this object in view, they have concluded the following agreement:-

ARTICLE 1.

The Government of the U.S.S.R. and the German Government establish, as the frontier between their respective State interests in the territory of the former Polish State a line which is marked on the attached map and which will be given in more detail in a supplementary protocol.

ARTICLE 2.

Both countries recognise as final the frontier between their respective State interests, as set out in Article 1, and will resist any interference with this decision on the part of other Powers.

ARTICLE 3.

The German Government will carry out the necessary State reconstruction on the territory west of the line indicated in Article 1, and the Soviet Government on the territory east of this line.

ARTICLE 4.

The Government of the U.S.S.R. and the German Government regard the above mentioned reconstruction as a reliable foundation for the further development of friendly relations between their peoples.

ARTICLE 5.

This agreement is subject to ratification. The exchange of instruments of ratification is to take place as soon as possible in Berlin. The agreement enters into force from the moment of its signature.
Moscow, September 28, 1939.

German-Soviet Declaration.

The German Government and the Government of the U.S.S.R. having, by the agreement signed to-day finally settled questions arising from the collapse of the Polish State and having thereby created a solid foundation for lasting peace in Eastern Europe, declare that in the opinion of both of them the liquidation of the present war between Germany on the one hand and England and France on the other, would be in the interests of all nations. Both Governments will therefore direct their joint efforts, in agreement if necessary with other friendly Powers, to achieve this object as quickly as possible. Should, however, these efforts of both Governments prove unsuccessful the fact will thereby be established that England and France bear responsibility for the continuation of the war; in this case the Governments of Germany and the U.S.S.R. will consult together as to the measures it may be necessary to take.
Moscow, September 28, 1939.

Letter from M. Molotov to Herr Von Ribbentrop.

Referring to our negotiations, we have the honour to confirm to you that the Government of the U. S. S. R., basing itself on and in spirit of the general political agreement reached by us, is actuated by the will to develop, by all means, economic relationship and exchange of goods between the U.S.S.R. and Germany. With this object in view, an economic programme will be drawn up by both parties, under which the Soviet Union will supply raw materials to Germany, in exchange for which Germany, on her part will supply industrial goods produced over a lengthy period. Both parties will thus draw up this economic programme; in order that the German-Soviet exchange of goods should in volume again approach the highest point attained in the past.

Both Governments will issue at once the necessary orders for the passing of the measures indicated above, and will ensure that negotiations are entered into and brought to a conclusion as soon as possible.

Moscow, September 28, 1939.

No. 94.

Estonian-Soviet Mutual Assistance Pact of September 28, 1939.
(Similar treaties were concluded by the Soviet Union with Latvia and Lithuania).

THE Supreme Council of the Union of Soviet Socialist Republics and the President of the Republic of Estonia, having decided to develop the friendly relations which were established by the peace treaty signed on the 2nd February, 1920, and which are founded on State sovereignty and on non-intervention in the internal affairs of the parties;

Recognising that the peace treaty of the 2nd February, 1920, and the Pact of Non-Aggression and the Peaceful Settlement of Conflicts of the 4th May, 1932, continue to be the foundation of mutual relations and obligations;

Being convinced that it is in the interest of both parties to fix the exact conditions of mutual security;

Have agreed to conclude the following mutual assistance pact, and have appointed as their plenipotentiaries:-

> The Supreme Council of the Union of Soviet Socialist Republics: The Chairman of the Council of People's Commissars and the Commissar for Foreign Affairs: Molotov;
>
> The President of the Republic of Estonia: The Minister for Foreign Affairs: Selter;

who have agreed upon the following conditions:-

ARTICLE 1.

Both parties promise to afford each other mutual assistance of every kind, including military assistance, in case of direct aggression or of a danger of aggression by one of the great European Powers on the maritime frontier of the Baltic Sea or on the land frontier through the territory of Latvia, as also on the bases mentioned in article 3.

ARTICLE 2.

The Union of Soviet Socialist Republics promises to afford the Estonian army assistance in the form of armaments and other war materials on privileged terms.

ARTICLE 3.

The Republic of Estonia guarantees to the Union of Soviet

Socialist Republics the right to possess on the Estonian Islands of Saaremaa and Hiiumaa and in the town of Paldiski bases for warships and a certain number of aerodromes for air forces on a leasehold basis and at a reasonable price. The exact sites of the bases and aerodromes shall be specified and their exact frontiers determined by mutual agreement.

For the purpose of defending these aerodromes and bases the Union of Soviet Socialist Republics shall have the right to maintain at their own expense, in the areas set aside as bases and aerodromes, a certain specified number of Soviet land and air forces, the maximum number of which shall be determined by a special agreement.

ARTICLE 4.

Both parties promise not to conclude any alliance or participate in any coalition directed against one of the parties.

ARTICLE 5.

The enforcement of the present pact shall not in any way infringe the sovereign rights of the parties, nor affect in any way their economic systems or State structure.

The sites which are set apart as bases and aerodromes (article 3) shall remain the territory of the Estonian Republic.

ARTICLE 6.

The present pact comes into force with the exchange of the instruments of ratification. This exchange shall take place at Tallinn within six days from the date of the signing of the present pact.

The present pact shall continue in force for ten years, but, in the event of neither of the parties finding it necessary to denounce the pact at the latest one year before the expiry of that period, the validity of the pact shall be extended automatically for a subsequent period of five years.

Made in two original copies, in the Estonian and Russian languages, at Moscow on the 28th September, 1939.

V.M. MOLOTOV.
K. SELTER.

No. 95.

Resolutions of the Assembly and of the Council of the League of Nations, December 14, 1939.

The Assembly:

I.

WHEREAS, by the aggression which it has committed against Finland, the Union of Soviet Socialist Republics has failed to observe not only its special political agreements with Finland but also Article 12 of the Covenant of the League of Nations and the Pact of Paris;

And whereas, immediately before committing that aggression, it denounced, without legal justification, the Treaty of Non-aggression which it had concluded with Finland in 1932, and which was to remain in force until the end of 1945;

Solemnly condemns the actions taken by the Union of Soviet Socialist Republics against the State of Finland;

Urgently appeals to every Member of the League to provide Finland with such material and humanitarian assistance as may be in its power and to refrain from any action which might weaken Finland's power of resistance;

Authorises the Secretary-General to lend the aid of his technical services in the organisation of the aforesaid assistance to Finland;

And likewise authorises the Secretary-General, in virtue of the Assembly resolution of the 4th October, 1937, to consult non-member States with a view to possible co-operation.

II.

Whereas, notwithstanding an invitation extended to it on two occasions, the Union of Soviet Socialist Republics has refused to be present at the examination of its dispute with Finland before the Council and the Assembly;

And whereas, by thus refusing to recognise the duty of the Council and the Assembly as regards the execution of Article 15 of the Covenant, it has failed to observe one of the League's most essential covenants for the safeguarding of peace and the security of nations;

And whereas it has vainly attempted to justify its refusal on the ground of the relations which it has established with an alleged Government which is neither *de jure* nor *de facto* the Government recognised by the people of Finland in accordance with the free working of their institutions;

And whereas the Union of Soviet Socialist Republics has not merely violated a covenant of the League, but has by its own action placed itself outside the Covenant;

And whereas the Council is competent under Article 16 of the Covenant to consider what consequences should follow from this situation:

Recommends the Council to pronounce upon the question.

The Council :

Having taken cognisance of the resolution adopted by the Assembly on the 14th December, 1939, regarding the appeal of the Finnish Government,

1. Associates itself with the condemnation by the Assembly of the action or the Union of Soviet Socialist Republics against the Finnish State, and

2. For the reasons set forth in the resolution of the Assembly,

In virtue of article 16, paragraph 4, of the Covenant,

Finds, that, by its act, the Union of Soviet Socialist Republics has placed itself outside the League of Nations. It follows that the Union of Soviet Socialist Republics is no longer a member of the League.

Argonaut Papers

The Theft of the Irish Crown Jewels, 1907
Peace in Tibet, 1903
Dealing with Josef Stalin, 1939
Dealing with Adolf Hitler, 1939

Moments of History

The British War in Afghanistan
The Irish Book of Death and Flying Ships
John Lennon: the FBI files
Marilyn Monroe: the FBI files
The Great Train Robbery 1963
Spitting Tacks: the building of the Scottish Parliament
Lord Hutton's Report
Lord Butler's Report

Uncovered Editions

Crime
Rillington Place, 1949
The Strange Story of Adolf Beck
The Trials of Oscar Wilde, 1895

Ireland
Bloody Sunday Lord Widgery's Report, 1972
The Irish Uprising, 1914–21

Transport
The Loss of the Titanic, 1912
R.101: the Airship Disaster, 1930
Tragic Journeys (Titanic, R.101, Munich Air Crash)

Travel and Empire
The Amritsar Massacre: General Dyer in the Punjab, 1919
The Boer War: Ladysmith and Mafeking, 1900
The British Invasion of Tibet: Colonel Younghusband, 1904
Florence Nightingale and the Crimea, 1854–55
King Guezo of Dahomey, 1850–52
Mr Hosie's Journey to Tibet, 1904
The Siege Collection (Kars, Boer War, Peking)
The Siege of Kars, 1855
The Siege of the Peking Embassy, 1900
Travels in Mongolia, 1902
Wilfred Blunt's Egyptian Garden: Fox-hunting in Cairo

Tudor History
Letters of Henry VIII, 1526–29

UK Politics Since 1945
John Profumo and Christine Keeler, 1963
UFOs in the House of Lords, 1979
War in the Falklands, 1982

United States of America
The Assassination of John F. Kennedy, 1963
The Cuban Missile Crisis, 1962
The St Valentine's Day Massacre, 1929

UFOs in America, 1947
The Watergate Affair, 1972

The War Facsimiles
(*Illustrated books published by the British government during the war years*)
The Battle of Britain, August–October 1940
The Battle of Egypt, 1942
Bomber Command, September 1939–July 1941
East of Malta, West of Suez, September 1939 to March 1941
Fleet Air Arm, 1943
Land at War, 1939–1944
Ocean Front: the story of the war in the Pacific, 1941–1944
Roof over Britain, 1939–1942

World War I
British Battles of World War I, 1914–15
Defeat at Gallipoli: the Dardanelles Commission Part II, 1915–16
Lord Kitchener and Winston Churchill: The Dardanelles Commission Part I, 1914–15
The Russian Revolution, 1917
War 1914: Punishing the Serbs
The World War I Collection (Dardanelles Commission, British Battles of World War I)

World War II
Attack on Pearl Harbor, 1941
D Day to VE Day: General Eisenhower's Report, 1944–45
Escape from Germany, 1939–45
The Judgment of Nuremberg, 1946

Tragedy at Bethnal Green
War 1939: Dealing with Adolf Hitler
The World War II Collection (War 1939, D Day to VE Day, Judgment of Nuremberg) (*see also The War Facsimiles*)

Titles can be ordered from
www.amazon.com
www.amazon.co.uk.
www.abebooks.com

www.ingramcontent.com/pod-product-compliance
Lightning Source LLC
Chambersburg PA
CBHW031251230426
43670CB00005B/129